IN THE FACE OF FLYING GLASS

Susie Parks, son Garnet Jr., and daughter Gwen, Columbus, New Mexico, August 1916

IN THE FACE
OF FLYING GLASS

Susie Parks, Border Town Hero
of the Pancho Villa Raid

SHANNON PARKS

© 2023 by Shannon Parks
All Rights Reserved
No part of this book may be reproduced in any form or by any electronic or mechanical means including information storage and retrieval systems without permission in writing from the publisher, except by a reviewer who may quote brief passages in a review.

Sunstone books may be purchased for educational, business, or sales promotional use. For information please write: Special Markets Department, Sunstone Press, P.O. Box 2321, Santa Fe, New Mexico 87504-2321.

Printed on acid-free paper

Library of Congress Cataloging-in-Publication Data

Names: Parks, Shannon, 1960- author.
Title: In the face of flying glass : Susie Parks, border town hero of the Poncho Villa raid / Shannon Parks.
Description: Santa Fe : Sunstone Press, [2023] | Includes reader's guide. | Includes bibliographical references. | Summary: "The story of the twenty year old telephone switchboard operator, Susie Parks, whose life beyond one fateful night on March 9, 1916 during Pancho Villa's raid on Columbus, New Mexico reveals her true strength"-- Provided by publisher.
Identifiers: LCCN 2023039912 | ISBN 9781632935540 (paperback) | ISBN 9781632935557 (hardback) | ISBN 9781611397291 (epub)
Subjects: LCSH: Parks, Susie, 1895-1981 | United States. Army--History--Punitive Expedition into Mexico, 1916. | Telephone companies--Employees--Biography. | Columbus (N.M.)--Biography.
Classification: LCC F804.C65 P37 2023 | DDC 978.968092--dc23/eng/20230831
LC record available at https://lccn.loc.gov/2023039912

WWW.SUNSTONEPRESS.COM
SUNSTONE PRESS / POST OFFICE BOX 2321 / SANTA FE, NM 87504-2321 /USA
(505) 988-4418

DEDICATION

To my aunts, my uncles, my mother and Dad, who bravely took them on with his tongue in his cheek.

My mother was my hero. No matter what was going on she always took action. That's just what she did and she told me: "Don't ever own something that you're afraid to lose or you'll end up a slave to it." —Barbara Parks Gay

AUTHOR'S NOTE

I was born in 1960, the same year that a stranger named George Sparks died at the Fresno, California Veterans Hospital. His daughter, Joyce, must have been confused when she planned for his burial. She knew he was a veteran of WWI, but when she applied for his veteran's marker, they told her no such man existed. She, her two sisters, and his five grandchildren were sure that he did exist. She didn't accept their answer.

After over a year of investigation, Joyce succeeded in getting to the bottom of part of the mystery. She at least achieved her goal of getting approval for his veteran's headstone. It seems she was able to match his Social Security number with his Army service number. The service number belonged to a man named Garnet E. Parks, who is my grandfather. She learned that Garnet E. Parks' birth date was August 3, 1890, not August 3, 1895, as she had always been told. Additional corrected data on the application matched up with everything my Grandma Susie knew to be true of her husband, who had left her and their children in June of 1929 with a promise to return. Joyce died in 1987 and never knew about us, the family he left behind. In fact, the image of the headstone application document, that proved George Sparks and Garnet Parks were the same man, circulated on ancestry.com for years before my cousin, Kelly Parks, found it in 2017. The discovery rocked the family and compelled me to uncover as many details as I could about what possessed my grandfather to walk away from his family and live a lie for 31 years.

If you are a Parks, several things are likely true about you. It is safe to assume that more than once you have been asked to keep it down in a public place. If two or more of you are in a room, you are prone to stay up well into the morning hours determined to convince the other which version of a song is better. You might show up at the door of a relative unannounced and leave just as suddenly as you came. There are two more things if you are a Parks, that are almost certainly true. At some point in school, you did a special history report about our Grandma Susie and The Pancho Villa Raid on Columbus. I don't know a cousin who didn't. Also, when you remember her, her adventurous spirit, and the quality of her laugh that could rattle windows, there is a deep warmth and sense of pride that wells up inside you. She affected us that way.

A need to pursue the unanswered questions of her life burned inside me. I began by thinking I would write the story of a woman done wrong, abandoned by her husband, and left to raise their seven children alone, but that's not the story that unfolded. The family stories I heard as a child had so many inconsistencies, I couldn't depend on them for accuracy. I would have loved the benefit of family documents, but my grandmother never kept anything. Her sister, Eva, was the keeper of most all the family photos and letters but her house caught fire in 1947 leaving those treasures lost forever.

What I had were the stories my mother, aunts, and uncles told throughout my life, each with a very specific point of view. I went to work finding court and county records, I contacted and visited local historical societies and hospitals, and I spoke to researchers and librarians in each of the towns where they lived. It was the newspapers, both my grandfather's and the surrounding papers, that provided me with the most consistent vehicle to paint a picture of their life. I spent countless hours reading through microfiche records of small-town newspapers from Washington to New Mexico and Oregon to Troutdale, Virginia. There is a year, starting in August of 1926, where news and records of their activities go almost completely dark. I believe this was a time they were just barely holding on.

Through the process, I got to know my grandfather and my grandmother better and their life together took on a shape I didn't expect. I came to realize that my grandmother knew more than she ever revealed about the circumstances around his leaving. The truth of their story revealed itself to me in layers.

My Grandma Susie was so busy living, it was going to be up to one of us to write down the story of her life and I was honored to do it. Also, it was a pleasure getting to know you, G.E. Parks.

PREFACE

My mother was the youngest of seven kids. When she was little there was a "crying crazy lady" who would storm into her house on occasion to yell at her mother. She later learned that the crazy lady was her oldest sister Gwen who was fifteen when my mother, Barbara, was born. Gwen wanted answers about the man she called "Papa." She wanted answers and she wanted action from her mother. "Are you just going to do nothing?"

It was a legitimate question. My grandmother didn't know the meaning of "do nothing" and Gwen knew that. They all knew it. But in the first week of June on a Portland, Oregon street, her six children were squeezed into the back of the family's Oakland sedan, and they watched their papa walk away while their mama did nothing about it. He said he would come back, but he didn't.

My mother's brother Lyle was older than her by nineteen months. Neither knew their father and they were curious about him. They asked the older ones, "What happened to Papa?" They had ideas, but it was all speculation. Maybe he got sick again and died alone or maybe he came into money and was robbed and killed. Gwen always said *Papa was the smartest man I knew.* The second born, Garnet Junior, avoided talking about him. Bill was the third. *I didn't like my father. I was afraid of him.* The fourth, Margaret Irene, remembered a night he popped corn on their wood stove upstairs for her and Jim and she got a little weepy. *He always called me Baby.*

Jim was the fifth born and seven years old when their Papa left. He looked like his father, they shared a birthday and, up to the day he died, kept one photo of him in his wallet and another photo of him on the shelf, wherever he lived at the time. To Lyle and Barbara, *Papa* was a vague idea, but he loomed large. The day he walked away, counter to her very nature, my grandmother let it happen. They say his last words to her were, *Susie, I'm no good for you and the kids. I'll come back when I'm cured.*

1

It was the first Saturday in June 1929 and Susie was distracted. Things had been difficult in the house for months, but they could always count on Saturday morning family breakfast. The five oldest kids staggered into the kitchen expecting to see their mama at the stove flipping pancakes, but the kitchen was empty. No coffee perking, no bowl of batter. No Mama.

Bill was the first to find her. She was pacing the living room floor and mumbling to herself as if practicing some sort of speech. He watched from behind the wall and studied her. The others fell in behind him and listened. Jim broke the silence.

"Mama. Pancakes! It's Saturday."

Baby Lyle cried from the back bedroom sending out a plea to be rescued. Gwen said, "I'll get him, Mama." She went to be helpful but also to cajole her mother to get on breakfast. It worked. Susie tuned in and herded the kids into the kitchen.

"Good morning! I'm late, aren't I?" Throwing out a forced chuckle she rustled through the cupboards then instructed Irene and Garnet Junior to set the table. "Bill, run to the coop and get us some eggs."

The meal was tense. Garnet Sr., their papa, joined late. He'd been in the back room with the door closed all morning. Not a word passed between him and Susie throughout the meal, and he was the first to excuse himself from the table. He told them, "You'll be driving me into the city today. All of you."

Irene and Jim loved a ride in town, but the older three had plans for the day. Gwen started to object but Susie's unusual seriousness gave her no footing to protest. Gwen yanked her brothers, Bill and Garnet Junior, to the side.

"What's going on?" The boys were equally stumped.

They scooted into the backseat of their 1926 Oakland sedan. Susie squeezed her pregnant belly and the baby into the passenger side while

Garnet locked the door of the house. He was dressed in his usual suit and tie with a Homburg hat covering his bald head. Junior whacked Gwen on the arm to bring her attention to the suitcase their father carried. He loaded it into the back of the car.

Portland was a 40-minute drive from their house in Estacada. Irene and Jimmie carried the conversation most of the way. Irene had questions about how they would make up the teams for baseball on the Fourth of July because she didn't think they were fair last time. Jimmie had some ideas for what they might do when they reach the city, mostly having to do with candy. They weren't far enough into the city to find a candy shop when Garnet pulled to the curb. "I'll get out here."

Susie whispered to him, deliberately muddling her words so they were hard for the children to decipher. He listened, shook his head, and gave no reply. Their tone wasn't harsh, but it wasn't warm either. Finally, Garnet addressed Susie clearly enough for all to hear.

"Susie, I'm no good for you and the kids right now. I'll check myself in and come back when I'm cured." He opened his door and stepped into the street.

He had to have felt the five sets of eyes from the back seat locked on him as he passed to get his suitcase. Gwen unrolled her window and, on his way back, he stopped and looked in. "Goodbye Sister." Sister is what he called her. He patted her hand that was clutching the car door. Then he leaned in. "Goodbye, kids."

Susie watched for any sign that he would waver as he faced them. Maybe he would realize that leaving them would be impossible. But there was no shift in his posture and watching only exposed her to the pain of their bewildered faces. Gwen welled up. Garnet Junior's expression was frozen. Irene and Jim were at the far end and slower to grasp what was happening. Bill looked left and right, searching for a clue as to what to feel.

Their papa stepped onto the sidewalk in front of the car and set his suitcase down. Inside the car it was silent. They watched him. Maybe he was having second thoughts. He took out a cigarette and lit it, then placed the pack in his pocket. He pulled out his watch and checked the time. It was the watch he had given to Junior five years earlier when, at the time, he believed he was dying. He must have decided he needed it now. He picked up the suitcase again and, without looking back, started walking.

"Gwen, take Lyle and get in the front." Susie spit the words out so forcefully that it was as if she were shouting. Gwen did as she was told. Susie got into the driver's seat and turned the car around to face the opposite direction. The children propped themselves up on their knees tracking their papa out the back window. He kept his pace, putting more and more distance between them until he disappeared around a corner.

Susie pulled out, onto the road toward home. Inside her was something sour mixed with a dull kind of emptiness. She felt thirsty suddenly and felt lucky that she knew the road well enough to make her way home automatically. Her attention to the road faded away, replaced by a memory of them dancing with the babies to Jingle Bells. Then, a memory of Garnet writhing in pain in the bedroom as she shoots him with morphine, calming him instantly back into sleep. Next a memory of the two of them, a younger Garnet and Susie, riding in the southern New Mexico desert and then them again, even younger, rolling into the prickly pear laughing together. Happy.

A rush of overwhelming grief drew her attention back to her driving and she pulled to the side of the road. Her fingers squeezed the steering wheel and she collapsed in an avalanche of tears. Bill leaned over from the backseat and spoke to her. "Mama. Why are you crying, Mama?"

The question came from such innocence and from a place of such goodness, she was afraid that this eleven-year-old boy might be tempted to try to take care of her. That would not do. She would have to figure this out like she had figured things out so many times before. *He's only a boy*, she thought. She owed him what she had at eleven, the freedom to be a child. She wiped her eyes and cheeks.

"I'm all right, Bill." She turned to Gwen, who had been watching her intently. She nodded, took in an ugly snort, and smiled.

"See, I'm all right. We'll go home and figure things out."

2

Susie Gregg and Garnet E. Parks began their lives on opposite ends of the country. He was brought up in the Blue Ridge Mountains of Virginia and Susie was raised in the Great Northwest. There she got what she wanted for her own children, the unencumbered freedom to be a child.

She was the youngest of seven children born to David Duncan and Eliza Jane Gregg who they called Jennie. David Gregg was a restless man. He was tired of farming in Nebraska and moved Jennie and their four children by covered wagon to as far west as you can get in Washington State. There, Jennie brought three more babies into the world, George, Donnelly, and finally Susie who was born in Cinebar on October 22, 1895. Susie was still a nursing baby when her pa got word that the federal government was parceling out Montana land to homesteaders. He hitched the wagon and Jennie now loaded up seven children to chase another hope. A year later, the Greggs packed up the wagon and headed west again away from the broken promise of a homestead, back to the damp and densely wooded land on Rose Hill in Kirkland, Washington. Susie's earliest memory was, at three years old, watching the rocking hind ends of the horses that pulled their wagon.

The Greggs loved the Fourth of July. Every year, starting at six in the morning, Susie's older sister Eva fired a rifle from her second-story bedroom and yelled, "Wake up, wake up. It's the Fourth of July!"

Susie woke to the excitement of a brand-new dress, sewn by Eva for her the week before. Rain or shine, it was a full day of celebration with food and games. Her pa's brother, Uncle John provided the music, and Susie was invariably asked to entertain with a song and a dance. Nighttime brought the bonfire and the smell from gunpowder loaded firecrackers. Shouting with excitement, the children would rush in to get as close as they dared. It invariably ended with Susie falling into bed in her Fourth of July dress peppered with burn holes.

Susie was lukewarm on school. She far preferred tagging along to help her brother while he worked.

"Out of the way, Susie, you'll get your hand chopped off," her big brother Lyle warned her.

"Let me chop 'em, Lyle!"

It seemed to Susie that Lyle could do anything. She believed him to be indestructible. There was nothing unique about looking up to Lyle. They all did. Lyle was talented and strong, and he didn't mind taking a minute out to show her how to do something if she wanted to learn.

"All right then. You can try a few. Start with the smaller ones and work up." Her brother Don often interrupted by smacking her from behind which sent her squealing after him almost always ending in him holding her down while she hollered for help.

Her pa was a practical man. "That's enough, Susie, stop your squawkin'. Get over here!" He had no tolerance for a girl's whining, so he fixed her by giving her boxing lessons. He knew what he was doing. He trained her in the style of Gentleman Jim Corbett who was famous for using sharp, quick punches to keep his opponents off balance. Susie loved it and practiced continually on fir branches, hanging laundry, and anything that could take a punch. Between training with her pa and a significant growth spurt that summer, she got to where she could hold her own against her brothers.

There was a problem with her pa. He could be mean and even meaner when he drank. She often woke in the early morning hours to the sound of the horses plodding up the gravel path with her pa passed out in the cart behind them. They all knew to stay out of his way if he was still staggering and not yet asleep. About her ma, she said, "My ma was just good. We weren't overly religious, but if there is such a thing as a saint, that was Ma." Jennie was small and sturdy and stood by her husband often when she shouldn't have. She loved all her kids, but Susie's happy, outgoing nature brought her a special joy.

They were all charmed by Susie's wit and adventurous nature. Her brothers and sisters called her spoiled, but she took that to mean she was just luckier than them by being born last. She spent those young years on Rose Hill trekking through the woods thick with sword ferns and salal and stuffing her belly full with wild huckleberries. Eva became exasperated at the fir sap that accumulated in her unruly head of hair, so she started braiding it for her in the mornings.

"Where do you go all day? Look at you, you're a mess!"

"You have to go deep in if you're going to get the good, juicy ones, Eva. I'll bring you enough for a pie tonight, I promise!"

Eva's sharp tone never softened for anyone, not even Susie. But she never pulled too hard on her little sister's head or missed a day to fix her hair so she could be off to grub about freely in the forest. Susie's sister Ida, twenty-two, was older than Eva by two years and Maggie was the oldest by two years more. The summer of 1906, Ida and Eva had both married and were out of the house. Susie was eleven. Lyle was eighteen, and he and Pa worked at the log boom on the north end of Lake Washington. When George turned fifteen, he worked there half days.

One wet, gray day in August, Eva decided to cook up a bunch of vegetables from her garden for a family dinner. Everyone arrived except Pa and Lyle. Pa came up the road from the lumber mill on foot. He entered through the back door with the color drained from his face. First his eyes lit on Jennie, then he averted them and spoke to no one directly.

"Lyle's been killed." That's all he said.

At first no one spoke. Then a noise came out of Ma. It wasn't a cry, but a coarse, involuntary sound.

Pa continued. "They were on the lake, and he was lying on the logs. Anyway, the logs rolled, he disappeared and didn't come up."

George said, "Why didn't they…"

Pa erupted. "There's no more to say! It's all I know. I'll not hear any more about it!"

Susie began emitting jerky sobs and Don whispered to her, "Susie don't cry. Not here." He pulled her outside to the back. Eva followed. On the porch the three caved to a grief they thought might swallow them whole.

Pa went to the shed and drank down the dregs of a bottle he had stored there. He lost several days to the bottle in the days that followed. A simple ceremony at the Kirkland Cemetery put their brother to rest but it didn't change how unreasonably long their days had become. Pa continued to forbid the mention of his son's name and, while it seemed cruel, it spoke to the gravity of the loss. After all, they believed Lyle to be indestructible and now he was gone. There were no words for such a thing so, in a way, Pa spared them from trying to put words to the impossible.

§

Quite suddenly one morning, Pa sat down at the table with renewed intention. He announced, "There are folks having success in Mexico growing bananas. I thought about it, and I think that's what we need to do." He waited for a response.

The idea was far-fetched but no shock. Picking up and leaving was what he knew how to do. He shifted in his chair preparing to make a stronger case. "We need a change. Your Ma..." His voice cracked. "...your Ma may need a change. Do you Jennie? Need a change?" Jennie gazed downward. She was holding back tears and he tried to talk through it. "We've had a loss here. A change might be what we need."

Jennie said, "Susie, boys, leave us. Your Pa and me need to talk."

The next morning, radiating a deep calm, Susie's ma told her, "Start packing up. I'm going to tell the boys that at the start of next month we're taking the train to Mexico."

Don and George decided they were grown enough at fourteen and sixteen to stay behind with Eva. This would make things harder on Pa and he knew that. The truth was no one believed his banana growing idea was about growing bananas. It was about getting to the other side of their loss and that's probably why the boys got no argument when they refused him.

So, it was Ma, Pa, Maggie, and Susie who boarded the train for a long trip to Michoacán, Mexico. Susie's role in the family would change without her brothers in the house. George pulled her aside and handed her his single-shot .22 rimfire rifle. She was thrilled. "Is it for me? Really?"

"I expect you to use it. Go hunting for, well, whatever game they have down there. Lions?" He joked.

She squinted down the barrel of the gun. "Okay then, George. I'll shoot me a lion!"

The ride to the train station would have been Susie's first car ride ever. If not for the circumstances, she'd have been thrilled with the novelty of her first trip in a real automobile, but her heart was heavy as they drove around the north end of Lake Washington where Lyle had taken his last breath. Maggie squeezed her hand.

At King Street Station they hauled trunks through the Seattle drizzle onto the baggage car. When the train rolled out, they waved out their passenger car window to the family they were leaving behind. Their number was depleted by more than half. How quiet it would be now.

None of the four of them had ever been tested by the kind of scorching heat they would find in Mexico. In the first two days of the ride, the colors out the train car window went from grey northwest skies and evergreen hills to the southwest reds, beiges, and browns. On day three they stepped out to put their feet on Mexican soil and look around the town of Chihuahua. The still air had them dripping with sweat. It was so dry Susie wasn't sure it was even air she was breathing and they still had almost 1,200 miles to go. Pa said, "That's enough. We're going back." His exhausted travel team gave him no argument. They pulled their crates off the southbound train and boarded the El Paso & Southwestern Line back north. Nine miles over the US-Mexico border, the train rolled into the depot of a barren little town called Columbus, in the US territory of New Mexico. It was no cooler than Chihuahua and it was still a long way from Kirkland, but David and Jennie weren't as young as they used to be, and they were traveled out so they stayed.

Bananas don't grow in Columbus so that part of the plan would have to be adjusted, but nothing was going to grow for the Greggs in Columbus without water. Anyone who knew David Gregg would tell you he could find water on the moon if he wanted. He began, as he always did in a new place, with his witching stick. Susie, Ma, and Maggie held picks and shovels and stood, shifting their weight on a nameless stretch of desert under the sharp, midday sun. The heat crawled up from the hard earth through the soles of Susie's shoes. They watched him as he made circles in the dirt guided by his stick. Gusts of hot wind sent dried brittle brush bouncing by, allowing moments of distraction. Susie was up for most things, but this exercise had her yearning for Rose Hill and the cool, soggy ground they'd left behind.

Finally, he called out, "Water!" As unlikely as it seemed, they knew he wouldn't say it if it weren't true. The three of them went to his spot and started digging. Sure enough, a dribble at first then a puddle. They had their well. It took them longer to get a house built but the Gregg work ethic produced a four-room tin house and a functional barn inside of two weeks. They added livestock, a cart, and horses and David Gregg traveled the county taking on building and repair work where it was needed. They were citizens of Columbus.

Susie suggested that she not enroll in school which was fine by her ma and pa. The boundless New Mexican desert was growing on her. When her work was done, she spent every spare moment riding her horse, Sam, and honing her shot with her .22 rifle. Those were among her happiest times: on her own, on the southwest desert, hunting with Sam.

§

Susie developed an appreciation for the desert and its strange relationship with life. The foliage was sparse and seemed to be hanging on by its last breath. Her heart went out to the lifeless, shriveled brush and the thirsty desert cactus twisting in and on top of itself desperate for a drink.

Her pa spent more days away from the house and Susie took on his chores. This notion of work being assigned to a man or a woman annoyed her. She thought it stingy of some men to claim so many of the best jobs for themselves. She did it all from trimming hooves to making repairs on the carts and wagon. Work was work and she seldom found it unenjoyable, but it was hunting that gave her the most gratification.

When she rode, she sang and kept an eye out for surprises in the grass. Sam's color matched the light caramel color of her braids that swayed back and forth to the rhythm of his gait. One good thing about the desert is that you can sing as loud as you want without bothering anyone.

"*In the good ol' summertime...*
in the good ol' summertime...
Strolling through a shady lane
With your baby mine.
You hold her hand and she holds..."

A rustle from behind the brush got her attention. Like a shadow warrior, she slipped off Sam's back and grabbed her gun, crouching low with her skirt in the dust. She followed the sound with her shotgun slow and steady. Something dashed behind a gray clump of brush. "Ahh, Sam! I lost my shot." Sam had been grazing on weeds and not listening. She kicked the dirt, set her gun back in the bag, and mounted. She cued Sam to a canter then spotted the critter from the other side. This time she could see, plain as day, it was a black-tailed jackrabbit. She took aim, pulled her trigger, and hit him.

"WoooOOHH-HoooHH!" She jumped off where the rabbit dropped and grabbed it by the ears. "Betcha neither Don or George coulda' gotten it done while running, huh Sam?"

Sam was back to his ragweed but must have sensed that she needed to mark her moment because he looked up. She reached to the sky and delivered a deep bow. Sam blew out his nose. She and Sam would bag game hundreds of times just that way on the desert.

No one worried when she traveled after dark. Her life there was sovereign and carefree, and she was fully capable of taking care of herself. On their way home, Sam often kicked it into automatic. She'd start singing but barely made it past the second line before nodding off. Slumped over Sam's neck fast asleep, he could hit a pothole and spill her out onto the ground which would wake her up quick. There she'd be in the dirt, shaking herself back to consciousness, then back in the saddle where she'd sing to the moon:

> *"In the good ol' summertime!*
> *in the good ol' summertime!*
> *strolling through a shady lane!*
> *with your baby mine!"*

3

By 1911, Columbus had tripled in size since the Gregg's arrival in 1907. This was due in part to New Mexico becoming the 47th state. It was also a consequence of the Mexican Revolution going on south of the border. Many Mexican families moved up to Columbus to escape the turmoil. The population in and just outside of town was 60:40 American settlers to Mexican residents. Columbus was peaceful, mostly, but the citizens worried about rebel armies bringing violence from over the border. This had happened to other small towns. In fact, the concerns traveled as far as the US capital inspiring President Taft to build a Post at Columbus across from the Columbus Train Depot.

Cavalry soldiers now came into Columbus regularly by train. From the window of a train car, the perpetual haze of flying dust might make one think Columbus was more an impressionist painting than a town. It was from this vantage point that a round-faced Private Garnet E. Parks first encountered Columbus and had him scratching his prematurely bald head in disbelief.

"This is it? I'm sorry, but...this is our post? This is the border we're here to defend?" The private sitting beside him looked out.

"Ha! Yeah. It don't look so good!"

Except for the unremarkable hills of Tres Hermanas peeking up from the northwest, Columbus was a sweeping stretch of tan flatness. Not a single tree. No grass. Just barren...*like hell must be*, he thought. "Where I come from a place where pines and red spruce tower over rolling hills. Virginia is rich with foliage. The only problem with it is, unless a man is content as a farmer, he has no choice but to leave...which is what I did, and this is what I find? Unfortunate."

A sour mood was not what Garnet planned to bring to this new chapter of his life. At twenty-one, he had a plan to use this post in Columbus as a steppingstone out of Flatridge and onward to a loftier occupation. He self-corrected. "Well, we'll have to find the glory in it, won't we? Ours is not to question or judge…"

The brakes squealed and brought the train to a halt. His nameless travel companion grabbed his bag with one hand and interrupted. "It's all the same to me, partner. I'll just be glad to get me some regular grub and a bunk to hang my hat." He started to tip his hat then saluted instead. Garnet returned a proper salute and braced himself for the scene that awaited him outside.

They were met at the foot of the steps by an orderly. "Welcome, soldiers."

Garnet again returned the salute. "Thank you. Glad to be here with the Cavalry of the 12th Regiment." The orderly took his bag.

"We're glad to have you. Let me walk you over to camp and get you set up with something to eat. Are you hungry?"

Garnet answered that he was while he scanned the landscape again, hoping to give the disappointing place some redemption. He wouldn't be leaving any time soon, so if this dust hole had no more than this to offer, he knew he'd have to write his own story.

§

Susie had a unique competency when it came to dealing with life's surprises. One of those surprises presented itself at a babysitting job in town. It was mid-morning and already scorching hot. Susie stood on the Bennet's front porch as an unexpected gust of wind lifted her dress and blew it clear over her head.

Mrs. Bennet answered the door. "Susie, is that you?"

"Oh, one minute…" she said as she worked to put her dress back into place. Pulling several stray hairs out of her mouth and eyes, she grinned. Mrs. Bennet's stoic expression compelled her to give an explanation. Nothing tickled Susie more than a surprising moment of indignity, especially if the joke was on her.

"It was the wind. Did you see it?" It was clear that Mrs. Bennet would not be joining her in a laugh.

"No, I didn't. Come in. We'll need to be going soon." Susie scooped up Baby Bennet and helped him wave goodbye to his parents.

"Don't stay away too long Mrs. Bennet," Susie teased. "I might be tempted to keep this one for myself." Neither of the Bennets were big on frivolous chatter.

"Okay then," Mrs. Bennet called back and stepped into the passenger side of their motor car. The wind picked up and this time threw both Mr. and Mrs. Bennet's hats into the backseat. Susie felt vindicated.

The older Bennet kids were occupied on the floor with Lincoln Logs, so Susie sat at the dining table to feed the baby. Suddenly, another breeze picked up and sent the window coverings flapping into the open flame of the wood stove. One panel caught fire and before she knew it, it spread to the other. She needed to get the children out. She grabbed the baby from his chair and herded the other three out the door with little Thomas tripping over his oversized feet all the way.

"Stay out here. Don't move," she ordered and they obeyed. She ran back to the house where the blaze was spreading and went to work on the fire. Back and forth, she filled a tin bucket at the kitchen pump and hurled water at the curtains. She worked at an exhaustive pace until all that was left was wet soot. Thankfully, she was able to keep the damage to only the curtains. She ran back to the children.

"It's out! It's finished! Are you all right?" She took the baby from the arms of the oldest girl, Sarah, and walked them all back to the house. Recognizing a combination of bewilderment and fear on their little faces, Susie provided a distraction.

"Come now, we're all going to help." She stooped down and met the little boy's eyes. "Thomas, can you help?" He was a bit stunned and could only muster a tentative "*uh-huh*." Susie grabbed some dry rags and handed them out.

"Whichever one of us sops up the most water wins." They went to work on the black puddles with rags and buckets. They played firefighter, princess and the dragon, and some nonsensical imagination game that Susie didn't understand but happily went along with anyway. Finally, they finished and collapsed onto the floor.

When the Bennets returned home, they found four intact children. The baby was fed and dry, all were safe, and had been well entertained. The kids fell over one another trying to be the first and the loudest teller of the story. 'Mother, you should have seen,' and, 'you'll never believe...' After several starts and stops, they could see they'd lost their mother's attention completely. She was absorbed in the display of her charred, wet curtains.

"What happened here?"

"That's what we were trying to tell you, Mommy. There was a fire, a real fire!" Sarah squealed. "Susie put it out! We all watched, and Susie did it! Just like a real fireman!"

"You did this, Susie?" Mrs. Bennet frowned.

Susie answered humbly. "I did, but I couldn't have done it if the children hadn't been so well-behaved. Sarah looked after them like a proper mama while I put the fire out. They all helped with the cleanup, so all credit to..."

"My draperies!" Mrs. Bennet interrupted. "Look what you've done to my drapes. You let them burn. They're destroyed!"

Susie was surprised by the woman's priorities and stumbled. "Uh, no, I didn't actually *let* them burn. They were burning and I uh..." Then she offered, "I suppose I might have saved more of the curtains if I hadn't been distracted with getting the children out of the house."

Susie's sarcasm sailed past Mrs. Bennet as she continued to address no one in particular. "Well, what will I do with these now? I'll have to have them replaced, won't I?" Susie had a salty suggestion as to what Mrs. Bennet might do with them but decided to address Mr. Bennet instead.

"Mr. Bennet, can I collect my last two weeks' pay before I leave? I have something special to buy at Miller's."

"Oh yes, of course," he said. "Here you are then."

He pulled out his money clip while his wife groaned in the background. Susie accepted her pay and prepared to leave. The children gave her hugs goodbye. Little Thomas added, "Let's play that again next time."

Susie turned to the sour, twisted face of Mrs. Bennet. "We cleaned up the best we could, but I'd be happy to come and help some more with washing or whatever you need."

On that note, she stepped outside and started into town. She had two goals. One involved her brother, George.

George was in town. He had given up logging and since tried several things from laying tracks to working in a Seattle foundry. Now he was looking to his next venture. Eva wrote often and complained that both George and Don had the same fickle disposition as their pa. Her husband, Jim Cathcart, had been working a solid job with the railroad since before she married him, and she far preferred that to the rambling ways of their family. Susie didn't share her opinion. She was entertained by her brothers' fluctuating goals and all the possibility that came with it. George decided he wanted to drive to Columbus so he bought himself a barely operating Buick 10 that he worked on until he was sure it could make the trip. He showed up without warning the night before and promised Susie he would give her a ride home in his Buick after she was done babysitting. This she did not want to miss but first, she had to make a stop at Miller's Store.

Susie didn't know a stranger. She clicked down the wooden walkway greeting friends as she passed.

In front of the Palace Café, Señora Vienda sat twisting a hunk of wool into string. "¿Como estas, Señora Vienda?"

The lady returned the smile and asked Susie where she was going. "¿Adónde va Susie?"

"Over to Miller's store. I'm going to start…" Susie slowed down in earnest concentration, "…falda nuevo para mi mamá." Señora Vienda was patient with Susie's Spanish and always offered her gentle corrections.

"Ah, sí, vestido nuevo."

Susie corrected, "Of course. Vestido nuevo. Gracias!"

As she walked along, she reviewed the absurd episode with Mrs. Bennet in her head and crossed the street past the Columbus Bank muttering. "Curtains…all that over curtains?" It struck her funny and she entered Miller's Drugstore giggling.

One thing Susie learned from Eva was that to make a dress for someone is to say *I love you*. By that example, Susie had a plan to sew her ma a new dress and take her to the community dance on Friday. As she saw it, if her ma was going to continue to work her hands raw, she could do it with the promise of a pretty dress and a night out. Mr. Miller had previously promised Susie that a new shipment of fabric was coming on this day, and she wanted first pick.

She entered still giggling. "Hello, Mr. Miller."

Charles Miller looked up from his till. "Good afternoon, Susie Gregg. What's given you the giggles?"

"Well, I just put out a fire at Bennet's house, and…well, we lived."

Miller gasped. "Oh my. Are you all right?"

"Yes, I'm all right. The children are all right. Only the curtains suffered." She spared Mr. Miller additional details. "Mr. Miller, has the shipment come?" There was a pile of new material on a center table. "Never mind, I see it."

She sifted through the fabric and found a pale green and rose print that grabbed her. She also found some ivory lace she thought would set it off. She slapped her money on the counter. Miller cut her three yards, folded it, and tied it up with twine. Thanking him, she bounced out set on finding her brother. George was parked, waiting for her in what she thought was a truly amazing automobile.

"There you are. Get in," he yelled. "What took you so long?" She was happy to have ol' George in town.

"You probably haven't heard, but the B.O.B. finally finished building the dance hall. They've promised us weekly dances starting this Friday." The Benevolent Order of Bees was Columbus' local men's organization established for the purpose of spreading happiness and goodwill in town. She imitated the growling voice of the vice president who made the announcement. "'*Everyone is cordially invited. We will have, at all times, the best music that can be obtained.*' Of course, by that he means the Cavalry Band because who else is going to play? I'm going and I'm taking Ma. That's why I bought material to make her a dress."

"Why didn't you just say that?" He winked. "Ma won't go, but nice idea."

"I think she's got a case of cabin fever and I've got the cure."

"Not likely. You'll have to knock her out and drag her to that dance of yours. Hey, I've got a cure for you though. Look at this." George reached behind the seat and pulled out a hand-carved maple violin.

Susie was awestruck. "Where did you get this?"

"Don's been working on it for a while. There's nothing he can't make these days out of a chunk of wood. What do you think? Pretty good, huh? He made it for you. He thought you would like it."

"Like it? Look at it! That old violin I got from that pawnshop in Deming is a piece of scrap next to this. Does it play?" He handed her the bow.

She sniggered, "Whose hair is this anyway?" Then she tried it out. "It's got a nice sound, but it's a little out of tune. I can fix that. Don is a good one, isn't he?"

George agreed. "Yup, he's a good one, all right."

He started up the car. Susie shouted over the motor. "Hey, we playin' five-card stud tonight? Pa's home!"

George talked to her like she was still a kid. "Not if you don't have money."

She sassed back like a kid. "I have enough...I want to play Split-Pot."

"Of course, you do. Split Pot's the only way you don't go broke."

She punched him. "Hey, George, let me drive."

"Horsefeathers. I'm not dizzy, missy. I just got this automobile running and you think I'm about to let you wreck it?"

"Nah, I 'spose not," she conceded. George drove and Susie picked out tunes on her new violin on their way back to the house.

§

Almost two years into Garnet's post at Columbus he had not crossed paths with Susie Gregg. He stayed close to camp and only occasionally took the train to El Paso when on leave. What he enjoyed most was writing. Before joining the 12th Cavalry, he wrote stories for a little newspaper in Troutdale, near his home, and found it very gratifying. He was a prolific letter writer and considered himself to be a skilled wordsmith. The story was that he was a flawless speller and took the spelling bee championship every year at his secondary school.

At camp, he shared a tent with four other cavalrymen. Most nights he was at the small wooden desk writing in some capacity while the others slept. Days before he would first encounter Susie, he wrote to his brother.

Columbus, New Mexico March 25, 1913
Post at Columbus

Dear Gurney,
I write you in a combined state of shock and admiration. You've taken a bride. What a surprise. All you have told me is her name, Colyer Swann, which is unusual if not glamorous. You described her mother and their farm in detail, but all I know of this young woman is that she is nineteen and has stolen your heart. Please tell me more.
As for the life of this cavalryman, assignments have been sparse. There has been trouble in the towns to the east and the west of us, but our post here has been as quiet as the Potomac. The 13th Regiment will be taking our place here. They tell me I'll be discharged in October.
Now, regarding the election of this president. I marvel at the swift work Republicans put in DC to ensure that they lost this election. It's baffling that the electorate allowed Roosevelt to split the party in two only to open the oval office to that anemic Governor Wilson. He is a Democrat to the worst degree and indecisive on most things, yet he wasted no time implementing his federal segregation policy. Further, I have no confidence in Wilson's policy in Mexico. He repeatedly changes his mind which only succeeds in agitating these Mexican rebels further.

They are a ragtag band, all of them intent on ruling Mexico and each taking their turns to unseat one another from Diaz to Madero and now Huerta. Wilson only stirs the pot.

As for the little village where I live. I'm finding it more agreeable, and I've decided to take in some music at the new dance hall this weekend. Maybe I'll find a farm girl of my own.

Please send me news of the family and send regards to our brothers and sisters. Love to Mama.

Your brother,
Garnet

§

George and Pa were outside the Gregg house dismantling machines. They had a way of taking things apart and putting them back together significantly improved. The Gregg women were inside. Maggie worked fibers for a floor mat while Susie pumped the pedal on her sewing machine. She was singing. "Sweet Ad—e—liiiiiiine..."

Maggie echoed softly. "Sweet Ad...e...liiinnnnne..."

Susie bellowed. "My Ad—e—liiiiiiine...

Maggie cracked and giggled. "My Ad...e...liiinnnnne..."

"At night, dearrrr hearrrrrt...For you I piiiiii—ne!" Susie interrupted herself. "Maggie, isn't Adeline a beautiful name?"

Maggie knew where this was going. Susie always hated her middle name and used any opportunity to make the case for changing it. She got louder to be sure Ma could hear. "A girl could be proud of a name like Adeline couldn't she, Maggie?"

Jennie yelled back, "Susie!" She poked her head through the doorway. "You know your middle name is important to the family. Of all your brothers and sisters, you are the only one named for royalty."

"Royalty? Ma. No one knows who Lord Ashcraft is. And what good is it to have a man's name if I can't do what men do? I can't go to war, I can't vote..."

"Oh my goodness, Susie. You can tell the folks in town your name is Anteater, for all I care. Your Pa would change George's name before he agreed to change yours."

The only name she considered more ridiculous than her own name was George's, who had the misfortune of being born on the Fourth of July. "Poor George would jump at the chance to change his name. George

Washington Independence Gregg. He should..." George entered, and the conversation came to an abrupt halt.

"What?" He said and got no answer. He washed his hands and left. Susie changed the subject.

"Look, Ma, I added lace round the neck. Here." She gestured toward herself near, but not directly to her breasts. "This is what they call a low Empire waist. It means the waistline is just under the, uh..." Susie had never so much as seen her ma's ankles, so she was always careful not to arouse her modesty. "...the chest area." She looked to Maggie for validation. "What do you think, Maggie?"

Maggie tried to answer but Jennie protested. "That dress is not for me. My goodness, I've got no business draping myself in lace. You can fit that dress for Maggie."

Maggie was visibly shaken by the suggestion and Susie diverted quickly. "No ma, I'll take care of Maggie when she's ready. This one's for you."

Jennie backed into the pantry with false urgency and began filling a tin pan with oats and kitchen scraps. She took a glance back at the dress. "Well, it wouldn't be right to deny you after all your trouble. If it is a sturdy dress, that'll do well enough for getting things done around here." She went outside to toss her scraps to the chickens.

Susie shot raised eyebrows at Maggie. Their ma loved music and dancing as much as Susie, but she had long ago abstained from enjoying them in public. David Gregg was jealous, and Jennie wouldn't subject the family to his displays of jealousy just to indulge herself in a night of fun. Susie couldn't abide the injustice, however. She was on a mission.

"You've got to help me, Maggie. Bessie and I have a plan to go dancing every Friday we can this summer. I want you to come too, Maggie, when you're ready. I'm keeping my promise not to push you till you are. But Maggie, Ma's not getting any younger."

Maggie nodded. "Susie, even if Ma said yes there's no way Pa will let her go. He's jealous as a cock pigeon."

"Why does he have to know? He'll be gone and won't be back till Saturday."

"But if he finds out..." Maggie quaked.

Susie answered her with the audacity of someone who had never taken a blow from him. "I'm not afraid of him."

Maggie fell silent and Susie knew she had run her mouth too long. To say such a thing to her sister was thoughtless and downright unkind.

Of course, Susie wasn't afraid of him. She was the only one of them who never had to brace herself against the force of his hand. This fact filled her with guilt, especially for Maggie who, when she was seventeen, made the mistake of taking the company of a young man without a chaperone. Susie was only four at the time. When Pa found out, he ordered Maggie to the shed and let loose till he beat the screams out of her. Ma, Ida, and Eva tended to Maggie's torn, unconscious body for weeks. They were sure she would not recover. As for Pa, the sight of his bleeding, broken daughter only inspired another drunken night in town.

Just as with Lyle, they were to never speak of it again, but in a private moment Eva told Susie, "It made no sense for Pa to go after Maggie like that. Ida was the wild one. Maggie was as innocent as a lamb." Maggie's body recovered and no one got beaten after that, but her spirit was broken. Now, thirteen years later, she only had strength enough to live through others. Maggie had paid the price so Susie could grow up safe in the house of their pa. Susie was ashamed for being so thoughtless.

"I'm sorry, Maggie. I didn't mean..."

Ever accommodating, Maggie smiled softly. "It's okay. See if you can get her to go, even if it's just once. He doesn't need to know."

Jennie returned and let the door slam behind her. Maggie took the dress and held it up to her. "Look Ma, it fits you. It looks like a sturdy dress that can be just right for going out this Friday to the dance."

Susie pinned the dress to her ma's waist and backed away for Maggie to see. "Oooo, pretty! Say yes, Ma. Please say yes!"

Jennie cocked her head. "Well, George and Pa built some sort of contraption out there that feeds and waters the chickens, so that's one less thing I've got to do." She lowered her voice. "I'll go. To hear the music."

"To hear the music," Susie teased and sent a grateful nod in Maggie's direction.

Maggie sighed. "It will be wonderful."

§

The B.O.B Hall was to the west of the Columbus Bank off Main Street, a block from the Livery Stable. Proudly painted onto its adobe frame was the title: "Order of The Benevolent Bees Dance Hall and Auditorium."

Someone had added a sign on the door, poking fun at the men of

Columbus who couldn't break their old west habit of wearing a holster. It said, "Don't Shoot the musicians, they're doing the best they can!"

One attendee read the sign and, looking for a laugh from anyone within earshot he quipped, "Our band is the Thirteenth Cavalry...they shoot back!" The people of Columbus were proud to have their own dance hall.

Music spilled out onto the street as Susie and Jennie Gregg arrived in the buggy pulled by Sam. The sweet and clever Bessie Bain waved excitedly to them from the entrance.

"Hello, Mrs. Gregg," she squeaked. "Oh, look at your dress. Don't you look pretty!"

Jennie twitched and shook her head in denial. "Oh, it's just a dress." She nodded to Susie. "A well-made dress."

"Both you ladies look pretty." Bessie tugged at her dress self-consciously. "Do I look okay? I tried to do my hair as you did for me last time, Susie, but I don't think I got it right."

Bessie was smart and did well at the high school in Deming. A little over a year younger than Susie, she was inclined to defer to Susie's judgment even if she could just as easily figure a thing out for herself.

"Let me see." Susie looked at the front, then at the back of Bessie's gussied-up head. "It is nearly perfect except for..." She adjusted a pin in the back. "There. Look at you. You look just like the Resinol Soap girl. Better even."

Bessie burst open to fill Susie and Jennie in as they entered the hall. "So, some boys from Deming showed up and they are in the back on that side."

Jennie took a seat near the entry door and worked to manage her discomfort about being away from home. At first, she scanned the room checking for signs of disapproval from town folks she might know but detected none. Susie and Bessie were already on the dance floor. Jennie settled in and, before long, the music and the lively atmosphere had her tapping and clapping contentedly from her chair.

In his cavalry dress, Private Garnet Parks crossed the highway and followed the music coming from the B.O.B. Hall. He claimed a spot near the door behind Jennie Gregg. Not quite 5'5", he had developed a habit of stretching himself up by the chin when entering a room to improve his height. He thought it odd that he was one of only a handful of soldiers there, but it was lucky because there were only a few younger ladies. Susie stood in a small group on the dance floor. He watched as she radiated her distinctive brand of unbridled enthusiasm. There's no doubt she was pretty, but it was her smile and vivacious energy that grabbed him.

Bessie and Susie squealed with delight when the band launched into a rag. At first, the town folk didn't know what to do. Some of them tried an awkward two-step.

Susie called out to Bessie. "This is what we've been waiting for." She launched into her version of the Grizzly Bear that she'd seen on the newsreels. She flopped her arms and threw out her legs. It was comical, which is what she was going for.

"Do you even know what you're doing?" Bessie laughed.

"Not really, watch my Camel Walk." Bessie copied her. When the band played *Alexander's Ragtime Band,* some dancers began stepping together in a Camel Walk across the floor and it ended in a burst of applause. The band leader must have sensed they needed to catch their breath and set up a slower tune *By the Light of the Silvery Moon.* Folks paired off and Susie and Bessie danced together. When they checked in with Jennie, she was all smiles.

Bessie bubbled over. "What do you think of your daughter out there, Mrs. Gregg? She can sure get a room going, can't she?"

Jennie beamed. "Oh yes, she really can."

Bessie caught a glimpse of Garnet at the wall and noticed he was watching them and smiling. She shot him a curious smile back, then excused herself. "I have to say hello to Mrs. Castillo before she gets away."

Susie asked Jennie, "Are you having fun, Ma?"

"Oh, I am. Think of me missing this. Good music and the band can really play."

"I know. Come on Ma, dance with me."

"Of course not."

"Just one?" Susie threw her arms up, doing the Grizzly Bear again. At the wall, Garnet laughed.

Jennie held Susie off with an affectionate hand. "Now don't go trying to ruin my good time by tempting me. Let me watch you. Go dance some more and entertain me." Susie started up a silly dance again but felt she was being watched and stopped herself.

"My oh my, don't stop on my account," Private Parks told her. "You are quite the hoofer." The band started *Let Me Call You Sweetheart.* He stepped forward, took off his hat, and introduced himself.

"I'm G.E. Parks. You can call me Garnet." He bowed to Jennie.

"Ma'am." She nodded shyly. He turned back to Susie. "I assume this is your sister?"

Jennie let out a gasp. "Oh no! That is my daughter."

Susie was on to him and rolled her eyes. "Hum, no fooling."

"Teach me some steps?" He offered his hand for a dance. His uniform and his confidence impressed her so much that she hardly noticed the three-inch difference between them. She did notice, though. They talked as they danced. Susie asked where he came from.

"I'm from the Flatridge area of Virginia."

"Have you always been a soldier?"

"Oh no, this is new. Before I came here, I went to Emory and Henry College in southwest Virginia and taught school in the Blue Mountains. For a short time, I wrote for the Troutdale News. That was my favorite occupation, but Grayson County was too small so I enlisted, and they sent me here. Besides, I thought it might give me more to write about."

"It sounds like you lived a lifetime already. After all you've done, what could you find to write about in Columbus?"

"I didn't think much at first. But the more time I spend, the more attractive I find it to be. Especially after tonight."

They danced several songs in a row and Susie lost track of time. She was fascinated by the way he spoke. He had a clear sound to his voice and an intriguing southern lilt that made her want to ask him to repeat himself.

"Say that again... 'the more time I spend'."

"The maww time I spend..."

"The maww. The way you say that..." Now she embarrassed herself. She felt a warm and unsettling flutter in her stomach.

As he turned her, she caught sight of her ma who was beginning to droop. "Oh no, my ma! She's never stayed up past eight-thirty. I've now kept her up..." She tried to calculate the hours in her head. "Well, I need to get her home."

"Can I walk you out?" *Oh, his manners.* Garnet helped them into the buggy, removed his hat, and held it to his chest. "Good night, ladies, it's been a pure pleasure."

Bessie attempted to sneak up from behind, but she failed to go undetected. He tipped his hat to Bessie then turned and walked away. Susie and Bessie watched him leave with gaping jaws. What they couldn't see was the triumphant smile on his satisfied face. He placed his cap on his head and walked back to camp. Bessie circled her own head with her finger and mouthed the words 'No hair.'

Susie whispered. "I know. Isn't it sophisticated?" That made Bessie giggle.

Jennie was too groggy to fully grasp their meaning. "How are you getting home, dear?"

"My brother Lloyd's here, he'll get me home. Good night Mrs. Gregg. I'm so glad you came. Night, Susie."

They said goodnight. Susie's heart raced with the unexpected excitement of having met a mysterious southern man, combined with the success of executing her plan for her ma. "We'll do this again, Ma, okay?"

Jennie was smiling and nodded. "Yes, we can do that, I think." They rode home under the starlit sky.

§

Maggie heard them roll up and closed her book. "How was it, Ma, did you have a good time?"

"It was an exciting night, Maggie," she sighed. "I wore myself out from tapping my feet. What a wonderful band we have in our little town." Susie came in after tending to Sam. "I'm going to say good night, girls. We have an early day of cleaning and getting ready for Pa to get home. Get your rest."

"Good night, Ma," Susie called after her. "I left you a hanger for your dress. Use it, so it doesn't wrinkle." She waited for the door to close, then crouched at Maggie's feet. "I met a man at the dance."

Maggie's eyes widened. "You did?"

"Not a boy, Maggie, a man! He's a soldier. He asked me to dance. In fact, he danced only with me."

"Of course, only with you. You're the best dancer there, I'm sure."

"Oh, Maggie. I never felt like this before. He made me dizzy. He's so smart. When he speaks, he looks straight at you." She leaned in to demonstrate. "Like this, with his eyes. He's nothing like Pa in that way. He said he's from Virginia, or maybe West Virginia. Is that the same?"

"Susie, you be careful that he calls on you proper. That he comes to the house and meets Pa."

"If I see him again. Also, Maggie. He's not tall." She illustrated with her thumb and forefinger.

"That small?" Maggie squinted, and Susie laughed too loud.

"Hey, pipe down. I'm trying to sleep," George barked from the back room.

Susie whispered. "No, more like," gesturing to her chin, "right about here."

Maggie laughed. "Oh dear, you might have to slouch."

§

One Saturday morning in January, Susie got the wind knocked out of her by Maggie. "John Bliss and I are getting married."

"Oh!" exclaimed their ma.

"What? John who?" Susie's head rattled. "You mean the chicken man from behind the schoolhouse?"

She had seen John Bliss lumbering across town on his stick-like legs that were held to his torso by a rope he used as a belt. He was friendly in his manner. Polite. He greeted everyone he passed with a "How-d'ya-do" and a nod from the head bobbling atop his narrow shoulders.

"Well, ol' John Bliss. He's got a farm," Pa praised.

Maggie confirmed. "He does. He's alone on that farm and he said he thinks I'd make a good companion. That's how he said it. He says he thinks I'm too pretty for him, but that he'd like me to marry him if I'll have him."

Susie prepared a protest. "Were you even seeing him? Does he even..." but seeing Maggie there, smiling with such novel contentment, she stopped herself. For the first time in Susie's memory, all members of the household were focused on Maggie, and she emitted a pride Susie didn't remember ever seeing before. Any judgment she was inclined to share would be selfish and Maggie deserved better. So instead, she took her by the shoulders and spoke earnestly. "Maggie, you need a dress."

The details of how and why John Bliss was becoming her brother-in-law would be answered over the hum of Susie's sewing machine. By the end of the week, she had turned four yards of white cotton lace into a dress fit for a bride. Maggie would begin a new life with her own home and her own man. As simple and odd as John Bliss appeared to be, it was perfect.

In the meanwhile, Susie and Garnet could not get enough of each other. They conspired so that each day guaranteed they saw one another. Susie invited him to join her for jobs and errands, he went with her to the Friday dances, and he sat and wrote during her practices with the small group of musicians she played with off the main room at the B.O.B. Previously those practices were the highlight of her week, but now it required that Garnet be near for her to keep the date. She took him hunting, though she had to slow her pace for him to keep up.

Riding with her in the desert left him nothing short of astonished. The way she moved through the world fascinated him. Her adventurous, unpredictable nature set him off balance but made him desire her all the more. She gave him a thrill and brought excitement to what he realized had been his otherwise conventional life. He wanted to learn everything he could about her and in appreciation, he showered her with affection.

On a chilly October evening, Susie sat crossed legged on a picnic blanket by the tracks. She was working out *Peg O' My Heart* on her violin. Garnet was stretched out beside her reading the *Columbus Weekly Courier*.

"Oh no! The B string's flat again."

"That's okay, come here." He tossed the paper aside and pulled her to him by her waist. "Give me a kiss." She did, then kissed him again and he tickled her to the ground into a flowering prickly pear.

"Oww!" She laughed. "Okay. Now, can you get those spines out of my neck?"

"I'm sorry." He pulled her up gently and plucked three needles from her neck and shoulder. The connection between them was strong. If not for their need to always be touching, it would have been enough to just talk together forever. The physical attraction, the pull that always hung in the air, was getting stronger. Susie had only a vague understanding of what a woman should know about her body. Her ma told her nothing and neither did her sisters. When she menstruated for the first time, she thought she was dying. Now, four years later, she was still making guesses on matters of women's health in general and sex specifically. They talked around it, but there was something she knew was older than her that pulled her to him.

"Garnet, you really are so…"

"So are you, Susie. When I'm with you I feel like I can do anything." His words humbled her. She knew she wasn't refined or educated. She took pride in living on her instincts and she trusted them, but a man like

Garnet was new, almost foreign. His education impressed her. He read to her from his favorite books and shared his views on politics and world events. She liked to get the dictionary out and pick out random words for him to spell. She quizzed him on book titles and their authors for her own entertainment. She wanted to learn from him and that had a very positive effect on him. It strengthened him. With her, he felt the courage to assert himself and quite possibly realize his potential, whatever that would turn out to be. He burrowed in, commanding full attention from her.

"You know I was discharged this month."

"I know. So..."

"Well, it's expected that I will return home or move on to establish myself."

"You mean back to Virginia?"

"I'd rather not. There's nothing for me there and I was thinking, well, you're almost eighteen now." He looked away, fiddling with the fringe of the blanket. "I think you should give me a reason to stay. I mean, I'd like you to give me a reason to stay." He hopped up on one knee and put his hat to his chest. Entirely outside of his character, he sang to her vaudeville style. "You made me loooove you, I didn't want to do it... I didn't want to do it..."

"Ahh, Garnet, you know Al Jolson is my weakness." He laughed, spun his hat in his hands, and popped it on his head.

"Susie, my dear. I think I'll need you to marry me."

Her eyes widened. "Marry you?"

"Yes, please," he repeated. "Marry me."

§

Columbus Weekly Courier, February 13th, 1914
Parks-Gregg

The friends of the bride and groom became very suspicious when it became known that Miss Susie Gregg and Garnet E. Parks departed from Columbus in Mr. Evan's automobile with Deming as their destination. It has since been proven and is not now denied that after a visit to the clerk's office they went to the Methodist parsonage where they were united in marriage by Rev. Morgan.

Both the bride and groom are well and favorably known in this community and we believe that all will agree with us in saying "it is well." May they live long, be happy, and prosper.

Edward C. Morgan married them on February 6, 1914. It was witnessed by Mrs. E.M. Morgan and was signed by the Probate Clerk and County Recorder, C.R. Hughes. That is all that we know about that day.

They moved quickly to execute plans for realizing their hopes and dreams. Garnet burst into their one-room box of a starter home with his plan to acquire a homestead. Most of the land in and around Columbus was taken, but he had found a homesteader who hadn't proved up his claim and was going to have to give it up. "His name is Albert Adler and he's a man with a homestead. More accurately he *was* a man with a homestead. He hasn't plowed the property. Has not fenced nor cleared it. All we have to do is apply, stay overnight at least two nights each month and do some work to prove it up."

Susie lit up. "That sounds like all the things I do best."

In this area, he was out of his comfort zone. "Exactly and I'll...well, I'll learn."

"We'll do it together," she said.

He had more to tell. "Also, I spoke to Lewis, at the *Columbus Courier*."

"Mr. Lewis, the editor?"

"Yes. I asked as to whether he was looking to add a reporter to his staff. I had my writing samples with me from my Troutdale days and also some recent pieces. He said that his little paper couldn't support a reporting staff but then he said something very interesting."

Susie realized he was fishing for a prompt. "Yes, what did he say?"

"He said even though he had just recently acquired the paper, he might be looking to sell it in the next few months. He was looking for someone to take over the publication completely."

"Take over?"

"Completely. And with my savings and experience, who else better to take it over than..."

"Than you, of course," she beamed.

"Yes, than me. I'll work with Mr. Lewis to learn his office and his equipment. It's a step up from the Troutdale News, there's no doubt there. And Susie, it has an apartment in the back so we can stay here in town and work out at the homestead a few days a month. It's just what we need, isn't it? What with..." and he wagged a nervous finger in the direction of her expectant belly. "...what with all of that and all."

She felt butterflies. How different he was from her pa and even her brothers. *He knows what he wants,* she thought. "Yes. It could be a very good thing. What with all of this and all." Susie held her belly and Garnet rocked on the soles of his feet, both grinning.

§

Bessie caused Susie acute anxiety when she left town for Clifton, Arizona. By leaving in December, she risked missing the birth of Susie's baby. Besides, when not in school, Bessie had been helping Susie move from their one-room box into the back of the Print Shop. Not an ideal time for her to run off to Arizona. But Bessie had fallen for a slight-built, pumper employed at the El Paso & Southwest Railroad named Milton James and they left for Arizona to be married at the home of her aunt. As it happened, she got back in plenty of time to greet Susie and Garnet's new baby girl, Gwenyth, who arrived on the 28th of December.

Bessie was leaving the back room living space of the *Courier* office as Susie's ma and Maggie came in. Susie jumped up to get a second chair for Maggie and her baby, Clarence. "See you tomorrow, Bess." Bessie threw kisses all around.

Susie grabbed a copy of the *Courier* from the table next to the bed. "Ma, did you read the announcement Garnet posted? Right here. Read."

Jennie read aloud. "'The stork paid the home of Mr. and Mrs. G. E. Parks a visit this week, leaving a fine eleven-pound baby girl.' Eleven pounds! Get off your feet, Susie. That's a lot of baby."

Maggie was dumbfounded. "Eleven pounds? How can that be? Clarence isn't even eight pounds last we weighed him. Let me hold her." Maggie passed Clarence to her ma. His head wobbled and Jennie grasped him protectively. Susie passed Gwen to Maggie, and she buckled under the weight. "My goodness, she's eleven pounds, all right."

Susie laughed. "I know. She's a load."

Jennie rocked Clarence. "Garnet didn't take up much space announcing his first child to the world, did he? Why not? It's his newspaper."

"Garnet doesn't use the paper to put attention on himself. He's more civic minded," Susie explained with pride.

"Civic minded. Listen to you," Jennie kidded. "Well, he could have at least reported her name. What is her name?"

"Gwenyth." Then Susie mumbled self-consciously. "Gwenyth Neva..."

"Neva? Her middle name is Neva? Now that's a middle name isn't it, Susie Ashcraft Gregg." Jennie Gregg nudged victoriously.

"Middle names are a hard thing for me, Ma. I thought it sounded sophisticated."

Jennie bounced Clarence. "Oh yes, we'll see how she likes that for a 'middle name', won't we Clarence?" He responded with a bob and a wobble. "Yes, we will see."

Maggie was lost in the softness of Gwen's little hands. "Aren't we lucky Susie? I thought I might never have a child and now we're mothers together. Ida's little Florence now has two cousins."

Jennie sighed. "Who she may never meet if she don't come to visit. But Eva does so want a child."

"Her time will come, Ma," Maggie said then Gwen spit up and covered her dress with nearly a pint of her mother's milk. "Well, little Gwenyth Neva, thank you very much."

4

By the spring of 1916, G.E. Parks had become a progressive voice in the community with his weekly editorials. Susie ran the press and wrote copy for the Locals section with Garnet's help editing her grammar and spelling. They worked well together but despite their hard work and optimism, the *Columbus Courier* had gone from an eight-page weekly paper down to four-pages within the year. G.E. was determined to rebound by increasing advertising before years' end.

Between the newspaper, filling print jobs, and chasing Gwen, Susie had time for little else. Not only that, Mr. and Mrs. Burton's telephone office had burned down in January. Susie and Garnet offered them to set up Columbus' only telephone switchboard in the *Courier* office. Mrs. Burton trained Susie to operate it so calls could connect after she went home for the night. In gratitude, Mr. Burton connected a phone line for them at their homestead shack eight miles out of town. Susie had never in her life spent more time indoors, but she was too engrossed in the activities of motherhood and all the new learning to miss her previous life too much.

Bessie and Milton had a little house half a block from them up on Broadway, and both Susie and Bessie were expecting babies in July. On a March afternoon, Bessie bounded into the print shop. "Susie," she called out then quieted herself quickly. She was always forgetting that Mrs. Burton would be at the far wall operating the switchboard. "Sorry, Mrs. Burton."

Susie stood sorting pages at the counter and chuckled at Bessie's blunder. Bessie tried again with a whisper. "Ah, embarrassing! Susie, I need eggs and I have to tell you something."

"Tell me what?" Susie whispered back.

"I tell you I think this baby is feeding straight off my good sense. Lately, all I do is worry. I worry about the baby, all the things I don't know, and what if something should happen to Milton or to me. And then there is all this talk."

"What talk?"

"Talk about strangers, looking suspicious. Walking around town, and into stores but not buying anything."

"Oh, that talk." Susie had heard these rumblings that came from concerns that rebel fighters from Mexico might come into Columbus. For several years, talk like that had come and gone in waves. Lately though, the rebel General Pancho Villa had been active in northern Mexico. He gained a reputation for being a kind of Robin Hood, a bit of a hero. Villa was at odds with Mexico's current Carranza government, had his sights set on another revolution, and enjoyed support from the United States. But the tide shifted in the latter part of 1915, when President Wilson decided to give US support to President Carranza and because of it, at the battle of Agua Prieta, Villa suffered a decisive defeat. He was furious and he blamed Wilson. Then, in January 1916, eighteen miners were pulled off train cars and executed at Santa Isabél, Chihuahua. It had all the features of a Villa job. That's when rumors started stirring up again. Some folks said that Villa had met with Sam Ravel, owner of the largest and most successful general store in Columbus, to buy guns and ammunition. Like Bessie, Susie had also heard that strangers were showing up in town, but these days she seldom left the print shop so she hadn't seen anything. Bessie continued. "I just feel it in the air. It's unnerving."

"I also heard he's gone into hiding, Bessie. It wouldn't make sense for him to come up here. Maybe you just have baby nerves." The conversation had gone long enough for Gwen to take an inked-up paddle and tried powdering her face. "Ahhh, Gwen no!" Susie scooped her up, managing to keep the damage to her nose and chin. She washed her up at the sink.

Bessie heaved a sigh. "Okay, well it does make me nervous. For now, I need to borrow four eggs cause I'm making corn pie for Milton's stepsister, Myrtle. She's coming in tomorrow on the two o'clock train. Ever since that little sister of mine came to live with us, I can't keep enough eggs in the house. Do you have some?" She eyed the fifty eggs warming in an incubator on the floor.

"Don't even look at those. Those are the South Carolina Leghorns Garnet's been advertising to sell. They're about to hatch. Here, I've got some of Maggie's you can have." She put them in a box.

"Good thanks. So, I'd better get home to cooking. Do you want to come with me to meet Myrtle at the depot?"

"I want to. Maybe Garnet will watch Gwen. I can't remember the last time I stepped out of this shop."

"You'll come then." Bessie was halfway out then turned and gave a sheepish wave in the direction of Mrs. Burton at the switchboard.

§

On March 8, 1916, Susie held Gwen near a boiling pot hoping the steam would loosen up her stuffy nose. Garnet sat at the table. He had established a morning ritual of breakfast with the family, a cigarette, and a giant stack of newspapers by his side. He was proud that he shared Teddy Roosevelt's ability to devour large amounts of print in seconds. He called it page reading and he started each day inhaling the news from a variety of sources through his cloud of smoke.

He read to Susie. "Here's something from the *El Paso Herald*. Listen to this: 'Villa was at Buques Grades ranch fifteen miles west of Palomas. Villa is reported to have between three hundred to four hundred men with him. They are all well mounted and, since arriving near Palomas, have been slaughtering large numbers of cattle.'"

Garnet reflected. "One has to wonder how slaughtering cattle wins a revolution."

"West of Palomas? That's close." Susie was right. Palomas was four miles south of Columbus. She held a rag to Gwen's nose and made a blowing sound for her to copy. Gwen blew back. "But why would he come to Columbus? There's nothing here."

Garnet's nose was back in his paper. "I'm not sure. Maybe horses? We know he can't get into the armory. That's locked up. Maybe he would do it just as a show of strength. Maybe I shouldn't do the overnight at the homestead tonight."

Susie got another blow out of Gwen. "Of course, you should go. I was just going to go to the theater tonight. They're showing *The Broken Coin* with Grace Cunard."

"That's tonight? That will draw a crowd. Okay, I'll go out just for tonight and do some work on the fence tomorrow." It was settled. Garnet would go to the homestead and put in one of their two required overnights per month. Susie would stay in town with Gwen and do her night shift at the telephone switchboard.

By the afternoon Gwen was breathing better. Susie set her up with Garnet and set out on the hot, windy afternoon for her walk with Bessie to the train depot.

§

The *Courier* office was on Broadway which spanned a block and a half from west to east. It was generously referred to as "the business district." Other businesses were Frost's Furniture Store, JT Dean's Grocery, a small curio shop, the Palace Café, Miller's Drug Store and the Columbus Bank. Behind Broadway to the north was Floyd White's Livery Stable, the brick schoolhouse, and the church. Just over a block on East Boundary was The Columbus Bank. It sat kitty-corner and over from Bessie and James' house. Both were across the street north and west respectively, from the Hoover Hotel.

Susie stepped down into the street and thought the sun might burn a hole right through her saucer-brimmed hat. She and Bessie were headed west to Taft Street where they would pass Ravel's Merchantile and the Commercial Hotel on their way south to the depot. Across the highway west of the depot was the Post at Columbus where the 13th cavalry boarded up. Any place a person needed to be in Columbus never exceeded a three-block radius.

The two fought the wind to Ravel's Merchantile. Through the dust Susie spotted her old friend, Mrs. Bennet, corralling her children into the car and expressing her thoughts. "Look at what has become of your trousers, Mister. I suppose I'll have to do an entirely new wash when we get home."

Susie gasped at the sight of Sarah, who was nearly a grown lady, the baby was walking, and it looked like Thomas had grown into his feet. They saw Susie and ran to her.

"What is this now?" Mrs. Bennet pulled at her children and then realized it was Susie. "Oh, Susie. I didn't see you." She scolded them. "Come on now, let her go. It's not very often we see Susie so well dressed. We don't want to spoil her frock." Few things were more dependable than Mrs. Bennet's capacity to offend. Susie gave them hugs and waved them off. Looking down, she saw it was true that the children had added handprints to the dust that was already stuck to her dress. *Dirt is dirt*, she thought.

On the wooden walkway outside the Merchantile was Louis, the second Ravel brother, shouting instructions at the youngest brother, Arthur. Arthur was unloading crates from a flatbed into the Ravel's storehouse that sat under the Commercial Hotel. Bessie called to him. "Good afternoon, Mr. Ravel. Milton sends his regards to you and Sam."

"Regards to Milton. Sam's not here. He's getting his teeth fixed in El Paso, poor guy. Hello Susie Parks. It's been a while since I've seen you about. You'll be running our usual ad this week, I hope."

"Count on it every week until you tell me different." Susie wondered if she'd ever seen any one of these three brothers take a rest a day or even a minute. The train whistle sounded.

"Oh my gosh!" Bessie pulled her by the arm. "Come on, Susie. We can't be late." Susie held on tight to her hat and they ran to the train depot.

Waiting there at the platform, was the skinny and boyish Milton James wiping grease from his hands. His sister, Myrtle, stepped down from the passenger car and embraced her brother. "Oh, look at you, Milton, Bessie's been feeding you."

Bessie stepped forward with her arms stretched. "Welcome to Columbus." She wrapped her in a hug. "I'm so excited you're here and I can't wait for you to meet my little sister, Ethel, who has been staying with us. Tonight, we're having corn pie for dinner. We'll just relax and visit. I'm sure we will all be such good friends." Susie thought it was sweet how eager Bessie was to impress her new sister. Then Bessie realized she hadn't made an introduction. "What's wrong with me? Myrtle, this is my dear friend I told you about. Susie." Bessie leaned in to whisper. "She's also having a baby in July."

Myrtle responded with a supportive, "Oh. Wonderful!"

Susie reached out her hand. "I'm so happy to meet you. I hope you learn to love Columbus like we do." Susie wasn't used to behaving so formally and she impressed herself with such a dignified greeting.

Milton, on the other hand, appeared a bit overwhelmed by his wife's exuberance and reached for Myrtle's bag to have something to do. The group went east along the railroad tracks to Main Street then turned into Milton and Bessie's home on the corner of East Boundary and Broadway. Susie joined them inside for a short visit but realized Myrtle might want to rest after her long trip, so she stood up to leave. "*The Broken Coin* is playing at the theater tonight. It's a mystery. Do you want to come?" They did and planned to meet at the theater at seven. Susie said goodbye then braved the winds up Broadway where Gwen and

Garnet waited for her and dinner in their little kitchen at the back of the *Courier* office.

§

The buzz didn't stop about Villa. A foreman at the Palomas Land and Cattle Company, Juan Favela, had evidence that it was likely more than just buzz. He tried twice to warn Colonel Slocum, the commanding officer of the 13th Cavalry, that Villa was coming.

The first time was a week before when he came across a band of Carrazanistas interrogating Villa fighters. They told him their prisoners had confessed that Villa planned to make a move on either Hachita or Columbus in a few days. Favela sent his most trusted cowhand to deliver the warning to Colonel Slocum. The cowhand returned and reported to Favela that Slocum seemed unimpressed.

Four days later, Favela was riding along the high mesquite and, from atop a hill, spotted men on horseback moving in the direction of the border. He studied them long until he was certain they were Villistas. This time he went himself and brought his friend, Mr. Reed, to alert the Colonel. They both reported that Colonel Slocum dismissed him, suggesting he 'settle down and go have a drink'. So that night, instead of posting up for a possible insurgence, the Colonel kept his plans to host his officers and their wives at a dance in Deming.

Before Slocum left for the Deming dance, as was his routine, he placed 220 men on patrol at the border. Most of them were posted to the west with no fortifications. The rumors were true that Villa had sent spies into Columbus in the days prior. Villa knew where the guards were and where they weren't. Villa's Captain Rodriguez had been in town a few times and made a map of Cavalry officers' homes, the horse stables, and the armories. Villa knew that, on this night, many of the soldiers and most of the officers would be out of town either on leave or dancing.

§

Susie helped Garnet saddle Sam and load a couple of extra blankets for what might be a chilly night. He kissed Gwen on the head, squeezed Susie's hand, and rode east off to the homestead.

With a military camp so close to town, Susie didn't need a clock. When the bugler sounded Taps, she knew she had about a half hour before the opening newsreels. She wrapped Gwen up and started toward the theater where Bessie, Ethel, and Myrtle were waiting. No Milton.

Halfway through the picture, Gwen became restless and clingy. Her nose was running again and when Susie felt her, she was extra warm. By the end it felt to Susie that Gwen had doubled in weight. Outside, Gwen's limp body draped over Susie. Bessie was worried. "She looks exhausted."

Susie felt her forehead again. "She's got a fever. She was like this about an hour into the movie, right when Kitty Gray went unconscious."

"Wasn't she amazing?" Though she was trying to be respectful, Bessie's little sister, Ethel, had been bursting to talk about the movie. "When she was captured, and Frederick was trying to save her, but she didn't need him! She figured her way out all on her own."

"Of course, she didn't need Fredrick," Susie asserted and adjusted Gwen on her shoulder.

Bessie moved the blanket over Gwen's head. "Well, you need to get her home."

They said good night in front of the *Courier* office. Inside, Susie dabbed Gwen's forehead and neck with a cool rag like her ma did when she was little. Finally, Gwen's eyes closed, and she was asleep.

Susie was still up when the Drummers and Drunkard's Special rolled in. It was a nightly train that came through at 11:45 bringing mostly soldiers back from their parties while on leave in El Paso. It was always loud.

There was a knock. Mr. Riggs, the Columbus Customs Inspector, was outside the door. "Evening ma'am. Sorry to bother you at this late hour, but I need to make a call to El Paso Customs."

"Sure. Come in." She led him to the telephone exchange and checked her book for El Paso Customs. The Columbus exchange had two connections beyond town. One was to Deming, the closest small city to the north of them, and the other was El Paso, Texas, 80 miles almost directly east.

He motioned a request to take her headset. "Hello. Riggs here from Columbus, New Mexico Customs. We just got a report, not yet confirmed, that 500 Villistas are heading toward our border...Yes, sir. He says just south of Palomas where they set up camp... marching north." He stopped to listen and then answered the El Paso officer. "A source sir. A local Mexican man came to our post less than a half hour ago." Riggs strained to hear through the headset. "Pardon? No, it's more like forty miles, they said... Oh yes, we heard that. That report puts him up in Valley of Caves, more than 120 miles from here." Listening again. "Yes, we like that better also. Either way, sending the alert." He leaned in. "Yes sir, that's all we have from here. We will hope to hear from you if you get anything. All right then, thank you, sir." He turned to Susie. "Thank you, Ma'am. Again, I'm sorry to bother you so late."

"Do you think there's a problem? I should keep the line open from El Paso," Susie prodded.

"That's a good idea, but keep in mind, I have to report everything we hear. It probably won't amount to a hill o' beans."

She laughed. "I'll count on that. Have a good night."

"I will Ma'am. You have a nice night."

She went out with him and stepped off the wooden walkway to study the street. The night was clear and the road was dimly lit by the quarter moon. The soldiers from the last train had settled down. Over toward East Boundary the stores were all dark except for one light flickering upstairs at the Hoover Hotel. Across from the hotel at Bessie and Milton's house, they were certainly sleeping and with nothing to do in the empty desert, Garnet had surely been asleep for hours. Nothing to see, it was time to go to bed.

§

Returning from an El Paso polo match, Lieutenant John P. Lucas came down the steps of the Drummer's and Drunkard Special dodging inebriated servicemen. He was sober and ready for bed.

Meanwhile, Villa and his band moved north from their hiding place at Sierra Prieta, Chihuahua. They cut the fence at an unguarded section of the border and continued on foot across a desolate stretch of desert where they could be neither seen nor heard.

They were a diminished force due both to battle casualties and the many defectors who lost faith in any chance of victory against Carranza. To rebuild his numbers, Villa instituted a "draft by gunpoint" adding to his ranks some indigenous Yaqui boys of northern Mexico along with other poor and inexperienced drifters. They say Villa delivered a skillful speech that night to ignite excitement among the shabby bunch.

"¡Esta noche nos vengamos!" he told them. *'Tonight, we get revenge!'*

They cursed and called back, "¡Venganza!"

He shouted, "¡Venganza contra el presidente Wilson!" *'President*

Wilson has betrayed our cause, left us hungry by siding with Carranza!' They hissed and kicked the dirt with their ragged moccasins and mule-hide boots.

He blamed the U.S. for their suffering. *'The hunger you suffer has been caused by American greed!'* "...esos americanos que viven en esta ciudad de Columbus!" *'...some of those Americans who live in this town of Columbus!'* This got them jumping and agitated. They pumped their fists and grabbed for their guns.

His voice lowered. *'One man in that town sold me faulty ammunition and we lost a most significant battle.'* He shouted, "¡Venganza, Sam Ravel!"

Though there was not likely one among them who had ever heard the name Sam Ravel, they called out in agreement. "¡Sí, sí, lo hará!"

Then he roared. "Muchachos! Escúchame ahora... *Boys! Hear me now! If they want to swallow Mexico...let's give them something to choke on!"*

It was effective. He convinced his ad hoc army that they were about to embark on a noble cause. He split them into three groups. One group would steal horses at camp and a second would create chaos by looting and harassing the township. He sent his commanding officer Cervantes to lead the last group with one objective, to find Sam Ravel. Three men went ahead along a three-mile ditch and slit the throats of two guards at the first outpost. West of town, on top of Coote's Hill, Villa raised his arm and shouted, *"Go ahead, boys!* ¡Vayanse adelante, muchachos!"

Men and boys waved Mauser rifles and lever guns shouting, "¡Viva Villa...Mata los gringos!" and "¡Viva Villa! Viva Mexico!"

Lieutenant Lucas woke up surrounded by the black high peaked sombreros of Villa's fighters. With no way out, he had to wait. When a young sentry guarding headquarters outside was shot, it caused enough of a distraction for Lucas to escape. In bare feet, he gathered soldiers from the barracks and made a sprint for the arms tent. They broke open the locked weapons cabinet, pulled out the Benet-Mercier 7 mm machine gun and took as much ammo as they could carry. They set up the only defense the little town had along the railroad tracks, one block from the *Courier* office.

§

Susie woke with a pounding in her chest and clutched her nightgown. *What's happening?* The noise came from outside, but it felt so close, like a buffalo stampede in the room. In the pitch blackness she felt for Gwen, who was still beside her too hot and sick to stir. Her heart racing, she carried Gwen to check out the window. Barely detectable silhouettes of riders on horseback were coming at her like sheep, their guns flailing in the air. Above the hammering hooves, she heard their screams, "Viva Villa, Viva Mexico!" Bullets tore through the walls of the little shop and she realized, *He's come, it's Villa.*

She detected the sound of rapid-fire bullets in the distance. *They have a machine gun!* Single fire shots flew into the room and embedded into walls and floorboards without mercy. The incubator of South Carolina Leghorn eggs was showing a light, so she unplugged it from the wall, then crawled to the switchboard with Gwen in her arms. Habit made her strike a match, but she quickly blew it out then ran her fingers over the connections in the dark. She had kept the line open to El Paso but the headset was silent. The line was dead. Villa's spies had found it and cut the line just before the attack.

Ranch nine...where's nine? She found it.

It rang for what seemed like an eternity. Garnet answered. "Hello?"

"Garnet! It's Mexicans..."

"What time is it..."

"I said Mexicans are swarming in the streets...like cockroaches. There are thousands of them. They're shooting!"

"Shooting from where?"

"At us! They're yelling, 'Viva, Villa!'"

"Get down low," he told her. "Just lie down. That's what you need to do. I'll come as soon as I can. Take the baby and get down on the floor!"

She slithered across the floor as flying bullets directed her course. One way, then another, that's how she went toward the bed. She laid on top of Gwen and stayed a good three, maybe four, seconds. That was all she could stand. *Well, I can't stay down here.* She felt under the bed for their .32 rifle and stood up just as a shell sliced into the floor where they had laid. Sent this way and that, she reached the switchboard again. This time she tried other numbers in town but got no response. *They're all dead.* She felt she might faint, and her body went numb.

Suddenly, the room lit up. She wondered if she'd accidentally turned on a light, but she hadn't. It was a flickering orange light coming from Taft Street. At the window, she pressed her cheek to Gwen's. "Gwen, the whole town is on fire."

§

On the north end of town, Susie's ma and pa had taken refuge in a neighbor's adobe house with their friends, the Deans, who owned the grocery store on Broadway. When Mr. Dean saw the fire on Taft, he went out into the streets to help.

Villa was looking for revenge on the United States on behalf of Mexico, but his grudge against Sam Ravel was personal. On Taft, at the Ravel Bros. Merchantile, two gritty raiders smashed down the door. Louis dove under a pile of animal hides. Little brother, Arthur, was not so lucky. They yanked him from bed out of a sound sleep. He pleaded to them in Spanish, "¡No me maten!" *Don't kill me.*

Shoving him toward the safe they motioned for him to open it. "¡Abre- Abre la caja!"

"I don't know it! ¡No se, No se!"

The tall one pulled him up and leaned in nose to nose. "¿Donde esta Sam?!" His words sprayed a stench of stale smoke in Arthur's face. He tightened his grip and demanded, "¿Donde esta Sam Ravel?"

"El Paso! Está en El Paso!" It was a long shot, but Arthur hoped that speaking Spanish might help endear him to them.

They were not charmed. "¡Mentiroso!" *Liar!*

"No, es verdad. ¡Sus Dentist!" Arthur pointed at his teeth desperate to be understood but they didn't believe him.

"¿Dónde se esconde?" One commanded while the other put a rope around his neck. *Where is he hiding?* "¿Dónde se esconde?"

Arthur told them, "¡Por ahi!" *Over there!* Arthur pointed to the Commercial Hotel across the street. He hoped they had no more use for him, but they pushed him across the street anyway. He was dragged up the stairs into the entryway of the hotel.

Villa's spies knew that Sam Ravel lived in room 13 at the Commercial Hotel above the Ravels' storehouse. The commanding officer, Cervantes, was already there and, when they didn't find Sam, he told his boys to take what they wanted. "No molesten a las mujeres, pero maten a todos los gringos!" *Leave the women alone but kill all the gringos.*

The hotel's proprietor W.T. Richie, his family, and hotel guests stood in the entryway shaking and frantically handing over valuables. It was an unusual robbery. The red, wilted faces of Villa's raiders revealed they had gone too many months without proper food or relief from the sun. They demanded items with the point of their guns then stripped down right there to dress themselves in the looted shirts, pants, and shoes. They stuffed their pockets with money, jewelry, and silver pieces. One rancher, Birchfield, was able to escape by handing out checks.

Having taken all they could hold and still no Sam Ravel, the looters lost their patience. "¡Diles que bajen las escaleras!"

Arthur translated apologetically, "They want the men to go downstairs to see the commander." William Ritchie and the other male guests descended the stairs with guns to their heads. One broke free and ran to his touring car that was parked in the front. He got as far as starting the engine when a spray of bullets through the driver's side door ravaged his body and he was dead. The other men were taken one by one and executed.

Sounds of machine gun fire by the bank, now, drew the attention of Cervantes' group away from the hotel and into the heart of the fighting where Susie was on Broadway. Arthur's kidnappers got an idea to rob the bank and used him as a human shield to cross Broadway over to Main Street.

Before they left, they set fire to the Lemmon and Romney General Store that stood behind the Commercial Hotel. The flames traveled quickly to Ravel's kerosene-filled storehouse and turned the Commercial Hotel into an inferno.

§

Susie stood at the window with her attention fixed on the light flickering orange from the next block. Outside, below her window, she heard men speaking Spanish and held her breath. Three men were illuminated by the fire. A bearded one in uniform was giving orders. From the photos and publicity Villa himself promoted, she was sure she recognized his face and the gold embroidered insignia on his hat. *It's Villa!* But she lingered too long. A force propelled flying glass from the window and pierced her neck. She dropped to the ground. What blood was hers and what was Gwen's she couldn't tell, but it was everywhere. She felt sure that this much blood could only mean death so she laid Gwen in a box of fabric beside the bed, gave thanks for the fever that sedated her and prepared to die.

§

The machine gun sounds Susie heard weren't coming from Villa's men or Lucas' group. Lucas was still barefoot and set up south at the train tracks. These sounds were coming from a second Benet-Mercier 7mm that a young, off-duty Lieutenant Castleman had snatched from the bank arsenal. At the first sounds of insurgence, he set up at the intersection of East Boundary and Broadway. This was the heart of the battle where Castleman and twenty-five soldiers fought steadily to hold them off at the north end.

It was Bessie and Milton's misfortune that the intersection was at their front door. Their little wood-frame house was being decimated in the crossfire. They and their sisters could not be more vulnerable. "We've got to get out of here!" Milton insisted. They knew that the brick schoolhouse and the adobe Hoover Hotel were nearly bulletproof if only they could get there.

"The schoolhouse is too far, Milton. We can try to make it across the street to the hotel, maybe." Bessie looked at Ethel's anguished face. She couldn't bear how frightened she must be. Milton led the four along the floor in the dark and Myrtle and Bessie held Ethel by the hand between them. He threw open the door and tried to hold onto Bessie, but they had to let go. Shells from both directions spit dust in their path. Villistas screaming, *Viva Villa* fell to their deaths in the street. Castleman's machine gun fire came at them from the east and Villistas' shot from the west. Milton was hit in his upper thigh. His leg faltered and Bessie and Ethel passed him. Ethel made it to the west entrance of the hotel and pushed open the door. Milton was hit again then, before his eyes, Bessie was lifted into the air by the force of a slug that struck her in the abdomen. For a moment she hung there, suspended, then she landed in the dirt at the front entrance of the hotel.

Ethel saw it just before she entered and screamed, "My sister is killed! Out there!" Mr. and Mrs. Hoover rushed to the window to see Bessie down, groaning in the dirt. Moments before the drugstore owner, Charles Miller, had tried to make a run for his guns and was shot in the hotel doorway. He lay dead in the entry. Mr. Hoover took a chance, opened the door, and pulled Bessie into the foyer.

Her blouse and skirt were saturated in blood. She was shot both in the chest and in the stomach. She turned and saw the dead man lying next to her and told Ethel, "That's Miller." Mrs. Hoover laid a blanket over her, and Ethel held her hand. The last thing Bessie said was, "I am safe." Then she was gone.

§

At the *Courier* office, Susie lay in the pool of blood waiting to die. Gwen seemed as still as death, but she still breathed. Susie could feel the night air seep through perforations in the walls amplifying the sounds of the slaughter outside. She had been patient, but death didn't come, so she decided to regard the pain and the blood as more of a complication than a death sentence. A call rang in from an outside line. She pulled herself up to stop the sound from attracting attention.

Her voice was low. "Yes?"

"Hello, Columbus? It's Mrs. Frost, Mrs. A.D. Frost from Columbus town...who is this?"

Wiping blood out of her eyes, she whispered, "Susan Parks."

"Oh, Susie, so glad I got through. I'm in Deming," she reported excitedly. "We barely escaped. Mr. Frost was shot! Twice! Once in each arm but we made it to the car, and he drove fast out of town. I had to steer while he drove full speed all the way to Deming."

Shooting and screaming from outside took no pause for Mrs. Frost's story and it was hard for Susie to be fully attentive. Then she realized, *she's calling from Deming!* "Mrs. Frost, I have to go." The line from Deming was still good. She pulled the plug on Mrs. Frost and put through a call to the Deming operator. The operator wasted no time connecting her with Captain A.W. Brock, Company 1 of the National Guard. By now, the switchboard was lighting up. Susie pulled all the plugs but the one that kept her on with Deming.

She described the scene to the captain. "I don't know what is going on. There are Mexicans all around. They're breaking windows and destroying the place. The telephone line to El Paso is dead. Buildings are on fire and bullets are flying. We're just thick in gunfire. There can't be any of our soldiers left here, otherwise, I don't see how they have gotten in?"

Captain Brock asked her, "Which direction are they coming from? How many of them do you think are there?"

"They came in maybe thirty minutes ago. I just don't know, hundreds...maybe thousands?"

"We are on our way, Mrs. Parks. Stay by the phone in case we call and try not to let your tail down."

§

What seemed like an eternity had been less than two hours of fighting in the dark. Unfettered by the conflict, the sun rose as always from the east. Light was a welcome advantage to the cavalry soldiers fighting from the north and south ends of town. Both groups had struggled with jamming machine guns and limited vision. The light made them more effective and put Villa's soldiers at a further disadvantage.

Not far from the bank, Arthur escaped his kidnappers who had been picked off at Castleman's intersection. Nearby in the Hoover Hotel entryway, Ethel wept inconsolably over the body of her sister, and inside the *Courier* office Susie had put on a coat and wrapped Gwen in a Mexican blanket. She sat at the switchboard holding Gwen and her shotgun, holding her post for any word from Deming.

Colonel Slocum was spotted by Floyd White walking along the road by the Livery Stable. It was the first time the Colonel had been seen throughout the battle. Floyd asked him where he was going and he answered, "Well sir, I'm going down to see what's going on." The Colonel was unarmed so Floyd offered him his pistol, which he accepted, then continued southward toward the railroad tracks.

At the tracks, officers Tompkins and Smyser were thrilled to see him and requested orders to follow Villa's mounted men who begun fleeing back to Mexico. Slocum hesitated. "Please, Sir," Major Tomkins implored him. After a long and painful silence, the Colonel nodded consent. Smyser, Tompkins' and thirty-two Cavalry soldiers chased Villistas from the south end. Villa's bugler sounded the retreat as the National Guard's Company 1 rode in from Deming to chase the rest of them out of town.

§

Susie heard the bugler's call. The incessant hammering of machine gunfire had quieted and was replaced by faint gunshots in the distance. Voices from across the street roused her to the window. It was two men at the curio shop. They were speaking English. She stepped out into the harsh morning light then backed up and took a sombrero from the hat rack to shield her eyes. What she saw on the street was unspeakable. Across Broadway as far as she could see, lay the dead and nearly dead bodies of men, boys, and horses. Ash floated through the air like grey snowflakes and there was the strong smell of gunpowder.

One of the men called to her. "Ma'am? We are here to guard this corner. We have the street secured, Ma'am. The Mexicans are on the run."

She nodded. She wasn't looking to be rescued. She had promised to stay at the switchboard and that's what she planned to do. As she turned to go back into the shop, a bullet flew past her so close she felt the air of it on her face.

The soldier approached her carefully, he didn't hear it. "Ma'am, you okay? You're bleeding pretty bad. Were you shot?" She marveled at the question. One look at the Swiss cheese exterior of the *Courier* office should have confirmed that she'd likely been shot. "We need to get you to headquarters, over at camp."

"No, I told..." The feeble quality of her voice startled her. "I told the Captain I'd stay by the switchboard in case they call from Deming."

It took some convincing, but she agreed that she and the baby needed medical attention. The second soldier offered to stay at the switchboard. Her chaperone took a gun from a dying Mexican on the street, handed it to her, and took the baby.

"But he's still alive," she said.

"Don't worry," he said with chilling indifference. "He doesn't need it now."

In her nightgown and coat, and a sombrero on her head she carried the rifle of a dying stranger and walked through floating ash to the anguished moans of dying men and horses.

The guard herded her toward camp while chattering on about the events of the night and what he knew of the plans of his commanders. In light of the scene, she wasn't listening. They passed an incalculable number of dead, and suffering men and boys with arms outstretched pleading for help.

She asked him, "What time is it?"

"It's coming up almost seven o'clock by now. Where were you shot, Ma'am?"

"In the print shop," she answered absently.

They passed Walker's Store where Mr. Dean's body lay after failing in his attempt to help put out the fire. He was peppered with bullet holes and his throat slit straight through. Susie reached for her own throat releasing a cascade of dried blood onto her coat.

They passed the site of Ravel's storehouse and the Commercial Hotel where the charred remains of executed men still smoldered on the ground and one man in front, draped across the front seat of his touring car.

§

Soldiers patrolled the streets and collected injured citizens to bring to Headquarters for treatment. Susie was apologetic to the cavalry medic. "We're a smeared, bloody mess." He assessed Susie and Gwen's condition and got a helper to clean and wrap them well enough to hold them over until a doctor was available to treat them.

Garnet arrived at eight o'clock. The sight of his wife and baby could not have been easy to digest. "I couldn't get in," he said. "I was dodging bullets all the way into town. They were flying when I got within two miles, so I tied the horse and went ducking behind buildings to make my way here. What happened?" She had no story for him. Like all of them who had been in the thick of it, she was exhausted. He said, "Let's get you to the doctor."

A friend, Bogey, caught up with them as they were leaving. "Susie!" He stopped short when he saw her sombrero. "Oh no, was that you? In front of the print shop? Were you wearing that sombrero?" She nodded. "I shot at you!"

"What!" Garnet spat in disbelief.

"I was on the roof of the bank building. We was fightin' a good bunch of Mexicans off from getting into the arsenal. There on the bank, we was shooting everything we saw. At daylight, I saw a Mexican goin' into the print shop...what I thought was a Mexican, but it was you. I guess I shot at ya, Susie. I thought you was an intruder, so I shot."

It pained her to smile. "I felt it. It's in the door casing."

"Oh! Well, it's my good luck I missed." Bogey released an awkward laugh.

"I think it's my good luck you missed," Susie kidded him weakly.

Before he got to Headquarters, Bogey had been helping move bodies into the bank which now functioned as a morgue. He shared with Garnet and Susie what he knew of the events at the Hoover Hotel intersection. Susie took the news of Mr. Miller's death hard. Bogey told it all. It wasn't easy to tell and it wasn't easy to hear. When he got to the part about Bessie, the ground fell out from under her.

§

March 9th was a frantic, distressing day of uncovering all that had gone on in the morning hours. Susie learned that her ma and pa had hidden successfully in the adobe house and Jennie stayed there with Mrs. Dean consoling her when the news came that Mr. Dean had been killed. Maggie and John Bliss were far enough out they only heard the disruption from a distance. As townspeople emerged from hiding, the uninjured joined the soldiers in finding the missing and helping the injured.

A train conductor found Milton James by accident at the railroad tracks. He was delirious, bloody, and begging for water. He had dragged himself there trying to escape the battle. He saw Bessie pulled into the Hoover and he believed she made it. His sister, Myrtle, was found shot in the thigh and unconscious by a stack of railroad ties. They brought her and several others to the Hoover Hotel which was now operating as an infirmary. Susie and Gwen spent the afternoon there. Bullet fragments still in her neck were too dangerous to remove. The doctor took out what he could, then left it to volunteers to go to work on removing the several hundred shards of embedded glass, one by one, from her and baby Gwen.

While they were tended to, Garnet assessed the damage at the Print Shop. The walls and floor coated in the blood of his wife and baby painted a grisly picture of what he had missed the night before. That he was spared the trauma sent a pain to his gut. He was unsure whether it was guilt or envy. He boarded up the windows, cleaned up the best he could, then took an inventory of supplies. There was certain to be an onslaught of news traffic and he wanted to be prepared.

§

Looking out the window of the *Courier* office, Garnet noticed a young man waving at a Dodge Touring car coming in his direction. The driver parked in front which sent the young man rushing to the car's passenger side to assist. Out stepped a rather tall, mustached man in an army uniform of khaki wool trousers, high boots and spurs. He adjusted his Montana-peaked hat and followed the excited young man toward the newspaper office. The driver waited. Before they could knock, G.E. was at the door.

"How can I help you?" He assumed they had come to provide a story for the paper.

"Hello sir." He held out his hand. "I'm J.R. Galusha. Is this where Susan Parks lives, sir?"

"Yes." G.E. shifted his posture to study the impressive man waiting patiently to Galusha's right.

"This is..." J.R. Galusha held out his hands, palms up, then stepped aside to present the commander, "U.S. Brigadier General John J. Pershing, just arrived from Fort Bliss."

G.E. unconsciously extended himself upward not sure whether to salute or offer a handshake. "G.E. Parks, uh, General Pershing. I'm the publisher and editor of this town's weekly newspaper."

"A pleasure." General Pershing returned his handshake and Garnet stepped back to make way for the men to enter. He was unable to hide his thrill in having addressed the General whose reputation for service during and since the Philippine War had made him a bit of a celebrity. "I assume Susan Parks is your wife? I am hopeful that I might meet her, is she at home?"

"Yes, she is. In the back." Both intrigued and confused, Garnet led him to the back room where Susie was taking slow steps to pack for an indefinite stay at the schoolhouse. All women and children were ordered to stay in the protection of the large brick building until further notice.

Garnet's voice startled her and she jumped. "Susie. This is General John J. Pershing here to see you." The General removed his hat and took a step into the room.

Susie met his eyes, started toward him and tried to reach out a hand but the bandages hindered her and he graciously called her off. "You mustn't strain yourself. I've come to assess the situation here in Columbus but I wanted to stop here first to pay you my respects."

"Oh, that's nice. Thank you." Susie was not aware of the stature of the man and her relaxed manner made Garnet tense.

"I understand it was an eventful night for you who were in town." Susie nodded. Garnet noted that he had not been in town. "Captain Brock briefed me on much of what went on. He said that it was you who made the call during the battle. I want to thank you." Susie smiled appreciatively. This was news to Garnet and he stood frozen in place. "The advantage you promoted in alerting us cannot be overemphasized. Because of your call, Captain Brock got word to me at Fort Bliss before he rode out. I was in touch with Washington in good time which allowed us to begin plans for a response to the attack on this town and our nation."

She shook her head abjectly. "I should have called sooner."

General Pershing raised his hand. "Oh no. Sharp thinking and decisive action is a rare commodity in battle. You kept your head, kept yourself and your baby alive, and you made the call to the outside for help. No more could have been asked of you. You were a soldier. Do not underestimate the import of what you have done for your country, ma'am." He thanked them both and moved toward the door in quick, decisive strides. He was in town for a purpose and this stop was clearly not on his preplanned agenda. J.R. Galusha skipped ahead to reach the passenger door before the General tried to do it himself. The driver put the car in reverse and they rode west to camp.

Garnet took a moment to incorporate the experience. That envy he'd wrestled with earlier came up again, this time accompanied with a combination of admiration and annoyance. He turned to her and, in all seriousness, he said, "I thought I told you to lie on the floor."

§

In the days that followed there was a change in Columbus. South of town, desert winds sent abandoned clothes, pillowcases, and paper money ambling without direction. Jewelry hung from snake brush and briars marking the path the looters took on their way out of town.

The community tried to pull together and organize themselves responsibly. The schoolhouse was packed with women and children. Every civilian man was armed and took shifts to patrol the streets whether they could handle a gun or not. Susie found it ridiculous that some of these men, who couldn't shoot a blanket off a clothesline, were guarding women who were far better shots. She shared a section of the common area with her ma, Maggie, and the babies. They had to rely on Garnet, John Bliss, and Pa to bring in news from the outside. The arrangement made her restless. "This is no good. I can't just sit here. Tell 'em I'll take a shift." Of course, even if the commanding officers had agreed to put a woman in the rotation, Susie's bandaged condition made her an unlikely recruit. She would have to stay put until orders changed.

John Bliss embraced his authority and checked in often. "They're fixing to gather up wood to burn the bodies." He said some folks were helping themselves to swords, rifles, pendants, and crucifixes off the dead to keep as souvenirs.

Word on the happenings outside revealed a darker side of the changed little town. Major Tompkins' wife admitted her thoughts to a group of women. "I passed any number of dead Mexicans. They were lying all through the town and, I'll tell you, I looked at their shattered bodies with only an unwomanly joy." Susie couldn't go there, but she understood the darkness that fear and helplessness could provoke.

The retired founder of the *Columbus Courier*, Mr. Mosley, wrote, "Mexican prisoners were just taken out of camp and turned loose. Our citizens were informed of what was to be done and they shot them as they fled."

To her ma, Susie asked almost pleading, "Will we become hard? This is awful. What about our friends here? They're not safe."

Jennie tried to offer comfort, but she had seen it before. "I don't know. People get scared and they only see red. Fear makes people do shameful things." Mexican residents were being questioned regarding suspicions that they may have been informers or sympathized with Villa. It would be hard for a while for Mexican families living in town.

Garnet did his part to guard the area and assist in the cleanup while gathering as much intelligence as he could. He expected to have a pivotal role as the town's central source of information at this critical time. When he wasn't on guard duty, he went to the depot to greet reporters coming in from across the country. "Welcome all. G.E. Parks here of the *Columbus Courier*. Welcome to Columbus!" He engaged in greetings and handshakes, provided the latest news, and corrected misinformation. "On the list of the deceased, you'll want to correct the name of the hotel proprietor A.L. Ritchie to W.T. Ritchie. That's his name. And where Milton James is reported dead. That's false. He has been injured, quite severely, and is being cared for at the hospital in El Paso." Newsmen formed a semi-circle around him, scratching away at their notepads as he spoke. He intended to be a reliable, firsthand source of news for his colleagues.

That role was short-lived, however. The officer in charge made an announcement to the Press. "We've got a problem with this flow of news leaking intelligence on the slightest movements of our troops. This won't do, so orders for censorship of all communications have come down from Major General Funston in Washington. We will take charge of the telegraph office and watch all automobile routes out of town. No print news until you hear from us."

Garnet stepped forward. "How is that sir? No news? But I have advertisers with ads that are paid for and notices that are required…by law."

"That shouldn't be a problem. Print that, just no news. Be on alert. If the order is evaded in any way, the next order will be martial law." He slapped G.E. on the back. "We don't want that now, do we? Just the advertisements until further notice."

Garnet was flattened. He thanked the captain for the information and left the depot dejected. He passed his friends transporting bodies to the woodpile and decided to lend a hand. There was no breeze. The stagnant air intensified the drudgery of loading and unloading dead bodies. Also, bodies of Villistas shot while fleeing still lay scattered across the desert and they were getting ripe. The stink of kerosine, rotting corpses, and burning flesh fed the dark underbelly of a scared and changed little town.

§

Embers still glowed at the pyre on Friday when the ladies and children were let out of the schoolhouse for a special sendoff at the depot. They'd planned a gathering to pay tribute to the eight soldiers and ten civilians who died, some of whom were leaving on this day in caskets. Despite the lingering odor, the attendees felt the relief of breathing outside air and what they thought was the freedom to gather safely together again.

The ceremony began then, as if it were a cruel joke, was interrupted by an orderly riding in from the west screaming frantically. "Fly for your lives, the Mexicans are coming!" Sure enough, an ominous dust cloud was seen from the south and it sent the crowd running in every direction with no place to hide. It was total mayhem.

It was also a false alarm. It was a harmless dust devil that came and went but it stirred up a township primed for panic. They took some time to collect themselves then regathered in front of the depot. Eleven caskets lined the tracks with Colonel Slocum at one end of the line and the Mexican General Pablo Bertani at the other. The band played "Nearer My God to Thee". Captain Lutz's voice trembled as he paid tribute to the men who died in the defense of Columbus and its citizens. Caskets and the injured were loaded into the cars. There was a cry of "All aboard" as the train pulled out and the trumpeters played Taps.

That same day Bessie was laid to rest in the Valley Heights Cemetery. Susie faced her loss with the people who loved Bessie most except, of course, for Milton who was still at the hospital in El Paso. She stood with Ethel and held her as steady as she could. To Maggie she tried to put it in words. "It's all changed, Maggie. I don't see anything the same anymore. It's like the world we know has died. Just two days ago I was happy. I felt lucky. One of the best things was that Bessie and I were both having our babies in July. Now, my friend lies there in a box with her baby who will never be born. What do we do now?" Susie had always believed if something needed doing, she would be ready to do it. This was a demoralizing kind of helplessness because Bessie was gone and there was nothing that could be done to bring her back.

5

President Wilson wanted Villa and he threw all the force the U.S. had available to that end. The operation to find and capture Villa was named, "The Punitive Expedition" and it was to be directed and executed by General John "Blackjack" Pershing.

A steady stream of soldiers and horses flowed into town by train and by highway. An impressive fleet of Dodge Brothers Model 30-35 touring cars and Jeffery Armored trucks rolled in like giant armadillos. They were the first vehicles ever used in combat. Also, first ever used in combat were the Curtiss JN3 airplanes flown and maintained by the ninety-six men of the First AeroSquadron. The 13th Cavalry set up a city of tents south of the train depot to hold troops that more than quadrupled the size of Columbus.

While fear from the attack sent many folks out of town, the notoriety it brought attracted even more. There were the soldiers, of course, but also gamblers, bootleggers, prostitutes, and tourists. New businesses popped up, many operating out of tents and temporary structures. Large generators were installed in the Crystal Theater to fill the increase in demand for electricity. News reporters flowed in and out of town and used the *Courier* as a base.

G.E. had since recovered from the disappointment of his censure and Susie marveled at the effect all the hoopla had on his energy. He darted around town, back and forth from the telegraph office ensuring that the story of the Columbus Raid stay vital. The telephone exchange had more than it could handle with communications streaming in from across the country, so the Deming Telephone Company sent reinforcements. When the press got wind of Susie's call to the National Guard, she became a central focus for reporters. This had Garnet bubbling over.

"This is it, Susie. This town is exploding with us at its center."

Susie refuted. "It seems to me it's the Colonel at the center and I'm sure he'd rather not. I overheard Floyd Wright on the exchange."

"Slocum?" Garnet didn't like being the second to hear news in town.

"They're teasing him is all," she said. "Floyd said that the Colonel woke up from his bed and heard the shooting. I guess he and Mrs. Slocum have separate bedrooms so he called to her from his room. 'Mother, what a hailstorm.' and she answered him back, 'Can't you tell the difference between hail and bullets?'"

"That sounds like someone's spinning a tale." G.E. was speculative. "Folks have it in for the Colonel right now."

Susie nodded and giggled. "Funny though, isn't it?"

"It is but I'm telling you, those newsmen outside don't want to talk to Slocum. They want to talk to you. You've found yourself at the center of this story, Susie. *Brave Little Woman*, they're calling you don't you know."

"I don't know what I'm supposed to say. What do they want? They seem to want me to tell a better story than I've got. Like I was on the rooftop like Bogey, picking off Villistas with a Mauser rifle."

"You could have if you'd wanted to. You're a good enough shot," he bragged. "They are asking about you seeing Villa."

"Oh no, see. I don't know. It might not have been him." All the attention uncovered an uncharacteristic shyness in her.

He put an arm around her. "You know it was him. You've seen enough pictures to know and that woman, Maud Wright, the one they kidnapped? She confirmed that he came into town." G.E. made the final pitch. "We're at the center of a national story, Susie. Columbus is one of the biggest little cities in the USA right now. They're in the shop now and they want to talk to you." He held out his hand.

"All right." She pulled herself up, still wobbling a bit unsteady from her injuries as well as her bulging belly.

Garnet called the reporters over. "Gentlemen, Mrs. Parks is available for an interview."

The reporters pulled out pads and pencils and began firing questions. She did her best while Garnet moved through the space orchestrating the exchange of information.

"Were you scared?" One asked.

"I don't know." She laughed dismissively. "I was dumb...or numb...I don't know whether I was scared or not. You don't know when you're scared like that. You're not thinking about being scared."

"You called Deming. Why not El Paso?"

"There was no connection," she answered with confidence. "Villa's people cut the lines to El Paso."

"Oh. So, you made the call."

"I did once I realized. What would I do, nothing? I don't think there was anybody in town on that night that just did nothing." She heard her own words and a picture of Colonel Slocum, who had been taking a lot of criticism since the day of the raid, appeared in her mind. She smiled, and one reporter said out loud what she was thinking.

"Even Colonel Slocum?" She was rescued by the next question.

"You say you saw Villa outside your window?"

"Well, when I was standing by the window looking out, about five feet from me was a uniformed man. From what little Spanish I know it sounded like he was giving orders. There was a bugler and a little farther off was a drummer. It might have been Villa. He looked like I've seen in pictures. And there was the way they came dashing up to him every minute or so for orders. I'd say I was fairly sure it was him." Nodding heads across the group sent the message that she had given them what they wanted.

On their way out the door, Garnet did his due diligence connecting with each one and making sure they had the essential facts. It would be a while before Susie was fully herself again, but it was clear that Garnet was born for this.

§

Garnet had given an interview of his own. A reporter named James Hooper filled six pages on the Raid for the April issue of *Collier's Magazine*. The article gave an interesting glimpse into what may have kept Garnet from getting to Susie and Gwen the morning of the Raid.

In the *Collier's* April 15, 1916 edition, Hooper reports that Garnet made it to Columbus in about three-quarters of an hour after he got the call from Susie. Hooper wrote, "But, of course, the town was not easily entered. The Villistas were swarming all about it and in it, under the fire's glare." He wrote that G.E. left Sam, "in an arroyo, then began working his way toward the exchange." This meant toward Susie and the telephone switchboard where, "fifteen minutes later he found his wife and child gone." He went on to say that Susie and Gwen had been rescued in the heat of the battle which, of course, was untrue as was his report of the timing. After all, Susie had called Garnet at the start of the attack, about 4:20 am. If he loaded up Sam, rode and got to the *Courier* office in an hour, that would have put him there no later than 5:30 am. Susie and Gwen were still there and remained there for another hour with Villistas well on the run by 6:45 after sunrise. Garnet didn't get to Headquarters until 8:00 am. As Susie read the article, she knew something wasn't adding up. She turned the page as the article continued with Hooper crediting Garnet with an act of what he viewed as journalistic integrity. Hooper wrote:

> *Collier's*, April 15, 1916
> "What did you do then?" I asked Parks when I had drawn this story out of him. "Oh," he said, "I telephoned the story to the El Paso papers, and then I went to the camp to my wife." G. E. Parks, editor of the *Columbus Courier*, is some newspaperman.

A call to El Paso would help explain the lag in time between Garnet's arrival in Columbus and his arrival at Camp. But there was no line from Columbus to El Paso. Susie had tried. Still, the idea that Garnet had prioritized getting the story out to the press over seeing his wife and child impressed Mr. Hooper so that was the angle he took. Susie was working through the effects the event still had on her nerves and she chose not to question Garnet on the details.

Nights were the hardest on her following the raid. She would have sudden fits of anxiety, shoot up in the dark, and dart wildly across the room. Garnet learned not to wake her after he took a hit to the gut and shoulder a few times. He learned instead to wait for a pause and then gently coax her back to bed. During the day, his optimism was a tonic to her and to their friends in town who were still struggling to find a way back to normal. She was grateful for his positivity and the hope it kept alive in her.

The Generals finally lifted the reporting ban on the *Courier* and G.E. had more stories stored up than space to print them. The tagline for the *Courier*'s returning issue:

> *The Columbus Courier*, March 24, 1916
> The Future Has Never Looked Brighter For This Section Than It Does Today

G.E. was back at the breakfast table with his stack of papers and his cigarette burning in a saucer beside him. "It looks like *The Deming*

Headlight has bought a Merganthaler Linotype." Holding the front page of the *Headlight* up for her to see, "Look at the quality of that print. I think it's time we get one." The Merganthaler Linotype was the state-of-the-art typesetting machine of the time. It required a mortgage to own. For a small weekly paper like the *Courier*, the idea was ambitious. "With so many new businesses popping up in town, we can pay for it with new advertising. I bet we can build the *Courier* to compete with the *Headlight*. What do you say?"

She drank in his intoxicating optimism. "I'd like to get back to work. You think we can manage it?"

He nodded. "I thought you might say that. Don't say another word. I'll see about putting in our order." Then he added, "Also, I wrote to the president."

"Of the *Headlight*?" Now she was kidding, there was no president of the *Headlight*. "Oh no, Garnet, what did you do?"

"President Wilson, since you ask, of the United States. He plans to come this way to visit the Elephant Butte Dam, so I wrote to him and invited him to come to Columbus. I didn't tell you because, well obviously, look how you quiver." He grinned and shrugged at his cleverness. "In any event, they responded and said they would be glad to keep us in mind 'in connection with any itinerary'."

"Garnet, you hate him. If he comes, you might say something horrible to insult him. You will, I'm sure of it." Garnet's fantastical thinking sometimes fooled her into forgetting that there was truly no chance of President Wilson "stopping by."

"Whatever gets us in the papers, Susie." He scanned the *Deming Graphic* as he spoke. "Well, look at this. Here you are in the *Graphic*. This one looks good."

Deming Graphic, May 26, 1916
BRAVE TELEPHONE OPERATOR
The heroine Mrs. G.E. Parks, the telephone operator at Columbus, New Mexico reminds us that American women are still the daughters and partners of the indomitable pioneers.

"They call you a heroine."
Susie asked, "What does *indomitable* mean?"
"It means *steadfast...determined.*"
"How do you spell it?" He gave her a wink and let the cigarette between his lips bounce as he read silently.

"Oh, they say that the Hoover Hotel was the first building to be looted and set on fire. Well, they got that wrong. One wonders if they even listen when they're given the facts. They go on:

'With her baby clasped to her breast, she clung to the switchboard even while Mauser bullets from the rifles of the raiders tore through the thin walls of the telephone station and showered her with flying glass from broken windowpanes. Through all the excitement and fierce fighting in the street, as well as conflagration within a stone's throw...'

"*Conflagration?*"

"*Fire...*

...a stone's throw of where she sat, she remained at the switchboard with the child in her arms and sent out the only calls of help that were sent out from the little border town during the Villa raid. It was she who got in touch with Capt. A.W. Brock of Deming and his men were the very first from the outside to come to the aid of the stricken town.'

He got up. "We'll put this one up." He tacked the piece to the wall to add to his collection of clippings, then collected his things. "You've got to get comfortable in the spotlight, Susie. There are benefits, but it takes initiative. And initiative is exactly what I have, so I am off. There are hands to shake and prominent halls to penetrate."

There he goes. She couldn't really wrap her head around his pursuits. If she could build it, hunt it, or fix it, that made sense to her, but he was a man living in the world of ideas and what drove him was intangible. "All right, you do that. I'm going to Ma's."

§

At the Gregg house, her ma and Maggie were at the table sorting news clippings. Susie nudged Gwen over toward Clarence who was playing on a blanket. She peered over Maggie's shoulder. A photo of her in an Indian costume stared back at her.

"What is that? Where did they get that picture? Where are my arms? Where did you find this?" Jennie wasn't sure which question to answer first. The clippings were from northwest newspapers that Eva sent through the mail. Eva was proud of her little sister's sudden notoriety, so she took it upon herself to call the *Seattle Daily Times* and offered them her version of the story. She provided them with a photo of Susie taken before a costume party. It made the rounds to several newspapers in the western states. Susie was mortified.

Maggie tried to help. "Susie, now the article is very flattering. Listen." Maggie read while covering a giggle.

"Heroine at twenty and girl wife of many adventures…"

Susie interrupted. "Girl wife? What's a girl-wife?"

Maggie laughed and continued: "…is Mrs. G.E. Parks, night telephone operator here who remained at her post, sent a warning broadcast, during the dreadful night when Villa and his bandits committed their historic outrage. With a one-year-old baby in her arms Mrs. Parks, formally Miss Susie Gregg of Kirkland, Washington, sat in the darkened exchange and telephoned the news of the raid to the neighboring town of Deming.

Many shots were fired through the windows of the building, and once the raiders entered the place, leaving because they thought it deserted."

Susie interrupted again. "Entered the place? No one entered the place."

"A life of pioneering has made Mrs. Parks an exceptionally courageous woman. In 1909 she made a brief trip alone through Mexico, returning to Columbus two and a half years ago to marry G.E. Parks."

"What? You've got to be kidding. Nineteen nine, I was fourteen!" Susie held her face in her hands.

Maggie continued. "On two occasions she frightened Mexican outlaws away by firing at them with her revolver."

Horrified, "I did not!"

"Another time she was awakened by a huge tarantula in her bedroom and killed it with a single shot. Her friends say she does not know the meaning of fear."

She couldn't bear it. "Did Eva tell them that or do they just make it up?"

Jennie tried to reason with her. "It's unimportant. Nobody believes what they read in the papers anyway."

Susie redirected her annoyance. "Well, thanks Ma. You know we own a newspaper, don't you?"

Jennie pivoted. "I'm just saying that I'm proud of you and what you did. Do you know Mrs. Elliot said her granddaughter thinks you are the bravest person she knows? Not Lieutenant Castleman. You."

"That's sweet, really." Susie shook her head. "What Castleman and his soldiers did can't be measured, that's certain. But maybe a little girl looks at me and sees herself." Then she flashed them a cocky grin.

"Besides, I did shoot the tarantula."

Her ma laughed. "Yes, you did."

Maggie added, "That spider didn't have a chance against you."

§

Columbus Courier, August 25, 1916
Telephone Operator Will Be Honored Mrs. L Bradford Prince Will Present Tribute for Bravery During the Villa Raid. Mrs. L.B. Prince of Santa Fe, wife of former territorial governor of New Mexico and State regent of the DAR, will be here Sunday, August 27 for the purpose of presenting to Mrs. G.E. Parks, the heroin of the Villa raid on Columbus, a material tribute for her bravery. The event is to be at the Crystal Theater right in the heart of Columbus. The gift is to be made on behalf of the Daughters of the American Revolution.

Mrs. Prince desires that as many of the members of the Silver City Chapter make the trip to Columbus Sunday as possible. Several motor parties are now being organized for the trip and Mrs. Ashenfelter expects to attend. Col. E.C. Abbot of the first Regiment New Mexico National Guard will have the troops on dress parade for the occasion.

Garnet Junior arrived on the 3rd of July making the Parkses a family of four. They didn't know that a New York City socialite and wife of the former governor of New Mexico, Mrs. Prince, had been preparing for four months to shine a spotlight on Susie: Heroine of the Villa Raid on Columbus. She planned to come to Columbus to celebrate her in August.

On the proud day, Mrs. Prince arrived with her chaperone Chaplain Vincent of the New Mexico National Guard. Susie was in the back nursing Garnet Junior before she turned him over to her ma who would watch him during the ceremony. Nursing wasn't Susie's favorite activity as a mother. She did it dutifully, but the sitting still of it always felt tedious to her. Not like Maggie who loved those quiet times with little Clarence. Once, Susie watched a mama cat just get up and go with her greedy little kittens hanging on and dangling from her underbelly and she thought, "Yup, I know how you feel."

Garnet borrowed Mr. Elliot's horse and carriage so they might arrive at the theater with a little style. Susie lifted Gwen into the carriage and the wind nearly carried her away. Warm, gusty winds were so much a part of Gwen's life she viewed them like an amusement ride. "Weeeee."

Susie smiled at Gwen's delight toward Garnet but his expression was bland, almost brooding. He snapped the reins and set out to get them there early for pictures. Susie fought the wind for control of the wad of paper that was her speech. She was worried about her dress. "This is all I have to wear, Garnet. It's all that I can fit in since the baby." Pushing on the pleats to work out the wrinkles, "It's no good, is it? Maybe I should get a coat." He shrugged, disinterested. "Garnet, what is bothering you?"

"Sorry. Don't worry about it. Practice your speech."

Mrs. Prince and her chaperone were waiting outside the theater. To Susie's relief, Mrs. Prince wore a bulky coat and a flower and plume-laden hat held tightly to her head with multiple pins. Not the height of New York fashion that Susie expected, but she was a lovely person who embraced the three of them like they were her own. A reporter from the *Silver City Independent* took photos and conducted a quick interview. He and Garnet stayed outside talking printing and publishing while Susie, Mrs. Prince, and Gwen went inside to the theater.

The 13th Cavalry band were setting up as people from town and distinguished guests of Mrs. Prince began filling the thousand-seat theater. Susie kept Gwen occupied by making a game of trying to spot someone they recognized. She pointed at Garnet standing in the aisle. "There's Papa!"

Gwen pointed at him. "Papa!" He sent back a salute.

Far to the back Susie pointed. "There's Grandma, Grandpa, Aunt Maggie, Uncle John Bliss, and little brother. Oh, there goes your Uncle John Bliss chasing Clarence." Gwen burst into a happy giggle.

The band opened with a lively tune, *In the Park*, then Mayor Dabney approached the podium. Seated in front was a line of fancy ladies wearing various versions of Edwardian hats. Susie decided they must be the *sisters* of Mrs. Prince, members the Daughters of the American Revolution. The mayor spoke the names of the dead and asked for a moment of prayer. Colonel E.C. Abbot made an address and then introduced Mrs. Prince. She began:

"This moment marks the culmination of the thoughts, the hopes, and the efforts, which have filled the period since my heart was touched by the relation of events of the night, or early morning, of the ninth of March that never to be forgotten reign of terror here, in what is now the peaceful little city of Columbus. A chivalrous spirit was aroused, and I determined that recognition in some form should be given to this brave woman." Mrs. Prince made a broad gesture toward Susie. "Who, although alone with her little child," she gestured again toward Gwen, "did not cry for help, did not leave the house and desert her duty at the telephone; who had the forethought not to light a lamp, nor, in fact, to make a sign nor a sound of any kind, which might attract the wild and savage bandits, bent only on theft, arson, murder and all other crimes of bestial character." *Goodness* thought Susie.

Mrs. Prince went on to describe the weight of organizing the tribute and that went on for quite a while. "Weeks passed and ran into months before my purpose was accomplished. Being in New York at that time, well-nigh three thousand miles away from the scenes which have made Columbus famous and 'far from wars alarm,' it seemed as if it might be an uncertain effort on my part, but friends rallied to my assistance..." She continued and went into great detail about what that assistance looked like then somehow found her way back to the focus of her speech.

"The main thing is that we are assembled to do honor to this brave American girl." Again, her large arm made a sweeping gesture toward Susie. "This is intended, not only as a tribute to her, but as an attention to the entire city of Columbus which suffered so terribly at the hands of that border ruffian Francisco Villa and his bandits. I have brought a substantial recognition of her heroism and I have come that it might be presented to her here on the very scene of her devotion to all of her townspeople in endeavoring to summon aid." Her words promised that she was nearing a conclusion but then no, there was the subject of the flag. "But we must also remember that we are here to render homage, not only to our fair Columbus heroine but to the flag of our country."

Uh oh, Susie noticed bodies below shifting in their seats and she whispered in Gwen's ear. "She'll have a lot to say about the flag, I bet."

She did indeed and then boldly threw her opposite arm out wide toward the American flag and held it strong waiting for the audience to erupt in applause, which they did. She then launched into an amazing tangent that recounted Francis Scott Key and his experience at the bombardment of Fort McHenry. On she went about love of country, love of one's native land, and then quite dramatically, nearly singing acapella:

"*Embrace it, oh mothers, and heroes shall grow,*
while its colors blush warm on your bosoms of snow..."

Susie solidified a smile onto her face like it was her only job. Her nerves wound tighter with each of Mrs. Prince's rhymes, but then low and behold Mrs. Prince said, "Assist me with both your patience and your interest while we pretend that it is Christmas time, and that merry old Santa Claus has come to fill the stockings of the good little girl."

Susie pointed to herself and mouthed the words, *Is that me?* Mrs. Prince waved Susie toward her and directed Chaplain Vincent to bring up a 46-piece set of sterling silverware. Susie held Gwen by the hand as Mrs. Prince presented a watch and gold chain. She read the inscription:

"Mrs. S. A. Parks in recognition of heroic devotion to duty,
Columbus, New Mexico, March 9th, 1916.
From Mary C. Prince and friends in New York"

To Gwen, Mrs. Prince presented a silver cup lined with gold and an inscription:

To Gwenyth Parks. Commemorating your mother's
heroism at Columbus, N.M., March 9th, 1916.
*   —from Mary C. Prince*

The audience applauded uproariously at the quality of the gifts and the generosity of Mrs. Prince and her unnamed friends in the Edwardian hats. Blood rushed to Susie's face and emotion seized her throat. It was time for her to speak.

The arms that Mrs. Prince wielded so liberally before now guided Susie to the podium. Gwen toddled beside her. Susie pulled the paper out from her belt and straightened it on the platform. Dreading the focus that was to be on her words she cleared her throat and began. "I am grateful to be here able to..." As luck would have it, the whistle of the evening train blew so hard and loud it shook the theater. To Susie, it was a friend that had come to her rescue. She read the rest of her prepared words delighted to be drowned out by the train and, as it faded, "... Thank you, Mrs. Prince. I am grateful to you and all your kindness and the kindness of your friends." The crowd applauded and some stood. The event was over.

They stayed at the theater greeting attendees to the closing music of the 13th Cavalry Band. The night ended with a reception at the Burton's house where Garnet and Susie saw Mrs. Prince off and then excused themselves early to put the babies to bed. Garnet returned the Elliot's carriage and walked home.

He entered the Shop still prickly and Susie confronted him. "You're upset about something. Did I do something wrong?"

From the far side of the room, he arranged books and papers that didn't need arranging. "No Susie. You've done everything right. Just ask anyone. Just pick up a paper."

"Pick up a paper? What do you mean? Was something in the paper?"

"There's nothing but you in the paper and you seem pretty comfortable with it all."

On that he was right that she'd decided to stop resisting the attention. She knew it would fade and complaining about it was just a different kind of fuss. "Comfortable? What are you saying? You're being a baby."

That hurt. She had never rebuked him like that before. It took him a moment. "I think you've forgotten what we were doing here. Let's face it, Susie, you always find a way to be all right. I'm working to build the paper and set us up. You're fine with or without it. Fine with or without me."

"That's not true. How can you say that?"

"Because you are. Because the celebrations and the babies and your family have taken your attention and here we are still only a four-page paper. We were starting to grow it together before all this. I'm thinking about our future, but it seems I'm alone."

Tears welled up and her heart pounded. She was under attack and flashed on images of the night, crawling in the dark with the noise of the raid in the street. "Like I was alone, Garnet? Like that?" He turned away feigning distraction. "I was alone, but didn't I call you? Because I wasn't all right at all and then I had to read..." She had planned to take all the questions she had about his late arrival that day to her grave. Now he provoked her. Still, she wasn't sure she wanted to hear his answer.

"What?" He challenged. "What? Read what?"

"I had to read in Collier's a full month later, that you were in no hurry to get to us...that you called in your story before you even came to me and Gwen?" Spoken out loud, she realized she was admitting to him and to herself that she doubted his concern for them that day and she couldn't stop her tears. "Why were you so late? That interview said you were in town at 6:30. We were still in the shop." He didn't answer and now she was pretty sure his answer would only make things worse. She broke the silence. "Collier's called you '*some newspaperman*' for calling in your story. I've got news for you, Garnet, there was no line out to El Paso. They cut the line."

She had him, though she still didn't know what she had on him. He had been untruthful and she had been letting him get away with it. Now he stared away blankly knowing he wasn't going to win this fight. If he dropped it, maybe she would too. He scratched his head. "All right, all right. We should take some time. Take stock. Maybe we need to spend some time together. We'll borrow the Dean's car and take a drive, just us. What do you think?"

There was relief in the prospect of dropping it, but now the question was out there. How could she pretend it wasn't? Maybe there was a compromise. "Will you tell me then, why you said what you said to Collier's? Will you tell me who you called?"

"I will. We'll talk about all that, just the two of us." He reached out to her and she started toward him, but Garnet Junior began stirring from the cradle ready to be fed. Time passed and things didn't ever slow down enough to take that drive or to get the story straight on that morning, the Collier's interview or the telephone line to El Paso. The unanswered question was filed away and they moved on with their lives.

6

Other than the military presence in town and the sporadic residual pain in Susie's neck, remnants of Villa and his raid began to fade into the background of their daily lives. A symbol of Garnet and Susie's rededication to their goals and dreams arrived in the form of an elephant-sized wooden crate with the words: *Columbus Courier – Columbus, New Mexico* stenciled on one side, and *Merganthaler Linotype* stenciled on the other.

Friends in town helped get it into the Print Shop. Their willingness to take on the enormous load was a testament to their affection for G.E. They had to remove the door jamb and bring it inside in sections. They left wiping the sweat from their faces. Garnet expressed his gratitude from the doorway. "Thank you, fellas. I couldn't have done it without you."

Gwen jumped in and out of the wooden crates while G.E. rubbed out fingerprints with a dust rag.

"What do you think, Sister?" Sister was his name for Gwen since the birth of the baby. It was evident that the machine didn't impress her nearly as much as the boxes it came in. "Susie! Come on in and take a look."

Susie stood at the doorway taking it in.

"They're calling it the industry's dominant printing machine of the twentieth century."

Susie said, "It is dominant. It really fills the space."

"That's because it does a lot of work." He patted it on the side. "We'll be able to replace all but the printing press with this workhorse." Garnet checked under the body of the machine like it was the hood of a car. "We'll grow the paper, and it will pay for itself before we know it." Signaling for her to come closer, "Now, look here. This is how it works. You press the keys which sends the characters down into this gutter, here, and the hot metal is sent through the wheel and casts the line of type... here. It even adjusts the spaces to justify our columns. Susie, it is just going to change the whole way we do business."

The challenge of learning the machine was invigorating but proved more complicated than he anticipated. Besides the learning curve attached to operating the linotype itself, Garnet Junior was now crawling and he had a fascination for the heating element. Plus, Gwen was three, a climber, and getting more creative about drawing her Papa's attention. She'd shimmy up his leg, plant herself on his shoulders, and pound on his head. "Go horsey go." It was time to separate shop and home, so they found a little house just off East Boundary, a short walk from the print shop.

On moving day, Susie had the doors and windows wide open. She was unpacking crates and noticed a man standing at the foot of her porch who held a striking resemblance to Garnet. He was in a green New York-style suit, a derby hat and he carried a suitcase in each hand. "Hello, ma'am." He took his hat off and bowed low. "Is this the Parks house? I was directed to this place by a helpful lady at the depot who said Garnet Parks lives here."

Susie emptied her hands and approached him for a better look. "I'm sorry, you could not look more like my husband." Gwen pulled at her from behind.

"You must be Susie." He squatted to meet Gwen face to face. "Which would make you Gwen." Gwen shivered with embarrassment and hid behind her mama. He offered a handshake. "I'm G.A., Gurna Albert Parks."

Susie was thrilled to set eyes on a genuine Parks and she threw her arms around him. Surprise visits didn't faze her. The Greggs never told anyone when they were coming. "Let me clean up and I'll walk you to the shop to see Garnet."

She led him up Broadway with Garnet Junior on her hip and Gwen double stepping along between them. G.E. jumped up at the sight of his brother. "For crying out loud!" He seized him up and held him in a warm hug. "Well, this is something to celebrate." He turned to his assistant, "J.B. Smith, this is my brother Gurna. G.A. say hello to John." J.B. was now living in the *Courier* office back room as part of his pay. G.A. returned a friendly nod and shook his hand. "What do you say I show you around? J.B., do you think you can handle the shop for the afternoon while I take my brother out?" J.B. obliged so they stepped out.

Garnet led the way with G.A., and Susie, baby Garnet, and Gwen followed behind. Garnet couldn't mask his pride while showing off Columbus and he didn't try. He pointed out their favorite spots like the B.O.B., the Crystal, and the half-built Columbus Theater and recapped the highlights of the infamous Raid. "But of course, Susie can tell you more about that." They passed a grocery with a Near Beer ad in the window which sent G.E. into a rant. "Now here's a hitch we've had in this town. Our Mayor Dabney has it in his mind to dry up Columbus to the extent that not even Near Beer should be sold here. We approved an ordinance at the Commerce Club that imitation and Near Beer should continue to be sold as long as it's taxed, but this fellow has an aversion to money. We're trying to grow this town but Dabney has us hobbled. It's infuriating."

"Ho, ho!" G.A. spoke to Susie. "Our brother Rex would sure turn your mayor on his head. Rex is a wild one. At just twenty, he's put on a bash in every bar east of the Mississippi." Susie looked confused. "I'm saying he's a drinker. There's not a mayor or a woman who can tame him."

"Rex is full of adventure, all right," Garnet acknowledged. "He does nothing halfway. He'll do something big someday, just you wait."

They walked over the tracks and south from the depot overlooking the ten-acre tent city. Garnet held G.A.'s shoulder and spoke with reverence. "All of this is Pershing's project. He and the troops are still in Mexico, but he'll be withdrawing soon. These accommodations, these tents, will house his 'helpers' as he calls them." Gwen stood in front of her Papa quietly, with her arms stretched out. He picked her up. "They are his Chinese and Mexican aides, scouts, and cooks. The Major-General wants them taken care of after the Expedition is over. What we'll do, the Commerce Club, the Red Cross, and the B.O.B., is coordinate a homecoming celebration for the soldiers and welcome his refugees."

G.A. was fascinated. "Pershing is withdrawing. Why?"

"By my estimation, it's about priorities. It's only a matter of time till American forces are called to the war in Europe. Wilson's going to want to send his best General and military equipment or send none at all. Villa is just one man but in pursuit of him they've tested the best tanks, the best Aerosquadron, and the best soldiers, so it's time to use them to the advantage of the allies on the front. With the power of this force, the allies will be unbeatable."

"There you are. I'll admit, Garnet, I wondered if you weren't overstating it in your letters, but this is impressive." He turned to Susie. "He can be prone to exaggerate."

She laughed. "Ha. Never!" She got a warm feeling from G.A. In such a short time she felt comfortable with him, and it made her feel closer to Garnet.

Garnet defended himself. "I prefer to think that I move the inevitable forward by proclaiming it before it happens. I'm a visionary."

§

G.A. and Garnet sat together at the kitchen table G.E.-style, each beside a chair stacked with newspapers.

The Columbus Courier, January 12, 1917
Gurna A. Parks, brother of G. E. Parks of the *Courier*, arrived Tuesday of this week and expects to become a citizen of New Mexico.

G.A. confronted the reporter sitting beside him. "What's this, Garnet? I expect to be a citizen of New Mexico?"

Garnet grinned. "As I said, I move forward the inevitable. That's the power of print, Gurney. Sometimes we report the news, and sometimes we create the news."

In the three days since G.A. arrived, he had yet to divulge what brought him to Columbus. He happily asked questions and shared all he knew about the Parks family back home in Elk Creek. Mostly he was content to let his older brother control the conversation with his thoughts on everything from the suffragette movement to the price of ice and bread. All they knew about G.A. was that he had been living on a widow's farm in Appomattox and had married her daughter. Finally, he told them, "I worked from morning to night. I don't know that farming can keep any sane man's interest for more than a couple of years and I was there for seven. It was time for me to leave."

Susie probed, "But what about your wife?"

"I couldn't compete with the mother." G.A. got up. "I think I'll take my cigarette outside."

"Well, that's sad. Poor G.A.," was all Susie could think to say.

Garnet watched him exit. "Humm. She's really gotten to him, it seems."

Later, G.A. returned to the table apologetic. "I don't mean to bring my troubles to you good folks. It'll all work out for me, don't you worry. Now, what else is in the news?"

Garnet continued. "Look at this. *The Headlight* wrote something about the arrest that was made here last week. Remember when the Parry father and son got arrested? It says, '*Deputy Thomas of Columbus was of great assistance to Sheriff Simpson...* Hold on now, '*great assistance*'? Simpson is from Deming. How is it they report *our* deputy has merely *assisted* a Deming sheriff in an arrest that happened in *our* town? It's insulting. Of all the smug arrogance!"

G.A. tried to subdue him. "Woah there, Garnet. Not your fight, I'd say."

"It is my fight! We're hard at work building a city of consequence and these high hats at the *Headlight* are deliberately trying to put us in the shadows only to shine the light on themselves."

"Uh oh." Susie knew the signs. Garnet was ramping up. A letter was inevitable.

He slapped the paper on the table. "They're getting a letter. What is the role of a community paper if not to be the voice of the people?"

She appreciated his sense of justice but sometimes wondered if Garnet shouldn't be choosier about where he applied his passion. After all, once it's in print, there's no taking it back. Nonetheless, his outrage flew from his fingers into his typewriter. It was a full page, single spaced, and ended in a threat:

> ...In short, the policy of the *Headlight* seems to be to take the credit to Deming for everything that happens worthwhile in Luna County, and the *Courier* has no objections at all, so long as they stay with the facts, but if they do not want a scrap they had better give the Columbus people due credit in the future. (*Columbus Courier*)

He mumbled, "That'll set them right," and pulled the sheet out of the roller then proofed it for errors. There were none. There was still time to get it to Postmaster Birkhead before the morning mail run, so he grabbed his coat and headed to Main Street.

§

In national news, February 1917, El Paso reported that Major General Funston and the Carranza advisor Alvaro Obregon met and agreed to a US withdrawal from Mexico providing Carranza take responsibility to control Villa. Wilson was tired of chasing him. Since the Expedition's launch in March, 10,690 US soldiers had been evaded by Villa and were now preparing to return home empty-handed.

Garnet and Susie were among the organizers of the biggest planned event in Columbus history: The Homecoming of the Punitive Expedition. The committee planned for a reception line that would begin a mile south of town.

Pershing's troops prepared that morning by disassembling the mud-brick huts that had been their sleeping quarters for eleven months and lowered the American flag for the last time in Mexico. Dressed in their regulation best, some of them boarded vehicles, armored trucks, and covered wagons while others mounted horses and donkeys. Many walked alongside the twenty-two Apache scouts, hospital corps, and the nearly 3,000 Mexican and Chinese refugees who had assisted throughout their occupation.

General Pershing had a reputation for acting on his principles and boldly objected to racist policies of any kind. Months before, he wrote to Washington requesting an accommodation to the Chinese Exclusion Act for the Chinese assisting his expedition in Mexico. The appeal was approved and "Pershing's Chinese," as they became known at the time, marched into Columbus enjoying full legal status. There was much to celebrate.

The Columbus Courier (Columbus, New Mexico) Fri, Feb 9, 1917
General Pershing Leads Thousands of Men Home.
For long years to come the date of February 5, 1917, will linger in the memory of all Columbusites holding second place only to the tragic date of March 9, 1916, for on this day, The Punitive Expedition returned through the international gate onto American soil and ceased to exist as an expedition after eleven months of struggle, trials, pain and sorrow in the "line of duty" on foreign soil.

Columbus' children stood in the beds and on the hoods of motor trucks parked along Coote's Hill prepared to sing. Cheers and hurrahs erupted from the sidelines as the procession into Columbus began. There was an uproar from the crowd as the regiment of the 24th infantry passed. These were Buffalo Soldiers who were to take the place of the 13th Cavalry as protectors of Columbus. Of course, arrival of the 13th Cavalry Regiment inspired adoring applause.

The children wanted to sing the Star-Spangled Banner but were dissuaded by their band leader. "Children, if you sing the Star-Spangled Banner, all the officers and servicemen will have to stop and stand at attention. It will halt the entire procession." So instead, they agreed to sing, "Red, White and Blue."

Susie, Maggie, John Bliss, and G.A. hooted and hollered while David and Jennie Gregg clapped and the babies jumped for joy. It was energizing and, in its way, allowed the community to take a collective deep breath.

Meanwhile, G.E. was distracted by his quarrel with the *Deming Headlight* whose editors had published a response to his letter:

> *The Deming Headlight* (Deming, New Mexico) Fri, Feb 9, 1917
> We do not think that the people of Columbus are looking for a fight because they are just as busy as we are earning a livelihood and would frown upon any effort to make capital from arraying one town against the other as the *Courier* has attempted to do several times.
>
> We believe that the citizens of Columbus must disapprove of such silly statements and old fashion newspaper methods. *The Headlight* has many friends, readers, and subscribers in Columbus who have been there, by the way, long before Editor GE Parks arrived, and we have not had the slightest intimation from them that diplomatic relations between Deming and Columbus were to be broken off.

Garnet was offended. He felt he could not let it stand, yet he knew he was in deep now and he also wanted it over. He tried to rouse outrage from folks around town but it fell flat in light of the celebration. Even Deputy Thomas was lukewarm on the issue. G.E. realized he was in this battle alone and that he and the *Courier* were more vulnerable than he liked to admit. Still, he felt a response was required. He decided to present a final defense and then use the power of diplomacy to duck out and set it up for publication the following week.

> *The Columbus Courier* (Columbus, New Mexico) Fri, Feb 16, 1917
> Now in the last issue of the *Headlight* they come out plain as day and accuse the *Courier* of using old-fashioned newspaper methods. We plead guilty, if the *Headlight* refers to speaking the truth, we

will most certainly remain old-fashioned, regardless of any stand the official county paper has taken or may take.

Furthermore, the *Headlight* charges us with trying to promote strife between the sister towns. It has been promoted long ago, and the *Headlight* has been the greatest factor in doing it. It was created when every influence was brought to bear to take the troops from Columbus and leave us on the border unprotected. Columbus has forgiven that. And Columbus would be glad to forgive and forget everything if she would be given a chance.

The Headlight never fails to take a slam at Columbus when the opportunity is presented. A little news story from Columbus published in that paper nearly always leaves a sting. Nothing is printed about our growth or development but if a gambling joint or a bootlegger is pinched it is worth front-page space. *The Headlight* appears to believe that Columbus has no real people.

Columbus is ready and willing to bury the hatchet. In the future, we will meet Deming 50-50 on anything that is for our mutual interests. Will the *Headlight* agree?

With hope he'd dodged a moral defeat, G.E. rejoined the homecoming celebration with his family and spent the rest of the afternoon offering greetings and firm handshakes to friends and neighbors. The celebration concluded with a flag raising in front of the new Columbus Theater. Columbus would never see a military presence like that again. Two months later, the soldiers of the Punitive Expedition, Lieutenant George Patton among them, followed General Pershing onto the war in Europe.

§

Susie decided it was time for Garnet Jr. to be out of his nighties, so she brought out the sewing machine to fix him up some britches. She stepped outside to empty her scraps and a kangaroo rat scooted under the woodpile over what looked to be a photo. She pulled it out and recognized the image of G.A. next to a young woman. *It must be his wife, Colyer,* she thought. In his arms, balanced between them was a round-faced baby, maybe ten to twelve months old. *There's a baby!*

Inside, Garnet was on a call and just hanging up. "Well, I've got a meeting in Deming with the *Headlight*. I'll be back before dark." He snatched his jacket from the hook and, with an impish grin, set his hat on his head and crossed Susie on her way back into the house.

"Was that the *Headlight*?" She asked G.A., but he was confused. "I bet we're about to see a make-up between your brother and the *Headlight*." Beyond their small talk, Susie studied him. *Was he suffering? Did he walk away from a family?* She struggled to reconcile this with the affection she had grown to feel toward him. *He is a good man. How does a good man walk away from a child?*

Garnet returned that evening in an electrified state. He sat at the table and lit a cigarette. "Well Susie, I'm Vice President of the Deming Chamber of Commerce."

"No fooling," she said grinning.

"Ab-so-lute-ly. We're building a bridge between our sister towns."

"That's remarkable. What about your fight with the *Headlight*?"

"That's just it. They wanted it over and I wanted it over. *The Headlight* has friends at the Commerce building, so they introduced me. Before I knew it, they offered me the position and there I am receiving handshakes of congratulations." He pumped his fist and hooted, "Ha-hah!"

"Atta boy, G.E. You did it again," Susie praised.

He bowed to her. "Thank you. Thank you very much."

§

The 24th regiment was now the official guard at the Camp of Columbus, now with the changed title Camp Furlong. These men had fought in Cuba and the Philippines and were lauded for their skill and commitment before ever joining Pershing's forces in Mexico. At Columbus, they settled into a quieter assignment.

The Courier was putting out beautiful newspapers with its linotype but the marvelous machine had not yet begun to pay for itself. Susie and Garnet took outside print jobs and hired a clerk, E.L. Carman, who would be dedicated to bringing in more jobs. Their family was young, and they had taken on a lot of overhead in a short time. Garnet reminded Susie often that a successful business requires investment. He expected the reward to come any day.

Exactly one year and a week after the 4:20 am Villa raid, Susie and

Garnet were roused from bed by the sound of gunshots. Susie ran to the babies' room. Garnet went to the closet to get the rifle. A call came from the street, "Fire!" while pistol shots repeated.

"Oh no, oh no, oh no, not again..." Susie scooped a baby up in each arm and collided with G.A. in the narrow hallway. In the street, backlit by flames and running toward them was Carman, the printing clerk. "Mr. Parks! Come quick! *The Courier*! It's burning!"

Mr. Carman had been asleep in the back room of J.A. Moore's real estate office which was next to the print shop. He woke up coughing, saw the flames, and shot his gun to sound an alert. It attracted the men of the 24th who were on the scene when Susie and Garnet got there. People in town came out to the road in their nightclothes. Susie handed off the baby to a friend and followed Garnet to the blaze where the soldiers pitched water from horse troughs. Garnet started into the shop determined to pull out whatever equipment he could salvage. G.A. and Susie were close behind. Before he reached the walkway an explosion from next door at the Jitney Lunchroom blew him back and stopped G.A. and Susie where they stood. In an instant, the fire more than doubled in force and size.

Garnet shouted, "The water tank! Can we tap the water tank?" It was too late. The flames swallowed the shop, most of Moore's Real Estate office, and were now finishing off the Jitney Lunchroom. Before the giant furnace, they wiped sweat from their foreheads and watched as their livelihood was reduced to a pile of melted metal and ash.

Garnet went in close once again to see if there was anything worth saving. "I saw a gas can on the floor of the Jitney. That must have been the cause. Not of the fire, I mean, but of the explosion."

"It just all went up so fast," Susie said in disbelief.

A soldier from the 24th added, "That wood is dry like tumbleweed. It's just kindling."

His shirt sleeves pushed to his elbows and black with soot, Garnet paced in the street. To those from the infantry still present he said, "Thanks. You did all you could."

Some nodded sympathetically and others offered a salute or a handshake, then went back to camp.

"We have insurance," Garnet uttered blandly.

"We do." Susie affirmed.

"I don't think it will cover it," he clarified.

"We'll figure it out." She said it and she meant it. Starting over was as natural as the changing of the seasons to Susie. *All gone,* she thought. *Time to simplify.* A part of her took pleasure in the expiration of a thing and the seed of potential that lay in the embers. *We'll start again.*

"I'm sorry, G.E.," G.A. offered.

"As am I," Garnet agreed.

They were filthy. Susie carried Garnet Jr. and Gwen walked on her own back to the house chattering. "Mama, Papa needs a bath."

The Deming Headlight (Deming, New Mexico) Fri, Mar 16, 1917
Three Columbus Houses Cleaned Out by Flames
Newspaper Loses Linotype

The building and plant of the *Columbus Courier* were completely destroyed by fire early Wednesday morning and the Jitney Lunchroom and the real estate office of J.A. Moore were also gutted at the same time. The fire originated in the lunchroom and quickly spread to the other buildings.

Practically the entire *Courier* office and contents were destroyed and editor G.E. Parks, who was in Deming yesterday estimates his loss at $5,000. One half of the amount is covered by insurance. The loss to the other buildings will not exceed $600.

Mr. Parks said that the members of the 24th US Infantry were on the scene shortly after the alarm was sounded and these soldiers did good work in preventing the blaze from spreading. *The Headlight* sympathizes with Editor Parks and our plant facilities are at his disposal if needed in assisting him in filling his orders until he secures his new equipment.

They set up a temporary office in the old post office building by the Columbus Theater. Every piece of equipment was lost in the fire. The goodwill Garnet had fostered with surrounding newspapers served as its own insurance policy. His colleagues at the *Deming Graphic* and even the *Headlight,* came through to fill the *Courier*'s outstanding print orders. Garnet rode to Deming weekly to set his four pages for the Friday *Courier* with assistance from the *Graphic*'s editor, W.E. Holt. They didn't skip an issue that month, but the fire took its toll on their finances. Susie wondered if she'd be smart to start looking for a job.

§

Garnet continued to serve at the Deming Chamber of Commerce and as the Village Clerk for the Commerce Club. He also put his hat in the ring at Luna County's state elections board to represent the Republican party. For several months, he led the fervent call to start a baseball team in Columbus. He and Susie continued to fill print orders daily out of the old post office and they used the *Graphic*'s machinery in Deming to publish the *Courier*. Both kept their eyes peeled for a new site for their print shop.

G.A. announced, "I'm moving to Sunnyside." He had bought a peach farm. "I've taken a five-year lease on a twenty-acre orchard." G.A. a farmer again?

In a rare moment, Susie and Garnet were alone in their temporary print shop while the children napped. Susie was baffled. "I thought he hated farming. A peach orchard?"

"I admit it's curious..."

"Garnet," Susie addressed him seriously, "G.A. has a child."

"What?"

"I found a picture of him and the wife, Colyer, with a baby. It's in my bag. He hasn't told you?" She rooted through the bag and pulled the photo out from the bottom.

Garnet studied the photo. "How did you come by this?"

"It was in the garbage. He had thrown it away. How does a man walk away from a wife and baby for a peach orchard?"

"He doesn't. There's got to be another explanation. It's unconscionable."

Susie nodded, "If that means unbelievable, then I agree with you."

However concerned they were about G.A., rebuilding was what needed their attention. Susie made a strong case for going back to the old-style typesetter and printer only to see Garnet's spark diminish. "What good is it to go backward," was his point. Besides, he had already spoken to the Mergenthaler people. The new linotype was in transit.

"Okay then," she conceded. "We'll make it work." Her agreement brought his spark back.

"You watch, Susie. We'll be the envy of the surrounding local papers. I'm putting the word out with an invitation for them to come and sample it for themselves." He moved through the world differently than she did and she had to remember that. How often did he remind her that success rarely comes without risk? She had little experience in this area, but she knew there must be truth in it.

The Columbus Courier (Columbus, New Mexico) Fri, April 20, 1917
The *Courier* is again equipped with a linotype machine, having received it exactly one month from the date of the fire. It was shipped from New York to New Orleans by boat and reached us in record time...The fact that Mr. Bacon completed the job so much quicker than the scheduled time is due to two things. The first is he is an unusually good machinist and the second was the unusually intelligent assistance of the *Courier* force. The linotype is one of the greatest inventions of the age...

In the meanwhile, President Wilson's Whitehouse decided the time had come to "make the world safe for democracy." Congress voted to declare war on Germany.

Santa Fe New Mexican (Santa Fe, New Mexico) Fri, April 4, 1917
President Wilson Proclaims War with Germany

§

Garnet and G.A. were among the first to register in May of 1917 and, never to waste a step, Garnet picked up a mining permit while they were there. He and G.A. planned to go up to the Three Sisters and see if they might get lucky enough to find some gold. "We've got to put every pot on the fire, right my brother?"

Susie questioned them both. "Gold? Where are you going to find the time to go searching for gold?" She heard herself as she said it, she sounded like Eva. In any event, the scheme fell away because the little town of Columbus was about to make the national news once again.

It was a hot one in July when Garnet threw open the door of their new print shop. "Hold on to your britches, Susie, this is a big one."

Susie stopped her page rustling and gave him full attention.

"Those boys from Bisbee, Arizona? The copper miners that have been striking since June? Well, it looks like the folks in Bisbee don't appreciate the Union stirring things up over there. The Bisbee sheriff deputized over a hundred people in town, and the group loaded the strikers in cattle cars by gunpoint. You'll never guess...the train just pulled in here to Columbus. Loaded with them, the copper miners. There must be two thousand of them. I'll tell you the smell coming out of those cars is enough to knock you out dead."

"What, here? Why here?"

"From what I can gather, Bisbee just sent the train off with no concern about where it ended up. So, they showed up here last night around nine o'clock but Dabney, being Dabney, sent them away to Hermanas. He sent the poor men to starve or suffocate while they stood on dung in those cars. When the Luna County sheriff heard about it, he called the governor who called President Wilson. That's right, President Wilson! That's when US troops were enlisted to escort them back here again because, of course, we have the tent city to house them. Dabney knows that. I imagine the men were pretty stale by that hour so it couldn't have been a pleasant ride." He went to the wall for his hat. "I'm going. They're not violent, but they're exhausted and dehydrated. Reporters will seek to crucify them because they're union. That IWW is not popular with the majority."

"IWW?" Susie's head spun at the sheer volume of his words.

"The Industrial Workers of the World. They organized them to strike. They're socialists and a lot of their strikers were immigrants. That Bisbee is a patriotic town and they don't like outsiders. My guess is that there'll be a problem of denying these strikers their civil liberties when it's all done."

"I'm going with you." Susie put a hat on Gwen, wrapped up baby Garnet and followed him out.

Susie, Garnet, and the children fought a particularly blustery windstorm on their way to the depot. The dust made visibility difficult. Once the scene came into focus, they could see hundreds of bodies dragging themselves down the steps of the train in a slow, steady flow. They were guided by Camp Furlong soldiers into the tent village that would be their home in the short term until further notice.

The news chain lit up on telegram and telephone lines demanding updates on the status of the strikers, commonly referred to as "the Wobblies." Due to the war, news agencies were short on reporters to send out on a major story such as this one. The Associated Press had no one to send to Columbus and G.E. got the call of his life.

The Columbus Courier Columbus, Luna County, New Mexico, July 13, 1917
Courier Handles I.W.W. Situation for AP
The deportation of such a large number of working men from Bisbee calls for much space in the newspapers of the country and in the absence of any regular Associated Press man in the section on the 12th and 13th, G.E. Parks was asked to cover for them.

Susie enjoyed tracking Garnet's movements as he darted about town. "Susie, this is going to require my attention around the clock." He prayed, "Keep the children out of my way. I can't afford distractions. I mean, this could mean a permanent assignment. It's a chance to show them what this newspaperman can do."

She took the children on playdates and snack breaks around town to keep him safe from distraction while he put his all into writing an informative, professional piece. Dispelling any doubt that he succeeded in the assignment, he received and published the following telegram:

DENVER, COLORADO, JULY 14, 1917
GE PARKS, COLUMBUS NEW MEXICO,
CONGRATULATIONS ON YOUR EXCELLENT WORK. YOU CERTAINLY MADE GOOD. YOUR STORY WAS FIRST PAGE STUFF ALL OVER THE COUNTRY. WE APPRECIATE THE MANNER IN WHICH YOU RESPONDED TO THE EMERGENCY.
 —THE ASSOCIATED PRESS.

Garnet raised eyebrows and confessed to Susie. "I'll level with you. I feel a little stuck up after being congratulated by the greatest newsgathering association in the world."

She commended him. "It's your right. You did great work."

Once the AP reporter, Walker was his name, was freed up he came into town and took over the story. Garnet traveled with Mr. Walker and assisted in any way he could maintaining his focus on landing a position with the AP. It had been a chance opportunity that could carve him a path and he wasn't about to let it go easily.

Garnet received several letters from his mother during all the excitement and he had yet to respond. In each letter, she reminded him of her patience with the fact that he had not visited once in the six years since he left Grayson County. More forcefully she expressed her disappointment that her grandchildren were growing bigger every day and were strangers to her. He had a brainstorm. "Susie, I think you and the children should take the train to Virginia while I follow up on this. I'll be taking this Walker fellow to lunch in Albuquerque. He'll want to introduce me to his people there. We'll hire an extra hand, maybe J.B., in the shop while you're gone."

It might have bothered her that he told her rather than asked her to go to Elk Creek, but the idea of taking a train to Virginia? She wouldn't need to be talked into that. Let J.B. stand over the printer for the next few weeks. "Gwen, Junior, we're taking a train ride."

§

Neither of the children slept more than two hours at a time on the 28-hour trip. When she wasn't sleeping Gwen either took names of the passengers, "*What's yer name?*" or stood on tiptoes with her nose pressed against the glass. Baby Garnet was not on board with the miracle of Mellin's baby food. Consequently, Susie had to squeeze herself, with Gwen, into a private closet every four hours to nurse him.

Finally, the train pulled into the Rural Retreat Depot. Susie stuffed her travel things in her bag and gathered up the babies to exit. She guessed that the small, white-haired man at attention on the platform was Papa Parks. He combed a white mustache that spread well beyond his jaw in both directions. "Mr. Parks...Wiley Parks?"

He raised his chin and nodded. "Uh-hum. You Susie?"

"I am." She approached him for a hug but sensed immediately that was not how they would be greeting one another.

He eyeballed Gwen and the baby. "These are my grandchildren, are they?"

There was nothing warm about him, but he wasn't entirely indifferent either. They claimed her suitcases and he led her to the wagon.

It would be up to Susie to lead the conversation. "I've never been this far east before. My family comes mostly from Nebraska and some from Ohio, but I've never visited. Garnet tells me it's beautiful here." She was glad for the clear evening because it would be another two hours before they reached Elk Creek in the open flatbed wagon. The bumpy ride rocked the babies to sleep. Long stretches of Appalachian pastures and the beauty of maple and pine trees kept Susie's attention during the frequent lulls in conversation. It was getting dark, but she could see well enough to recognize that there were walnut trees. "That's a walnut tree, right? What are those there?"

"That's an elm. Those are birch," he reported blandly. As taken as she was by the scenery, she lacked his strength to endure the silences and broke them every time. "Garnet is a real expert on the linotype. It's a difficult machine and he's especially good at it."

"Is that so?" Mr. Parks was remarkably incurious. The last leg of the trip was a long dirt road with a country house scattered along rolling hills every hundred acres or so. Mr. Parks pointed toward a vague outline of buildings indicating they were approaching the Parks' place. Even in the dark, she was impressed by what she could make out of the outbuildings and the big barn. What stood out to her most though, was the tall wooden house confirming the permanence of several generations who stay in one place. Kerosene-powered light flickered from the front window. Wiley stopped the wagon a few feet from the front porch. He pulled the suitcases from the back and lifted Gwen down from the wagon.

"This is beautiful country. Did you build all this?"

"Some." He nodded. "Some my pa. And his pa." Susie would have been interested in the details of it all but Wiley Parks was no chatterbox. *Garnet must be more like his ma*, she thought.

They entered the house and she was met by a receiving line of Parkses waiting along the wall expectantly. Susie encouraged Gwen. "Oh boy, Gwen, these are your aunts and uncles. Go on. Go hug your grandma."

Laura Jane Parks stood up from her chair, arms outstretched. "Oh my!" Her eyes welled up as she squeezed her granddaughter for the first time.

The oldest girl, who could only be Jettie, approached Susie timidly. "May I hold the baby?" Susie passed him over and scanned the group before her. Seated on an overstuffed sofa were the two teen boys, Raby and Carl, gawking at her like she was a unicorn. The girls, Opal and Lela, sat in one chair, grinning and giggling into one another.

With an arm around Gwen, Laura Jane offered Susie relief from her long trip. "You must be exhausted. We can catch up tomorrow. Jettie, take Susie and the babies to her room." She followed Jettie down the hallway to a bedroom where she changed the baby and put Gwen in a nightie. She had no memory of how she put them to bed. That night's sleep was the deepest she remembered having since she was a child.

Susie learned quickly that offering help in the kitchen was the best way to endear herself to her mother-in-law. Laura Parks was a traditionalist and she found Susie's lack of inhibition a little scandalous. Wiley and the boys liked a game of cards after the evening meal while the women cleaned up. Susie made a point of setting the table and helping at the front end of the meal to earn herself time for cards with the boys. She got side-long stares from Laura, but the fun of cards was worth it. Carl and Ray were captivated by how she shuffled like a club dealer. "Have you played split pot?" She dared them.

"Well," Carl shrugged. "We like poker." Opal and Lela perched themselves on top of the sofa to watch. "Split Pot is poker." She laughed loudly while she taught them the secrets of split pot like her pa taught her. The boys got a kick out of playing cards with a lady, especially a lady who could beat them.

Over the several weeks of her visit, they settled into a routine of chores and recreation. Two more babies were no burden to the Parkses and Susie was a real help around their place. She took on chores in the barn and hunted several nights to bring in grouse and wild turkey for dinner. She wished Garnet could be there to enjoy his family with her, but she surprised even herself with how the ease and freedom of farm living caused her to go hours, even all day, without thinking about him.

Columbus, New Mexico June 29, 1917
Courier office
Garnet E. Parks
Dear Susie,

I hope this finds you and the children well. I have spent the week collecting samples of writing to offer an AP editor Walker connected me with in Albuquerque. I've telegraphed San Francisco as well. As of this date, I have not heard back.

I decided to let go of the house to concentrate our finances on the print shop and payments on the linotype. I moved our furniture to the back of the shop where I've been sleeping. Next week I travel to Santa Fe to inquire about an opportunity there. Also, Kniffin has begun drilling for oil just as he promised. I'll be on the committee. Another prospect that, if it comes through, could put us ahead in our finances. Also, I received a letter from my brother Rex who mentioned a job prospect up north. He is in sales in the northeast states and wrote that he knows a man I can call about a well-paying job in Pittsburgh. I'll let you know which fish bites.

Some good news. It looks like we are going to get our baseball team here in town. I hope this news brings a smile to your face. It has mine. How I've missed days at the ballfield, and I think Columbus has enough talent that we might win some games.

Send my greetings to my younger siblings and my dear mother. Please tell her I heard from my brother Dean and he is well. Better that you tell her only and not my Pa. He and Dean didn't part on good terms. Kiss my son and give Sister a sweet. Tell her it is from her Papa.

Sincerely,
Garnet

None of Garnet's prospects in New Mexico panned out. The AP had more talent than they needed and G.E. had to accept that the praise he'd received for his reporting on the Bisbee strike was the last he was going to hear from them. Having exhausted all his better options, he contacted Rex's man in Pittsburgh and leased the *Courier* to J.B. Smith who had been itching to try his hand in the editor's chair. He bought a train ticket for Pittsburgh and would start on the assembly line at a chemical factory. He sent word to Susie to join him there.

After four weeks in Elk Creek, the ink stains on Susie's hands were faded and replaced by country farm dirt. Sitting on the Parks' front porch, she picked garden soil from under her nails and thought about how hard it would be to say goodbye. If Garnet hadn't communicated so clearly his intentions to never return to his home in Virginia, she would have been happy to start a life here. She was only twenty-two, but something about riding and working a farm in this country felt as if she'd reclaimed her childhood.

Time to leave. Opal and Lela had grown attached to Gwen and Garnet Junior and they cried. The boys took turns giving Susie awkward handshakes but, with Jettie and the girls, she shared unrestrained hugs. Laura Jane's hug was subdued but sincere and she was unable to conceal how her heart ached to say goodbye to her grandchildren.

Susie climbed onto the flatbed wagon and reached out to receive Gwen and Garnet Jr. Wiley snapped the reins to begin the two-hour ride back to Rural Retreat Depot. "There's those walnut trees," he offered almost as if reminiscing about their old times together.

She was touched. "Oh yes, I'll miss them. It's beautiful country here, Mr. Parks."

"Yes," and he approximated a smile. "I'm glad you like it."

§

When Gwen saw her papa at the train station she jumped into his arms. Garnet navigated around baby Garnet and laid a kiss on Susie that rivaled the passion of their courtship days. It was a happy reunion.

Susie stopped outside the Pittsburgh station to take in the scope of where she was, but the view was blocked in every direction but up. Tall steel pipes coughed out billows of smoke that replaced every inch of what would otherwise be sky. Susie drew in a deep breath. "The smell is like nothing I've ever..."

"That's the smell of progress...and profit." Garnet scooped up Gwen and the larger of Susie's two cases. Smokestacks lined the streets all around them and Susie felt assaulted by a rank odor. "Ew, what is that?"

"That, I think, is coming off the river," Garnet deduced. "Sewage maybe?"

They took the short walk toward a one-room apartment G.E. had rented for his stint at the factory. Susie thought it looked like this city floated on water with its rivers coming in from three sides. They made their way along the street stepping aside and stopping often to let others pass. Everything seemed so close with hills holding them in from every direction. It was amazing how rails and metal structures dominated nature here, especially in contrast to where she had just been. What impressed her most was the oddest sight of the Monongahela Incline climbing up the side of Coal Hill. What an awkward contraption it was. Boxcars, set at an angle moving up and down the steep hill simultaneously carrying people and freight. From the looks of them, they should have tipped over but no, it was an engineering marvel. Susie walked in time with the perfect up and down rhythm of the boxcars and embraced the sounds and smells of the city.

It was a four-floor walkup to their apartment. The space amounted to a box no bigger than the little room they'd started in back in Columbus. Garnet found a mattress for Gwen and cleared a drawer with a pillow and a blanket for the baby. It was a dull little place that smelled musty from mold, and from the butts in his loaded ashtrays. There was a small table, a couch, and a room with a bed. Nothing on the walls and no covering for the one thin window that bled noise from the streets below.

Garnet bounced on the bed. "Here we are."

"Here we are, all right." Susie laughed and ribbed him. "You're living like a prince."

"You can fix it up if you want. I bought toys for Sister." In the corner, there was a box of blocks and a wooden train car.

"I'm teasing. It'll do us just fine for the time we need it."

"That's what I thought." He slouched. The exuberance he derived from their reunion had diminished. "Not where I thought I'd be at this time."

"This is temporary, Garnet. You're doing what you need to do."

"The A.P. job was just this close…" he lamented.

"Not the time for it right now, that's all. You're an editor and a publisher. Maybe a job as a reporter was too small for you." She went to the window. "Look at this. We're living in a city. This is something altogether new. Let's have some fun while we're here."

Garnet soaked the encouragement up like a dry sponge and it gave him the strength to muster a smile. "Come here, Sister." Gwen hopped in his lap and gave him a bear hug.

Living in Pittsburgh was indeed altogether new. Garnet was gone sometimes ten hours a day which left Susie to walk the streets with the kids. The pace of the smoky city energized her. The boats, trucks, railcars, and people dropping off and receiving goods on every street sharpened her senses. Many of the workers were new to America and spoke the language of their homeland or an eastern European English thick with an accent that reminded her of the Ravel brothers back at home. There was a noticeable number of southern black folks in the northern city wrangling little ones in one direction or another. They had come to Pittsburg for the promise of work and equity from the northern states. Due to the war, strict limits on buying were rigidly enforced but even that was no hardship. Wartime through the lens of this melting pot metropolis made her feel a part of something…it made her feel more American.

Manual labor was already taking its toll on Garnet. The fact that he was not putting a tie on in the morning was in itself depleting. It simply didn't suit the man he aspired to be. For his sake, Susie felt they needed to meet their earning goal as soon as possible and return home to Columbus. She found a part-time waitressing job at a café up the block and the building manager, who had taken a liking to the children, agreed to watch them for a portion of her tips. Serving the diverse population in the city required that she sharpen her awareness of entirely new approaches to English. Her challenge became a running joke with her customers. *"You say you want a hum sundavich?"*

"*SundVich, Susie! SundVich. Vith Peekels!*" This banter over food orders sent them into a fit of laughter that rattled the windows of the little café.

After a full day at the plant, Garnet came in dirty, sweaty, and hungry. One cold December evening, Susie fixed a stew. Garnet was in the bath when there was a knock on the door. Susie answered to a man with an unlit cigarette hanging off his lip. He reached into his pants pocket for a light, looked up, and flashed her a grin. "Humm, you Susie?" She saw from the look of his suit he spared no expense dressing himself. He was more stylish than G.A. in his fancy New York duds. "I have the right place, don't I? Looking for my brother. Garnet."

Having met them all now, except Dean and Rex, she was sure as she could be that this was, "Rex?"

"Sure as shootin'." He skipped the greeting, pushed past her and entered the room. "Now where's my brother?"

"Right now, he is in the bathtub. I'll tell him you're here."

Rex took it on himself. "Garnet. Get out here ya dewdropper. Your brother's come to see you." Gwen stayed frozen in place and watched the noisy man.

From the bathroom, Garnet called out, "Rex? Is that you?"

"You can bet it is!" he called back. "I've got a pack full of Lucky Strikes and a load of dough and I'm looking for someone to spend it on, Brother." Water splashed and made it clear Garnet would be out soon.

"Little brother." Still buttoning up his trousers, he threw his arms around his much taller brother and then pushed him off. "Look at you. Just look at you." He shook his head in amazement. "Six, no going on seven years…I left you when you were fifteen. You were shorter than me."

"Ha! Who's the little brother now, big brother?"

Garnet let out a hearty laugh and hugged him again. "Sit down, sit down. You found me! What brings you to Pittsburgh?" He led Rex to the table.

The joy of seeing his brother knocked the fatigue right out of Garnet. It was clear there was a special bond between them and their energy didn't leave much room for a third voice, so Susie left them to eat her stew and catch up. Gwen crawled into her papa's lap while Susie cleared the dishes.

"Here, we're just a walk to Forbe's Field. Too late in the season to take in a game, of course."

"You wouldn't want to. They finished at the bottom of the league.

The only hitter worth his salt is Carey. The bums have pitchers who look like they're playing for the other team." Both burst out laughing then collapsed into giggles. "Hey, let's go out and see the city. You and me." Susie and Garnet were both stopped by his apparent lack of awareness of the wife and two children there in the room, but Rex was unfazed.

Garnet's diplomacy managed it fine. "It's getting pretty late on a work night. What if we stay in?"

Rex looked distinctly at Susie as if he'd solved a crime, then focused back on his brother. "That's all right then." He stood up, pulled a bottle of Hirsch Whiskey from his back pocket, and handed it over to Garnet.

"Susie, can you get us a couple of glasses?" *Okay, this is new.* Susie had not seen this Garnet ever before. She wasn't sure yet what to make of it but smiling at the novel prospect of her husband about to get rummy, she brought them over two glasses.

"I know, I know..." Garnet launched into reminiscences of their earlier days together. Susie settled the babies in for bed then joined the men at the table. "...you were so surprised when you came out from under that bush and there you were, face to face with that groundhog."

"All I could see was teeth..." Rex sucked his lower lip and mimicked the animal.

Garnet was loosened up and leaned over to Susie. "You think I'm awkward in the wild. Rex doesn't know a bush from a warthog." He pointed at Rex. "But he's a heck of a salesman. You could sell sawdust in a lumber mill."

"That's right I could." Rex slapped the table and poured another round, emptying the bottle. Susie was curious that neither of them thought to offer her a drink. "Hey, Susie. I bet you don't know about us brothers. We're all curses." Rex nudged Garnet with a wink.

"He's right. I'm Darnet because it rhymes with Garnet...."

Rex added, "And Gurney, he's Durnit, of course. Our brother Dean is Deanit." He leaned in. "And I'm Rex but my real name is Cammit." Susie nodded knowing where he was headed but she wasn't about to steal his thunder. So, we're Darn-it, Durn-it, Dean-it, and Dammit!" They exploded in belly laughs.

Intrigued and confused, Susie tried to repeat it. "Darnet, dangit... galdurnit?"

"Dean-it and Dammit!" Garnet corrected.

Then from her mattress, Gwen called out, "Dammit!"

"Oh, okay," Susie interjected. "Rex, how about I get you some blankets and set you up on the couch?"

"You don't mind if I crash your party? I have to be gone first thing 'smorning." He tried again. "In *thuh s'morning*. I have to get to Ohio. For a call...in... Ohio." He was fading.

"Not at all. You sleep here *'slong* as you need." Garnet slurred and stood to give him another hug.

Susie and Garnet crawled into bed to the sound of Rex's snoring. He whispered to her. "What about that brother of mine? That was a great surprise."

"He's a live one all right. He's different from the rest of the family. But then you're different from the rest of the family..." She had more to say on the subject, but Garnet was already out, on his back and sawing logs.

§

From July through December, Garnet continued working at the factory and Susie continued to earn as a waitress. The plan was to work and try to return to Columbus by spring, but a telegram from their friend J.R. Blair altered their timeline.

COLUMBUS, LUNA, NEW MEXICO 1918 JAN 02 PM 7:05
G.E. PARKS
   URGENT STOP MR. SMITH HAS ABANDONED COURIER STOP EQUIPMENT MISHANDLED AND NEEDS REPAIRS STOP MR. SMITH MAY HAVE LEFT TOWN STOP WILL WAIT FOR YOUR REPLY
J.R. BLAIR

It seems that J.B. had made a real mess of things while G.E. and Susie were away. He had done something to the printer that destroyed the quality to the point of illegibility. This would have been crisis enough if not for the additional problem that he had printed no viable news to speak of for several weeks, and then severed his communication with the Parkses and disappeared.

When the telegram arrived, Garnet happened to be sick in bed fighting off some nasty stomach pains. He pulled himself together, got approval at work for a short leave, and bought a round-trip train ticket to Columbus. Within twenty-four hours he assembled a skeleton crew of trusted friends, including Blair, who agreed to hold things together in the short term. He published a letter of explanation to go out in each of the January editions:

> ATTENTION
> *Columbus Courier*, January 18, 1918.
> Due to circumstances which were unavoidable, no complete issue of the *Courier* could be published this week and we very much doubt if it will be possible to give the readers the paper they are entitled to for two or three weeks, possibly longer. J.B. Smith, who had the paper leased from the owner, severed his connection on very short notice. The owner was in Pittsburg, Penn, in bed sick when he received a telegram from J. R. Blair informing him of Mr. Smith's intentions. The telegram was received last Wednesday evening at seven o'clock. He managed to catch a train departing exactly two hours later and is here in charge of the paper and as soon as some absolutely necessary repairs can be received from Dallas, Texas, the *Courier* will be built back to its usual standard and if hopes amount to anything it will be made larger and better than ever before.

Garnet felt compelled to rationalize his absence and padded the truth about his purpose in Pittsburgh to the readers of the *Courier*:

> G. E. Parks owner has been in the east during the past six months and has held positions on two large newspapers and in addition has had experience in job printing shops where only the highest class printing was turned out, and he believes that the readers of the *Courier* and those who buy printed matter will appreciate these facts when he has had an opportunity to "show them" and prove them correct by actual results.
> There is more enthusiasm in evidence today in regard to the future of Columbus than ever before and there are more and better reasons for enthusiasm than ever before and we are sure going to impress hard upon the minds of the readers of the *Courier* just as soon as the repairs mentioned above can be received. Until that time we ask that you remain as patient with us as possible. We thank you.

Garnet was back in Pittsburgh by the time his letter went into circulation. As for his embellishments, he had told white lies before and his need to do this always perplexed Susie. "Why did you say that, Garnet? You could have told the truth or not told anything at all."

"I just want the readers to know I'm still a newsman, to maintain their confidence. It's not entirely untrue, Susie. I have observed print practices. From a distance maybe, but I have. We'll make it all good when we're back."

Susie asked, "Who's running the paper?"

"It's not J.B," he assured her. "We can be confident on that count. What kind of man walks away from his responsibilities and disappears completely? He owes us money. Before I left, I went to the Justice Court and filed for garnishment backdated to December. Sixty-five dollars and ninety-three cents for his trouble. That doesn't cover the damages, of course, but it's the least we're entitled. He has 30 days to make good. As for who will run the paper?" He pondered the whole calamity for a moment then nodded to himself. "It's you, Susie. You're the only dependable man for the job. You need to go back. I'll write the editorials and send them to you. You've got to go back and set us right."

Susie was all too happy to be tagged 'the man for the job'. It tickled her and flattered her all at the same time. She knew he was right and if it meant her part of the adventure was over, she could live with that. She loved the challenge of putting the paper together. Now the whole operation would be under her control. It could be fun, as long as G.E. made it back to them before too long. Susie wasn't altogether confident she wouldn't pull a J.B. Smith and mess things up herself. "You're right. I'll pack up the kids and you finish here. I'll get us back on track 'til you come and take the engine." Train references came naturally to them now.

Garnet asked that Gwen stay in the city with him. He rationalized, "If anything, you'll be so busy, it's enough to have the baby." Truer for him was that Gwen would keep his morale up while he finished the job that, if he didn't get out soon, threatened to sap his spirit. They calculated his earnings and set the date when they would have enough that he could safely quit the factory and return to Columbus. Susie said her goodbyes to the owners of the café and her patrons.

The Columbus Courier (Columbus, New Mexico) Feb. 15, 1918
Mrs. G.E. Parks and little son Garnet E. Jr. arrived here Wednesday afternoon from Pittsburgh, Pa. having been away from Columbus

about six months. She spent several weeks visiting in Virginia, West Virginia, Ohio and Pittsburgh while away. She left the smoky city Sunday evening, and says the mercury registered several degrees on the wrong side of zero, and now that she's back where such weather is unknown she believes that New Mexico is the best place to call home after all.

The Heatless Mondays, Meatless Tuesdays, Wheatless Wednesdays and Porkless Saturdays are being very rigidly enforced in the east and no purchaser can get more than one pound of sugar, and there are restrictions upon the amounts allowed on a great many articles, she states, and that she is very much surprised that these proclamations and orders are regarded so lightly by many of the people here.

When Susie stepped down from the passenger train onto the hard dirt road of her hometown, she had Baby Garnet in her arms and was five months along with number three.

The Columbus Courier, February 15, 1918
Beginning with the next week's edition Mrs. G.E. Parks will take complete charge of the news part of the *Courier* and will endeavor to give you all the local news. We solicit your cooperation and will thank you for informing the office of anything you may know of news value. If you know anything call phone 8 and Mrs. Parks will be on the job.

In the month and a half that followed, she managed the repair of the printing press, put the linotype back in optimal condition, and moved them into a small house in town ready for Garnet and Gwen's return. Reacclimated to clothes and hair coated daily in layers of dust, she and little Garnet knocked on the doors of businesses and neighbors to gather the news that connects a small town. It was a comfort to be among friends and running the paper, but the memories of that fast-paced city and the green hills of Virginia occupied her imagination while she worked.

At the table of his room in Pittsburgh, Garnet smoked and read a letter from Susie. The news that things in Columbus were starting to shape up gave him relief. When he reached her report that their dear friend J.R. Blair had thrown his hat into the Columbus mayoral race, he let out a chortle. "There you are, Sister! J.R. is running for mayor. Between your mama and J.R., Columbus is back in business."

§

The Columbus Courier, June 21, 1918-W.S.S.
A baby boy was born to Mr. and Mrs. G.E. Parks on Thursday, June 20th.

G.E. returned a few months before the baby was born. Little Billie Jo was smaller and not as hearty as the first two Parks babies. Susie believed mother's milk would strengthen him in time. The brutality of the constant dust in Columbus was hard on the little guy.

He had a raw cough that was concerning and it brought the doctor to the house for regular checks. Gwen was a tall four and a half years old. She could easily pull her toddling two-year-old brother onto the wood box to spy through the window while the doctor checked the baby. She studied him. "Is he gonna die, Mama?"

"He's not. The doc is helping him. You keep saying prayers." Susie hadn't really taught them prayers outside of the memorized verses of, *Now I lay me down to sleep*.

Gwen folded her hands and said a prayer. "Make him better, God. Amen."

The almost constant disturbance in his throat and chest was unsettling and he cried often throughout the night. Susie couldn't help but notice Garnet's grimaces and it made her defensive. In those early days, Billie's discomfort didn't allow him to bond with anyone but Susie.

Cooler fall temperatures calmed the dust and eased Billie's symptoms some, but he still had fevers. When Susie found blood in his diaper, the doctor felt sure they were dealing with dysentery. "This climate is no good for the boy, Susie."

For Susie, it was settled. They would move north to Washington and the cooler, damper climate. Garnet resisted. "It's not a good time, Susie. Columbus is prime for development. Kniffin's drilling and bound to hit oil any day now. Why we've secured a hundred members in our Columbus Chamber of Commerce without even conducting a membership campaign. With Holt on publicity, we're bound to double that number."

What a *string of gibberish*, she thought. Pots of gold and building business contacts were not going to take priority over their baby's health. She wasn't swayed. "The baby won't wait for Knifflin to strike oil, Garnet. It's time to go. We haven't gone to the homestead in over a year. Talk to Holt. He'll buy us out. We could buy two town papers in Washington for what he would pay us for the *Courier*." She was already packing.

Garnet entered a living area of stacked crates and boxes, some that had not been unpacked since before Pittsburgh. "I've been named General Manager of the Oil Commission. Oil is coming to Columbus." *When pigs fly,* she thought, but as determined as she was to get her baby out of Columbus, the US government had other plans. Garnet's draft number came up and he would have to go to training camp in Texas. Still, Susie continued packing.

September 8, 1918
Columbus, New Mexico
East Boundary
Dear Eva,

I think about you every day. I know you've canned enough to fill three pantries by now. Send some down to us. Ha-ha.

Garnet has been talking about striking oil in Columbus. Sound like George? Ha-ha! Have you heard from George or Don? Ma got a letter from Don, and he said George is okay. We know he isn't a guy to pick up a pen if he can help it. Let's hope they stay in Cuba until this war is over, but I hear Marines are the most needed in France.

Garnet was called up to Camp Stanley for training – no sign he'll go to Europe. So anyway, I'm running the paper. Again. I don't mind, I like writing the news and I get better each day on the linotype. Between the paper and chasing the kids, I fall into bed in a dead sleep.

The Spanish Flu has come to Columbus. We have had 60 cases if you include the cases at camp. The soldiers have to rinse their mouths with salt water several times a day and wash their teeth after each meal. We do the same to be safe, especially for the children's sake. As fragile as Billie is, we don't want that. Our friend George Krebbs died of it just last week. It's very sad.

Gwen is tall. She talks nonstop. She talks more than Ida. Ha-ha! Little Garnet follows her around like she's a mother duck. Billie Jo is a sweet baby but not well. I hold him all the time. It would be better for him if we were up there with you. I am packing with plans to be there before Spring. I know you have a full house, so I've written Aunt

Sophrie to see if she can keep us for a few weeks at Anacortes. I miss the smell of the rain and fir trees. Send my love to Jim and Uncle John and family.
  With love, your sister,
  Susie

Garnet's enlistment date was October 27th, 1918. News of the signing of the Armistice hit the press just two weeks later on November 11, 1918. The war was over.

Washington D.C., November 11, 1918. Great War End!
Armistice terms have been signed by Germany, the State Department announce at 2:45 o'clock this morning.

Garnet was honorably discharged and sent home from Camp Stanley on December 5th. All the crates and boxes stayed stacked and ready to go. Garnet returned bustling around town conducting business, but his denial did not deter her. She carted furniture over to Maggie's and Ma's and paid off all outstanding debts.

Then oddly, their house was broken into while they were out visiting. The burglars took several items including a broom.

New Mexico State Record, February 9, 1919
Burglars Make Way With Broom.
The home of Mr. and Mrs. G.E. Parks was entered sometime between dark and eleven o'clock Wednesday evening and several articles were taken, including a broom. This fact proves beyond doubt that it was no ordinary burglar. Why anyone should take such a chance to steal an article like this is a puzzle. However, it is possible that he had an idea that a broom was never used in this home. (*The Columbus Courier*)

With the enthusiasm of a man who had thought of the idea himself, Garnet pontificated. "Susie, we could wait our lifetime for Columbus to grow into a town worthy of what we have to offer. If William Holt wants to buy us out, I say it's time we take him up on it and make a bid up north, what do you say?"

"What do I say?"

G.E. continued. "I just think with the ports up there in the Seattle area and what we know about the publishing business, I'd say we would have the circulation to have a real newspaper. A daily paper yet."

The June 6, 1919 issue of the *Columbus Courier* named W.E. Holt Editor and Publisher.

"It's a great idea, Garnet. Why didn't I think of it?" So, with a common purpose, they walked away from a homestead left not much better than when they acquired it and left for Aunt Sohrie's in Anacortes, Washington.

7

Susie and Garnet bought a used Ford, packed only the essentials, and made the drive to Washington. The benefits of moving north went beyond Susie's initial incentive. Waking up to the smell of fresh rain on fir trees was a luxury she had never wholly appreciated as a child. Also, Washington women had been enjoying the right to vote for ten years already, even though the 19th Amendment was passed that same summer before they arrived. The move offered them much in the way of possibility, most importantly, the calming of Billie's breathing. After only two weeks, his coughs were softer now and fewer between. Thanks to Jennie's sister, the sweet and generous Aunt Sophrie, they had a place to catch their breath after a long trip and within days found a cottage for rent up the way.

Susie didn't know why, but she felt nervous about the drive to Rose Hill to see Eva and the family, and the sight of Eva's walkway sent Susie's stomach swirling. Her pa and brother Lyle had helped Jim Cathcart build that house as a wedding present to Jim and Eva twelve years before. She remembered how proud Jim was of how Eva looked in her wedding dress. The whole day he repeated to anyone who would listen, "I can put my hands around her waist and touch my fingers." It felt like a lifetime since then. Every inch of its familiarity sent waves of warmth, grief, love, and pain all at once. Now, Garnet would meet Eva and Jim for the first time. George and Don were home from the war so he would see them too, not Ida though. Susie and Ida seemed to never be in the same place at the same time.

Don appeared first. Susie didn't wait for Garnet to come to a full stop. She jumped out screaming, threw her arms around him, and then screamed again and again as her people came out the door. When she saw her Uncle John and his wife, Goldie, she knew there would be music tonight.

Talking at Gregg get-togethers was always loud and simultaneous. The Greggs were yellers more than talkers, and Garnet found he could join and leave a conversation at will with little notice. Eva put out a spread of food and pulled out instruments she had in storage. Prepping to play was the surest way to quiet the noise. Susie and Don got on fiddles and George had his banjo but he also grabbed the guitar. Uncle John called the tunes from the piano and counted them in. "George, get on banjo. You'll be doin' a solo. Okay now, Turkey in the Straw. Ah one, a-two, a-one, two, three..." George grimaced. He was out of practice, but he knew that excuse never flew with Uncle John. They were a forgiving group and applauded anytime the band played a respectable number of notes together and in a row. When they didn't, that was okay too. George's solo went as expected and he was laughing most of the way through until the end, when he pulled off a lick that sounded downright professional. He bowed. Susie was also rusty but it didn't show and her solos inspired some *Ooos* and some *Ahhhs*. As she played, Gwen and little Garnet danced to the old songs she learned as a child. She thought her heart might burst.

Don and George had to get up early and made a bid to wind it down much to Uncle John's relief who, left to himself, would have gone all night. He and Aunt Goldie said good night and Susie laid the kids in bed. Quiet now, she joined Garnet, Jim, and Eva in the front room. Eva had questions.

Over the years, Eva had expressed concerns in her letters about Garnet's ups and downs as a newspaperman. She believed a man should invest in a firm piece of land and a labor job to provide for his family. Never one to hedge, she addressed him directly. "What are your plans for work, Garnet? Now that you've worked a stable job at the factory, I assume you'll do right by your family and get a position at a plant in Seattle? There's lumber and the railroads, of course. Jim has connections there." *Oh, dear.* Susie knew exactly how far Eva would get with Garnet on this subject. Why Eva was starting in on the first night she didn't know. She wished she had thought to warn him.

Garnet handled Eva. "Funny you ask. I read about a paper that is struggling in a small town by the name of Napavine. It's in Lewis County. Do you know it?"

Jim nodded. "Sure, that's just north of Centralia or thereabouts."

"Well, the *Napavine Independent* is looking for a buyer, a publisher. I'm thinking we'll make a bid on it." Eva's rolling eyes revealed the measure of faith she had in a plan like that, but she had no sway. No sway with Garnet anyway.

§

Happenings Worthwhile in Columbus:

Columbus Weekly Courier, October 24, 1919
It will be of interest to the many friends of Mrs. Garnet Parks, whose husband was at one time editor of the *Courier*, to know how pleasantly situated she and her family are in Anacortes, Washington on Puget Sound.

In a letter to Mrs. J.H. Cox she describes the place as an old city well-kept and it is nearly surrounded by water. She speaks of the reasonable cost of living. For the small sum of fifteen dollars she has a six-room cottage, nicely furnished, along with beautiful roses and all kinds of shrubbery. She also has a good garden with even berries. Quoting her: "you cannot drive me away from here with a club," expresses a good deal.

§

"Well, the country's gone officially dry," Garnet announced to Susie from behind the Sunday issue of the *Bellingham Herald*. "They signed the Volstead Act. They'll be no more drinking." He began chuckling at his own joke before he told it. "Poor Eva's going to have a harder time taking a toot from her pantry closet."

"Garnet! Eva only drinks her own homemade cordial."

"I'm kidding. Anyway, it's not illegal to drink it. Just to make and sell it. That's an idea. She'd make a firm profit selling cordial out of the back of her wagon."

"Okay. I'll let her know you thought of her. You should keep on her good side. She offered for us to stay with them, in their carriage house, until we find a place closer to Napavine."

Gwen had been listening from the next room. "No. Mama, no! I don't want to go there, Mama!" She pulled Garnet Junior into the kitchen for back up. "She doesn't like us. Not at all."

Susie answered. "Gwen, that's not true." Garnet raised an eyebrow.

Gwen scowled intently. "She made me and Garnet wait for dessert and then we had to split the last piece of pie."

G.E. corrected. "She made Garnet and ME wait for the last piece of pie."

Despite Gwen's protests, they packed again. Thank yous and hugs went out to sweet Aunt Sophrie, and they moved into the tight quarters of Eva and Jim's carriage house. Despite Eva's protests, they bought the barely breathing small-town paper and renamed it the *Lewis County Independent* with a plan to develop and expand its circulation. Baby number four was conceived in that little carriage house, and they found a forty-acre farm in Napavine. Their reputation followed them when a Chehalis reporter connected their name to the stories written on the Columbus raid four years before. The *Bee Nugget* provided G.E. with his first bit of publicity before the release of their first issue of the *Lewis County Independent*.

> *Chehalis Bee Nugget,* February 6, 1920
> GE Parks, until recently a resident of Columbus NM, has purchased the Korkan place south of Napavine and has taken possession. Mr. Parks was editor and Publisher of the *Columbus Courier* at Columbus and he and his wife had exciting experiences with Mexican bandits, Mrs. Parks having been wounded in the neck by a bullet fired from a gun in the hands of an outlaw during the memorable raid on that town by Francisco Villa on March 9, 1916.

Susie gave birth to a baby girl, Margaret Irene, and inspired an enthusiasm for babysitting in Eva she hadn't expected. Sometimes she, or she and Jim, would take the two-hour drive to Napavine and pick up the children so Susie and Garnet could set up the business and the new farmhouse without interruptions. Eva spent most of the time tending to the baby inside while the children played in the garden.

Gwen and Garnet Jr. burst through Eva's back door with two-year-old Billie toddling behind. Garnet whined, "I'm hungry."

"Well dinner's not for two hours," Eva told them.

Garnet began to cry and Billie copied him.

"All right, all right. You can each have a chunk of buttered bread." Eva pulled three hunks of bread off a hard loaf on the counter and spread soft butter on each.

Gwen took a bite and spit it out into her hand. "Eww. It's sour. It burns my mouth." Eva had a steadfast policy that no fresh butter should be brought out until the old butter was eaten. Too often it turned rancid before it was finished. "Don't eat it, Garnet. It burns!"

"Why you ungrateful little...." Garnet and Billie dropped their pieces on the ground and the three ran out the door. They hid until Susie and Garnet came, then waited in the car while their mama and papa got an earful from Aunt Eva. "Margaret was a perfect angel though," she was careful to clarify.

On the way home Garnet commented, "Eva really likes our baby, doesn't she?"

"Well, yes. She does like the baby."

§

Carving out a presence in Lewis County was G.E.'s top priority. He was elected Chief Financial Officer at the Napavine American Legion, was inducted into the Chehalis Elks Lodge and was elected President of the Napavine Citizens Club. So happy to be back in the northwest and on forty acres of farmland, Susie had more stake in their success than ever. She was determined to do her part and that meant joining local society circles like the Napavine Women's Literary Club and attending the ever so tedious Women's Society meetings. Even with long nights away and his right hand worn raw from shaking the right hands of businessmen from Pierce to Clark County, Garnet barely added thirty subscriptions to his circulation.

He planted himself mornings at the kitchen table with his cigarette smoldering and a stack of weeklies from across Western Washington. He had begun drinking a cola rather than coffee to keep his sensitive stomach calmed down. Shaking his head, "As far as I can tell, Napavine is proving to be nothing more than a greener, wetter Columbus." Susie saw it too. If experience taught them anything, it was how to spot a dead end. They needed to think more critically this time if they were going to make this work. "I'm going to make some calls." He grabbed his hat and coat and prepared to apply some strategic impatience to the problem.

It was well into spring and Susie had been trying to work out how to skip a ladies' meeting or two so she could prep her garden which was late as it was. The chickens were making do with a lean-to shelter. She was pregnant again and she knew all too well that the bigger she got, the harder it would be to finish that coop.

Eva showed up that afternoon with an arm full of cut flowers. She pushed past Susie to the cabinet where she knew there would be a vase and began arranging.

"Ahh, look at your peonies." Susie was envious. She knew she wouldn't have the indulgence of flowers for several seasons at the rate she was going.

"I put them on the south side of the house and they're coming up like gangbusters," Eva crowed. Irene napped and Gwen and Garnet had Billie outside doing some chicken catchin'. Susie needed Eva's advice, so they walked the property solving and planning. As egregious as she was to some, Eva calmed Susie. They viewed things similarly when it came to work and family. No one was more loyal than Eva and Susie appreciated her. Eva, like Susie, wasn't afraid of a hard day's work and she could easily see the potential of an undeveloped stretch of land. "You can do so much with this place." She picked up a handful of dirt and let it fall through her hands. "But you don't have a husband of a mind or with the skill to do it with you. He doesn't know the first thing about working this land. This is a nice piece of property, Susie, but you're not the family for it."

"He wants to make it work."

"Susie, have you been chewing snuff? He's got softer hands than you or me. He wears a tie in the house on weekends. That man is no farmer."

Garnet's car came coughing up the driveway. They met him at the porch. "Eva, hello." He removed his hat.

"Why are you home, Garnet?" Susie prodded.

"Couldn't do it. It's no use. They're friendly enough, but these Napavine people live hand to mouth." He laid his hat on the counter and pulled at his tie. "Do you know what *The Morning Olympian* gets for a page two, four by two ad? They're collecting four dollars and seventy-five cents for an ad that size. That's what they get in the city. That's where people understand the power of print."

"Did you go to Centralia?"

"I did not. I went straight to the shop and set three pages. My stomach was bothering me again, so I went to the drugstore to get a cola. I filled the car with gas and headed to Olympia."

Predictably, Eva's eyes rolled. Irene cried so Susie went into the house, calling back to him. "Why?"

Eva interjected, "You drove that run-down scrap to Olympia? It's a wonder you didn't break down."

He diverted. "Is that a new hat?" Then he answered Susie. "I went to the *Morning Olympian* and asked them about work and what they knew about papers closer to the city. The assistant editor there was interested in my history, and he was forthcoming with advice."

Eva took Irene from Susie's arms. "What was his advice?" Garnet was annoyed at her interest and continued to direct his answers to Susie. Eva dangled a spoon in front of the baby.

"What was his advice?" Susie repeated.

"He says Tenino is selling their weekly. He says I can probably get fourteen-hundred dollars to fifteen-hundred for the *Independent* which is a three hundred dollar profit. Tenino is fifteen miles from Olympia, far more access, more revenue, and more business. It's just that…"

"That makes sense to me." A supportive response from Eva was the last thing he expected. He and Susie were both surprised. "There's oil there in Tenino, you know."

Garnet lit up. "Yes, that's what I understand. Oil and sandstone. Sandstone for as far as you can see, and a railroad to move it."

Garnet met with the *Tenino News*. They weren't selling but he returned from the meeting with an idea. He told Susie he'd like to meet with Eva and Jim. Garnet thought he had enough goodwill banked to sell Eva and Jim on an investment proposition, provided he could make them a foolproof argument. She was prickly, conservative, stingy even, but Jim's steady living at the railroad provided them with a healthy nest egg. They had means.

Garnet made his case. "I've decided what is most prudent, rather than to sell, we should move the *Independent* from Napavine to Tenino. We'll establish a second paper in Tenino and call it the *Tenino Independent*. Why a second paper in Tenino you ask? Well, we can offer something the *Tenino News* cannot. We'll utilize the most modern method available to produce the *Tenino Independent* with a brand new Merganthaler Linotype, a machine that I have the unique knowledge and skill to operate. I think it's safe to say that no small paper has the benefit of such a commodity as this. Consequently, our product will stand out above all others in production and quality. The *Tenino News* won't see it coming." They were listening. "For such an investment, I'll need a little more cash than I have on hand. What do you say to putting up the down payment on the machine? On the Linotype? You'll be named co-owners of the business and you'll collect a percentage of the profits as we go. I believe we'll make the money back in no time."

Neither Eva nor Jim responded beyond head nods and *hums*. They told him they would think about it. At Eva's next visit, she sat with the two of them and laid it out. "Jim and I discussed it. We will put the money down for your machine, but you will need to sell this place and move the family into town…put your full attention into making a success of this newspaper of yours with no distractions. No digging for oil, no farming. Just newspapering." No doubt Eva had her sister's well-being top of mind. She was determined to bring Susie's fanciful-dreamer-husband down to earth.

Garnet made a convincing show of submission. "I hate to give up this place." Eva relayed a look to Susie revealing how preposterous she believed that to be. He hadn't lifted a garden tool since he signed the papers on the property. "But if that's the condition, Eva, I can agree. Susie?"

Susie, on the other hand, was genuinely disappointed. She had finally gotten the coop done. Out the back window, she watched as their kids ran the property with boundless energy in only their second summer there. Yet, she saw as clearly as Garnet and Eva did that the *Lewis County Independent* was already dead before it got off the ground and she had come to Washington with a firm commitment to make it work here. Their success had no chance in Napavine no matter how many Women's Society meetings she attended. And one thing Susie knew better than anyone, from the Greggs who came before her, was how to pull up roots and start again. "You're right, we have to do it."

> *Tacoma Daily Ledger,* June 18, 1922
> Volume 1, No. 1, of the *Tenino Independent* made its appearance yesterday. G.E. Parks, who recently suspended publication of the *Lewis County Independent* at Napavine, is publisher of the new paper, and Charles A. Berst is editor. The *Independent* gives Tenino two papers, the *News* being a long-established publication.

"We can do this Susie. You know, President Harding started as a publisher just like me. When he ran for president, his wife ran the paper just like you and now he's in the White House."

Susie smiled, eying the crates now waiting to be unpacked in their Tenino house. "Humph. Well, Garnet, if it comes to it, I'm willing to make one more move if it's to the White House."

§

Those pains that sent Garnet to his bed in Pittsburgh were coming more often now. Everybody's doctor in Tenino was Dr. Wichman and he ordered Garnet to bed rest and a schedule of Pepsid syrup. The doctor believed it was stomach acid produced from the stress of starting a new business. He told him to take several weeks off, but G.E. had only put out four issues of the new *Tenino Independent*. He rested three days but was in the shop Thursday night to make sure it went without a hitch.

Chas Berst had come on as an assistant editor. The three worked together. Susie was wearing a cotton dress and printer's apron that concealed her belly which was now nine months in the making. The three got acquainted as they worked. "Guess what, Charles. Today is Garnet's birthday." Susie gave him a nudge.

Chas set down his ink paddle and saluted. "Well happy birthday to you, G.E."

"Thank you, sir. Susie tried to talk me into a party, but I told her we can have cake on the weekend. All that bedrest set us back and I want this paper out." Garnet let out a grunt and doubled over the linotype and shouted, "Good night nurse!"

"Garnet." Susie dropped her pages. Another sharp pain caught him. "We have to take you in." Garnet shook his head no. She told Chas, "He's better when he's lying down. Let's get him back to the house."

Garnet pointed at Chas with his free hand. "You. Take me home. Let Susie finish printing. We're almost done."

Chas checked Susie for confirmation. She nodded for him to go. They helped Garnet into the passenger seat of the Ford and Chas drove the two blocks to the house. There, the kids were preparing to terrorize a sitter they hardly knew with an after-dinner wrestling match. When they saw their papa enter in the arms of his assistant, they sobered up. Chas and the nervous sitter put him to bed.

Back at the shop, Susie began to feel the familiar pull above her groin. She was printing the last copies they would need for the morning when Chas returned. The two collated, folded, and stacked to make the August 4th edition ready for delivery. The intensity of her contractions now had her heaving deep breaths and clutching the arms of a desk chair. She noticed Chas blinking nervously. "Ma'am?"

He was puzzled. *Uh oh.* She realized he probably didn't even know she was pregnant. *Poor guy,* then she let out a yell. "Woa! Okay, Chas, we're done here. I'm going to need to get home."

"Should I drive you? Did you and Mr. Parks eat the same thing for supper?" He didn't get an answer. He tried to accommodate while trying not to pry and made his second two-block drive to the Parks house. The sitter earned her pay that night. She took Susie into the back bedroom and, a few minutes past 11:00 pm, helped her deliver their eleven-pound baby boy.

Gwen was eight now and served as a traffic director permitting and denying her brothers and sister access to the new baby brother and their papa. "Not when Papa's sleeping!" She demanded. "You can see the baby if you wash your face."

The baby made funny faces that Susie knew was gas, but it reminded the kids of faces their Uncle Jim Cathcart would make to get them to laugh. They agreed his name should be Jim. Officially he was James Parks and they called him Jimmie.

§

On a sunny Tuesday afternoon, Garnet adjusted static on the dial of the radio with serious intention. Gwen was struggling in the hall to push their wicker baby carriage through the door and into the main room. In her best mommy voice, she consoled her imaginary baby. "Don't cry little Liza, we'll be out of here soon." Garnet Junior came from behind and gave her an unhelpful shove through the doorway. "Oh." She cried and then made more fuss over her baby. "Dear baby Liza, are you okay?" As she passed a side table, she picked off a pair of wire-rimmed spectacles, placed them on her nose then tossed Susie's scarf that was already tied around her head.

Susie fed Irene in the kitchen. "Where are you going, Gwen?"

"Baby Liza wants a walk, Susan."

Oh no, I'm Susan today. "All right. Don't go too far."

"Of course not, Susan. We're going to visit the ladies in town for tea and probably cookies."

Susie knew she should check on Gwen, but she was soaking up some rare uninterrupted time with Irene who was talking her ear off with nonsense words.

"Wonderful!" Garnet called Susie from the main room. "Do you hear that? It's the Indians' game."

"Hold on." Susie wiped Irene's face and carried her in. "What are you saying?"

"Opening day. Seattle Indians playing the Seals at San Francisco. Listen. I mean the announcer is...do you hear him?" Sure enough, through static and whistles, she could hear a voice reporting on a game. "They're telegraphing to him from San Francisco and he's announcing it, play by play. Listen."

A sports broadcast over radio. Susie leaned in. "What fun. Irene, you sit here with Papa. I'll get the baby and we can sit together and listen." Susie went to the crib, but no Jimmie. "The baby. Where's the baby?"

Gwen had already passed Billie on the walkway, who was squatted on the neighbor's grass working on a box of matches. Still in her mommy voice, "Young man!" She snatched the matchbook from his hands. "Good boys don't play with matches," then commenced making tracks up the street.

"Hey!" Billie tried to chase her down but she, and the buggy on only two wheels, had already cleared the corner. He turned back and met his mama on the sidewalk.

"Bill, did you see Sister?"

"She's being a mama," he sneered, then pointed up the street in alarm. "And she got matches."

"Matches! What is she going to do with matches?" Billie shrugged. Susie tied a knot in her skirt and went running for her. "Gwen! Gwen, get back here!"

She caught up to Gwen who pretended to be startled. "You've scared me, Susan."

She admired Gwen's commitment to the character when she was likely about to get paddled. Inside the buggy, under the blanket was a dolled-up but contented Jimmie Parks, painted up with pink cheeks and red lips, wearing a beaded necklace and Irene's frilliest pink dress.

"Gwen, do you have matches?"

The seriousness of the question caused Gwen to switch to her real voice. "I did, but I threw them in the bushes back there. Bill was lighting them on the lawn, so I took 'em."

"So, he had the matches?" It wasn't the first time. Billie's fascination with fire was concerning and having put more than one fire out in her short life, she couldn't figure what would make her own son want to start one. "Okay then, thank you."

"Well, you're quite welcome Susan." Gwen cocked her head and resumed her walk accompanied now by Susan.

Back at the house, Bill was watching Garnet Junior throw his hardball against the steps. Susie took Jimmie from the carriage and spit in her hand to rub off his rouge. "Papa and I are going to listen to the ballgame. After the game, Bill, you and I will have a talk. I'd love for you three to stay out of trouble."

"What did I do?" Junior asked legitimately.

Perched on the top step, Bill confronted Gwen. "Where's my matches?"

She barked back. "I threw them out! You're in trouble with Mama."

"I wasn't gonna do nothin'. Besides, you stol'd the baby."

Gwen glared. "You don't know anything. I was taking care of him."

Bill was indignant. "You don't know 'bout babies?"

"I know," Garnet chimed in. "I know that babies don't grow up from the ground like you told me, Gwen."

Gwen glared harder. "Where do they come from then!"

Garnet paused his throwing. "Papa said it's a bird that brings 'em and drops them in a cabbage patch." Garnet started throwing again. Bill sat, thinking.

Gwen considered it. "Cabbage patch? I never heard that."

From his perch, Bill spoke up. "That isn't what happens at all. There isn't no bird and isn't no cabbage." He had their attention. "The mama swells up, there..." He pointed his finger at Gwen's belly. "...and then she coughs." He coughed to demonstrate, "...and coughs and coughs, then she coughs out a baby."

§

Summer was over and Gwen and Garnet Junior would start new at the Stoney Point School. Gwen had done first and second grade in Napavine and she was now starting third. Junior would be in first grade. Susie had been pulling late nights at the sewing machine to make sure they each had something new to wear. She walked with them to meet the Model T school bus that transported the in-town kids across the way. At the stop, she pulled a loose thread from Garnet's britches. "Find a friend to sit next to at lunchtime. The ones sitting alone are usually the most interesting."

Susie was always so awkward about school and worried that it might hold them back. She noticed how involved other mothers were with their kids' learning and made a promise to herself to ask them to tell her about something they learned when they got home.

"Inside the house, G.E. stood at the kitchen counter swallowing his tablespoon of Pepsid. He lifted his coffee cup to wash it down then doubled over as if he'd taken a punch to the solar plexus. Susie found him folded onto the chair, pointing to his ribs. "It's higher this time...up here."

"Okay, let's get you to bed."

He resisted. "Nooo. Ah! It's..."

Susie called out, "Billie!"

Bill came in from the bedroom and sized up the situation quickly. "Papa needs the doc!"

They now had a regular "hired lady", Mrs. Chansky, to watch them when Susie worked, but she wasn't there yet. "Go get Mrs. Corbin." Billie ran full speed to Mrs. Corbin's house. She came and took the baby. Susie hadn't tested the speed of that old Ford before, but his moans were only escalating so she floored it all the way to Seace Hospital in Centralia. The nurses there wheeled him off and told Susie to wait. Waiting was not a strength of hers.

After several trips back and forth to the counter, the doctor appeared. "It's his gallbladder, Mrs. Parks. We're going to have to take it out." They took him back to surgery to cut him open. Susie waited.

At home, Mrs. Corbin was relieved by Mrs. Chansky who held things together. Irene was having a visit with Aunt Eva and Uncle Jim in Kirkland so, once Gwen and Junior returned from school, she only had the four of them. The September sun warmed the house up quickly by afternoon and Jimmie was getting fussy. Mrs. Chansky bounced him on her hip and checked the wall clock impatiently.

Billie was at her feet scooting along the floor in a pie tin and blowing spit bubbles pretending he was a car. Junior and Gwen barreled in from the backyard, with a crash and a bang and slammed the screen door.

Mrs. Chansky gasped and then covered Jimmie's ears to holler at them. "Kids, don't slam that door."

Gwen answered, "We can slam it..."

Then Junior added, "... if we want to."

Mrs. Chansky was in shock at their insolence but she kept her head and made it a teaching moment. Pointing to Billie, who was still scooting along on the floor she said, "Why can't you be more like your brother here? At least you're a good little boy, Bill."

Billie waved his chubby arms at her. "Ah, suttup. You isn't the Mama." Gwen and Garnet Junior knew they had been bad but they didn't expect their little brother to talk back. They were speechless.

Susie stayed through the surgery, which the doctor confirmed went well, then Garnet was admitted for rest and observation. She drove home alone and was able to relieve the sitter before dinnertime. Considering their family health crisis, Mrs. Chansky didn't burden Susie with the story of her ill-mannered children, but Gwen and Junior were more than ready to spill it. "Billie told Mrs. Chansky to shut up."

"What!" *Impossible,* she thought. *Not Bill.*

"He said, 'sut up'," Junior clarified. "After we told her that we didn't have to listen to her, and we could slam the screen door if we wanted."

Billie added, "She was yellin', Mama, but she can't yell. She isn't the mama!"

Susie was mortified. "No Bill, you can't..." Then she turned to the older two. "And you were talking back? Where do you think Billie learns it from?" They ate whatever was left over from the icebox and practiced their apologies so they were ready for Mrs. Chansky's return the next day. That took up the time until bed. Susie did not remember to ask Gwen and Junior about their learning.

§

Garnet was monitored for five days then sent home. "Papa! Papa!" Gwen and Junior ran at him ready to lunge but were stopped by the slow and careful pace Susie used to guide him into the house. She helped him to the couch, and he patted the cushion as an invitation. Irene was home now too. She crawled into his lap.

Susie noticed Billie hanging back as usual, always reticent about being near his father. She guessed he was scared of him, and it troubled her that Garnet didn't make an effort to reach out and make him more comfortable. "Go on Bill. It's okay. Go sit with Papa." She led him to the couch and he sat himself uneasily on the arm of the sofa.

"They cut you open didn't they Papa?" Junior's eyes bulged with intrigue.

"Yes, they did. They call it a cholecystectomy." Billie sat still, expressionless.

Junior leaned in closer. "Can we see it, Papa?"

"Sure, you can see it." He unbuttoned his shirt and showed the bandage on his right side. Irene pulled at it. "Careful, now." He pulled the bandage away revealing an incision lined with thick threads tied in knots across the wound.

Susie blurted, "Eckk..." Billie laughed and leaned in.

He touched the scar with his index finger and traced the path of it along the bumps and pits. "Wow, Papa."

Garnet tightened and pulled his shirt closed. "All right, that's enough. We don't want to get it dirty and infect it."

"No, Garnet, it's okay." She was sick to see Billie's apprehensions validated. Bill hopped off the arm of the chair, itching to get outside.

"No, the show's over. I could use a nap before dinner."

She helped him up and walked him into the bedroom. "You should have let him look at it, Garnet. He was interested."

"Who?" He asked her.

"Bill. You need to give him attention." But she realized it wasn't an ideal time for a lecture. "Okay, get some sleep."

§

The Tacoma Daily Ledger, Nov 9, 1922
Mrs. Molly Burnett returned Monday after a week visiting in Tenino, Centralia and Chehalis. While in Tenino Mrs. Burnett called on Mr. and Mrs. G.E. Parks who until last May published the *Lewis County Independent* in Napavine. Mr. Parks was very ill following an operation several weeks ago. He is now at home but is still confined to his bed, recovering slowly.

The first week Susie expected Garnet to sleep a lot. She ran at full speed between the print shop, the bus stop, supply stores, and home to care for Garnet, the kids and to keep the paper afloat. Since the move to Tenino, she only saw Eva when she came to pick up Irene and it annoyed her a bit but, with all that was on her plate, Eva's preference for Irene was a background disturbance. How could she complain about the special attention Irene enjoyed over there? If she had her choice, each of her kids would have an Aunt Eva and Uncle Jim all to themselves.

Garnet smoked and kept up on the news from his bed. At first, he would get up in the afternoons to join the family but, as days became weeks, he only made it to the kitchen for a few nights' meals. He was getting worse, not better. "What is it, Garnet?"

He indicated to the left of his abdomen and handled himself very gently. "It's tight here. Very uncomfortable. Like pressure and then sharp pains." His back ached and he still had stomach pain that was lower now. He simply could not get comfortable and hadn't slept for several nights.

After three successive bouts of vomiting, Susie called Dr. Wichman. "I don't understand. Why is he still hurting? He doesn't want to eat."

The doctor didn't like it. "This is certainly not what we expect. We should have seen improvement since the cholecystectomy. I know a specialist up at St. Peter's in Olympia. I think you should take him there. We may have missed something."

Garnet was shrinking in size. She noticed his belly had protruded and his complexion was yellowing. It was scary.

Dr. Wichman called ahead to St. Peters. Preparations were made for a series of tests and Susie and Garnet were alerted that they should pack for at least two days. Eva and Jim drove down to stay overnight with the children. Before she left, she locked in on her three oldest. "Aunt Eva and Uncle Jim are coming. You are going to play *Angels in Heaven*, the game of perfect children. Do you understand?" Junior nodded emphatically but Gwen and Bill seemed to be thinking about it. "Sister? Bill?"

Bill answered. "I will, Mama."

"Okay," Gwen conceded. "Will she be cooking?"

"I packed a box of fruit and bread and put it in your closet. You can say, 'no thank you' if you aren't sure about something." She hugged them and hoped for the best.

At St. Peters they poked, prodded and performed a series of x-rays. Nurses took his blood and swept his mouth for samples. He was rolled out of the room and then back again multiple times. On day two, a tube was inserted out the left side of his abdomen to drain the fluid buildup causing his swollen belly. The miracle of painkillers allowed him the relief of sleep. There was nothing for Susie to do but hold his hand and wait. Finally, a very serious Doctor Mowell entered the room. "Mr. and Mrs. Parks." His earnest manner was distressing. Susie sat up.

Garnet tried to adjust himself to greet the doctor with some dignity. Susie squeezed his frail hand as the doctor spoke. "We've studied the x-rays and discussed your case at length. One thing we know is that you are suffering from chronic appendicitis. This may be why you continue to complain of pain in your lower abdomen even after your cholecystectomy."

"His appendix?" Susie asked. "So, now he needs to have his appendix out?"

"I wish it were that simple, Mrs. Parks. Unfortunately, your husband's trouble is compounded by a hepatomegaly. What I mean to say is that his liver is enlarged." The doctor leaned in and held a light to Garnet's eyes. "See the yellow pigment showing here in the whites of his eyes. This is caused by an increase of bile pigments in the blood."

"Jaundice," Garnet suggested.

"That's right. It is the result of a liver that is compromised. I regret to tell you that we believe we are dealing with cancer of the liver."

"Cancer!" Susie choked, but she didn't cry.

Garnet remained stoic. He looked at Susie but addressed the doctor. "How long do I have?"

"We don't know Mr. Parks. Maybe weeks, maybe months. We aim to make you as comfortable as possible. Some of your discomfort is caused by the fluid buildup in your abdomen and that's common with liver cancer. Maybe you know it as dropsy. The tube there will drain the fluid and reduce the swelling. It should make you a little more comfortable."

"So, I'm dying." Garnet looked at the doctor almost accusingly. "What's your name again, sir?"

"Doctor Mowell."

"Doctor Mowell, I'm dying?"

"I wish it were not so but it's true Mr. Parks. You are dying."

§

On the day Garnet was to be released, Susie drove alone to pick him up. She planned to get Garnet home and set up in the bedroom before Gwen and Junior returned from school. She wanted the house quiet and wanted him settled before the kids saw him. Eva and Jim took Irene to Kirkland and Bill and Jimmie were with Mrs. Chansky. As she drove, she wondered what she should be feeling. Nothing was coming up. Her impulse was to just be still, like being still might suspend time somehow. She remembered feeling that way while at the switchboard holding Gwen and her rifle. *Just be still.*

At the entrance, she stayed in the car taking just another minute before entering, but the nurse was already wheeling Garnet toward her. The disease had diminished him so that he was nearly swallowed up by the wheelchair. The nurse lifted his eighty pounds with ease. She settled him into the seat of the car and handed Susie the drain tube and bag she would be changing out with enough Laudanum to last several weeks. The Laudanum was his only comfort now and she was grateful for the supply.

They tried talking on the way back, but Garnet kept nodding off, so Susie left him without interruption for the rest of the ride. Once home, she was anxious. "How is this for you, Garnet, on this side of the bed?" She fussed. "Is it better on the other side away from the window?"

She tried to ignore the extent of his fragility but she felt enormous next to him. "It's fine," he told her. "It's okay, I can do it." He landed on the edge of the bed and nearly slipped off.

She caught him and saw that her hands were shaking. "Here, let me get your shoes." She untangled his tube and wrapped it around the bedpost.

"Will the kids be home? Help me comb my hair. My hairs..." he chuckled weakly. "The ones that are left."

"Okay. Stay there. I'll get your comb." She put the Laudanum in a shoe box and set it on an upper shelf. The doctor had said five drops should keep his pain under control, but she shouldn't hesitate to increase if he needed it.

She returned with his comb and a hand mirror and handed it to him for the sake of his dignity, but he couldn't manage it. *I've brought him home so they can watch him die.* "Here, Garnet, let me get that." She held the mirror. He pushed the comb around his ears. This seemed important to him. "That's good. You look good. Are you hungry? Or thirsty?"

"Water would be good. Is there coffee?"

"I'll get you a paper and put the pot on. You rest." She came back with the paper and a coffee that she had cooled with water from the tap, but he was asleep so she stood in the doorway and sipped his lukewarm coffee. She knew the kids would be home soon. She wondered how she should contact his family, by letter or telegram, and how to handle Chas. *Do I let him go?* She worried that the children might always remember their father this helpless, that Bill would not connect with him before he was gone forever, that Jimmie would never know him, and also, she wasn't sure how and when to give him the shots.

What she didn't worry about was how she would manage once he died. It didn't enter her mind. Then, standing in the doorway, she realized that the date today was October 22nd. Today she was twenty-seven.

§

They tried, but it didn't work to have the children in the room with him. He was so easily fatigued, and they were more work than comfort to him. Also, as Susie feared, the change in him scared them. The first look at him caused Gwen to go white. "Mama, what happened to him? Why is he so small? What's wrong with his skin? He looks like a pumpkin." Being near his dying father made Junior fidgety and caused him to shake the bed and agitate him. Susie was not surprised that Billie avoided the whole thing altogether and spent his time in the yard or up in a tree. At night though, Bill would slide out of his bed and peek into the bedroom from a corner of the hallway.

"Susie!" Garnet yelled. "Susie, bring me the..." She jumped out of bed. "Gimme a shot! The itching. I can't..." The itching would come on suddenly and it was intolerable.

"I'll get the Calamine."

"No! The shot! The shot!" Squirming in the sheets he was desperate for relief. "No, never mind. Get me up! I need to go to the toilet." She pulled him up, but then he dropped to the floor. He did it on purpose trying to make more effective work on the itching by rubbing his body on their braided rug. She reached down to help him up. "Not yet!" Helpless to offer him even the tiniest scrap of relief, all she could do was wait.

"Mama!" Irene called out.

"I'll get her, Mama." Gwen was always listening and assessing these days, seldom getting a full night's sleep herself. If letting Gwen help was putting too much on her eight-year-old, Susie would have to answer to that later.

She called back to her, "Thank you, honey!" Then to Garnet, "Now?" He nodded. She lifted him and gave him the shot he needed. Doctor Mowell had replaced the Laudadum prescription with a Squibb morphine syrinette. The tubes came with the needle attached that injected straight into the muscle. It was faster, more effective, and Susie now dispensed the doses like a skilled nurse.

He scratched as she helped him to the bathroom. No sooner was he seated, that the baby started crying. Susie pressed on to the babies' room and noticed Bill on the floor. "Are you okay?" He nodded, which would have to be good enough. She went for the baby.

She returned to collect Garnet, who held onto her and shuffled back to his room. In a novel moment of awareness, his gaze lit on Jimmie. "Oh, hello," he said as if he were meeting him for the first time.

Susie helped him to bed, reattached his bag then carried Jimmie with her to nurse him. She wondered how Gwen handled Irene and if Bill was still hunkered down on the floor of the hallway. She imagined Garnet Junior pulling the covers over his head to make it all go away. She thought she must be exhausted but she wasn't sure. One thing she noticed, she felt gratitude for her nursing baby who required her to sit still. *Just like Maggie,* she thought.

§

As a courtesy among neighbors, the *Centralia Tribune* took over the *Independent*'s printing and distribution "until further notice." Susie found a way to pay and keep Chas Berst on to run the print shop. She cut back Mrs. Chansky's hours and worked with Chas as much as she could. It wasn't the hard work that drained her energy so much as the joylessness. Before, even in the darkest times, she'd find a way to light a spark to keep her going. Now, there was no room for such a thing. No family outings, no dances...her violin collected dust on the shelf of the closet. These were indulgences, sure, but a life of going from feeding to earning to fixing to caretaking was a life that pained her to see in her ma. Now, this was her and she felt ashamed of her selfishness.

Laura Jane Parks wrote almost daily and signed the letters, *Ma and Pa*. Since Garnet's gallstone surgery two months before, G.A. had moved back to Virginia and wrote his brother from there. There were letters from Dean and Jettie, but no one in the family seemed to know what had become of Rex. As death neared, the last words Garnet would have with his Virginia family would be by mail.

He wanted to give something to Gwen and Garnet Junior to remember him by. He asked Susie to bring them in. They entered cautiously and then planted themselves at his bedside. Susie left a crack in the door to listen.

Standing before their papa, Gwen took her brother's hand and the connection released a flood of tears from them both. "Sister. Son. You know that I'm not well. Soon, I'll die. Do you understand what that means?" Even in his compromised state, he fancied himself a teacher. Junior tried to answer but his words got caught on the way up. Gwen nodded. "It may be tomorrow but if not, it will be soon."

"Papa!" They squeezed one another's hands harder. Susie wiped her eyes from outside the room.

"I want you to have something to remember me by." He tried to reach the table but resorted to pointing. "The watch there, Garnet. Pick up the watch." He did. The watch fob fell through his fingers. Junior gathered it up anxiously and then held it to his ear. "Yes, it works. It's a quality watch. You'll have it a long time."

"Th-thank you, Papa."

"You like it. Good." Susie knew it satisfied him to see Junior holding it. *He loved...loves that watch.* "Now, Sister."

"Yes, Papa."

"Remember when I told you about my award from secondary school? I never misspelled a word. Remember?"

Choking for breath, "I... I remember." It was harder for Susie to hear Gwen vulnerable somehow. Even at eight, it didn't fit her.

"They awarded me this pen and pencil set." He gestured toward it. Gwen took it from the table, but she didn't look at it.

"Thank you, Papa."

"I'm tired. I need to sleep." He reached out to them. Their fingers touched his hand, but they didn't grasp it for fear he might break.

In the hall, Susie reached out for them. There was pleading in their eyes and she knew they wanted her to fix it. She closed his door and steered them away to get some distance. It was enough reality for one day, but she knew they were in for more to come. "Go on, now," she told them. "Go find Billie."

§

Garnet's last days were closing in and both doctors, Wichman and Mowell, encouraged Susie to dispense his morphine liberally to keep him as comfortable as possible. His appetite was inconsistent. He asked for Mrs. Corbin's rice pudding and took some tastes of Susie's potato salad but most days he didn't eat at all. Susie came in to check on him and he surprised her. "I smell bratwurst."

"Yes! I'm cooking bratwurst. Does it smell good to you?" Eva had brought bratwurst and a jar of the best sauerkraut any of them had ever tasted from the Market at Pike Street. "I'll bring you some."

He breathed it in, and Susie fed him a forkful. "Mmmm…" Then he let out a moan.

She cautioned him. "Take it slow."

"Just a little more of the sauerkraut." He took two more bites, then his eyes began to droop. Susie pulled him down flat and adjusted his blanket.

Then she noticed the oddest thing in his tube. In the drain tube, floating through it and down into the bag were little threads pale and yellow. Stringy pieces maybe an inch each in length going down the tube into the bag. She watched them swimming along and it struck her how curious it was, the resemblance of these little floating threads to Eva's Pike Street Market sauerkraut. "Garnet! The tube! Look!"

He muttered unconsciously. "Hum?"

"I'm calling the doctor." Dr. Wichman came over and examined the bag. He emptied it through a strainer at the kitchen sink. With the help of a magnifier and the original jar of sauerkraut, he confirmed it. "It's sauerkraut, all right. Somewhere between his stomach and the large intestine is an open door. We need to get him to Olympia."

§

The Centralia Tribune, still serving the *Tenino Independent*'s readership, reported on G.E.'s condition and the incredible discovery.

Tenino Independent, November 24, 1922
G.E. PARKS GOES TO ST. PETERS HOSPITAL
Dr. Mowell in Charge of Case, No Cancer Indications G.E. Parks was taken to the St. Peters Hospital Sunday morning November 19 and is under the care of Dr. Mowell of Olympia.

Mr. Parks has been suffering for the past four months from what was thought to be cancer of the liver. An x-ray picture was made Monday evening which shows indications of chronic appendicitis and slightly enlarged liver, and the main trouble since a thorough examination has been made, is thought to be a punctured bowel due to a mistake on the part of the doctor who performed the operation for gallstones, which occurred about twelve weeks ago at the Seace Hospital in Centralia. Mr. Parks will probably remain in the hospital two weeks.

It was truly a remarkable thing. There had been no cancer at all. G.E.'s bowel had been poisoning him from the inside. The doctors at St. Peter's closed it up and watched him slowly come back to life. He started putting on weight and, before long, was taking walks around the hospital. The better he felt, the antsier he got about getting back to work. By the end of his hospital stay, his leathery complexion softened and his previous color returned. He continued to receive doses of morphine with a plan to decrease the frequency and volume of his injections over time. It was such an odd and unlikely series of events they hardly knew how to react.

"We've got to get a telegram to your family. They won't believe the news." Susie was beside herself with happiness. It was a kind of happiness she had begun to believe she'd never feel again. The Napavine Women's Club, neglected by her since the summer after they moved to Tenino, insisted that they should throw him a dance to celebrate. Susie offered up her Uncle John for the music. "I've got to tell Don and George. We've got to call Ma and Maggie." She now dared to imagine a future and a long life together and she dared Garnet to imagine the same. She held the mirror up to him. "You're getting fat. Look at you." It was true. His energy was still catching up to hers, but he also had begun to reintegrate the possibility of hope and a future as well.

He wrote to his brothers and his mother with the tongue-in-cheek announcement that he had been resurrected. His idea of celebration was different from Susie's. He called out, "Sister, Junior, Bill. come into the kitchen. It's time for a Bee." It had taken some explaining and even some convincing, but they understood now that their father was going to be okay. They bounded in and took their places like they'd done whenever he called them six months before. "Okay Sister, the word is 'nickel'. The winner of this spelling bee will get a nickel. Nickel."

Gwen squinted her eyes hard. "Nickel. N. I. C. E...No, no...N. I. C. K." Then, with a big nod, "E. L...Nickel."

Susie looked on at the odd tradition of quizzing their children that had always perplexed her. Watching it now, she felt she could never again live without it.

§

The ladies from the Napavine Women's Club prepared the Tenino Grange for a celebration. They provided Susie's Uncle John with a piano and space for his friends and nephews to set up an authentic country dance band. George and Don came ready to play for folks from Chehalis, the *Centralia Tribune*, and Napavine and Susie's family who came from across western Washington. They came to wish Garnet well and to dance on a Friday night.

Eva loved parties. She danced with such liveliness it made Susie seem a wallflower in comparison. Don entertained the kids by playing his fiddle between his legs and behind his back before he got onstage to join the band. Jim Cathcart sat near the stage keeping rhythm with his dancing eyebrows that moved independently to the beat of the music.

Garnet went through half a pack of cigarettes while receiving friends and community members happy to welcome him back and inquire about his health. Susie asked the band to play "Let Me Call You Sweetheart" which got him up for a dance. It wasn't his favorite thing, but he couldn't refuse her a dance to the song that first brought them together. Garnet Junior got up after Gwen threatened to punch him in the gut if he refused. Billie needed no coercing. He turned and twirled to the music with or without a partner throughout the night.

The event marked the end of an ordeal that was nothing short of terrifying. Now it was over. By Susie's estimation, they were recipients of a divine intervention that came in the form of sauerkraut. They would treat it as a hiccup, happy to put it behind them with no residual damage done.

Dean, G.A., Jetty, his Ma and even Carl and the girls wrote relating the relief they felt to read the news of his "resurrection." There was still no word from Rex and all they knew was that he was somewhere in California. They were not aware of the ripple Rex had cast down there that was to find them in due time.

The Sacramento Bee Marriage Licenses, January 26, 1923
PARKS-REX-In Sacramento, January 25, 1923, Camet R. Parks, 24, and Lena M. Rex, 17; both of Stockton, San Joaquin County.

3

After six months away G.E. was back in the publisher's chair. Like the goodwill offered after the *Courier* office fire by the *Deming Graphic*, the *Centralia Tribune* had offered aid those six months for the *Independent*. Because of the *Tribune*, they had a paper to come back to.

> *Tenino Independent*
> On February 2, 1923, After an absence of over six months from the office, due to illness, I am back on the job as the publisher of the *Tenino Independent*.
>
> I shall endeavor to now carry out the plans for the paper made last summer.
>
> I desire to express to the people of this community my sincere appreciation for favors of the past six months. Your loyal support of the newspaper during this period has been far more liberal than I could have possibly expected.
>
> More deeply than words can express, I appreciate the assistance rendered by the people of this community, the Red Cross and the Chehalis Lodge of the B.P.O. Elks.
>
> It would be next to impossible to enumerate names of all those to whom I feel so deeply indebted. I want you to know that your favors are appreciated, and I sincerely thank you.
>
> I can't overlook this opportunity to mention Mr. and Mrs. George Dempsey. Night after night, for many weeks Mr. Dempsey sat by my bedside and did everything that anyone could do to relieve and cheer a sufferer. To say I wish to be able to return the favors would be equal to wishing Mr. and Mrs. Dempsey in like circumstances. I only hope to be able to let them know in some way how deeply and sincerely their efforts were appreciated.

Susie asked him. "This is such a nice tribute, Garnet, but why didn't you thank the *Tribune*?"

"I thought of it but out of respect I kept my thanks to volunteers. They enjoyed profits while they published our paper and I assured them we would do them the same courtesy if they ever needed it. I don't want to put a rift between us and other local papers by highlighting the *Tribune*."

Like all the highlighting that went out to George and Mabel Dempsey? Sometimes his capacity to turn a blind eye baffled her. Billie passed them. *Case and point*, she thought, and pulled the little guy in for a hug.

G.E. had papers to sell. He ended his return letter with the pitch forever in his back pocket for whichever town was the focus of his affections:

> Before deciding to come to Tenino, almost one year ago, I fully believed that it was the best town of its size in the country. I am more fully convinced of this fact now than ever before. I believe in its future; I believe in its citizenship.
>
> I fully appreciate the patronage and cooperation given the *Independent*. I hope it may be of service to this community. I want every citizen to know that it is their paper, an organ for the expression of public, rather than individual, opinion at all times and under all circumstances. Again, I wish to thank you, one and all for past favors.
>
> Sincerely yours,
> G. E. Parks

It wasn't all strategy. G.E. truly believed that conditions in Tenino were ripe for his influence. The number of homeowners in town had more than doubled much to the credit of an investor named Wilson who bought the sandstone quarry on Lemon Hill. Garnet had a vision of Tenino as a bustling center of commerce.

As if addressing a gathering of stockholders, he spoke from his kitchen chair to his audience of one. "This town needs a sense of community. Remember the spirit in Columbus during the Expedition Celebration? Tenino has jobs, investors, and families coming in droves... let's establish a baseball team. I see no reason why the Thurston County Fair shouldn't be held right here in Tenino."

G.E. was back to a steady schedule of club meetings and planning committees. Susie knew the positive effect a big project like a county fair could have on channeling his energy and she encouraged him. Also, no one was ever hurt by having a baseball team in the neighborhood. "A baseball team and a county fair? Great idea, Garnet."

On the other hand, Susie felt the ladies' clubs could do just as well without her. She began treating herself to one night a week of band practice with a small group of musicians. She needed the break but she had a concern about leaving Garnet on his own. Since their return from the hospital, there had been no noticeable decrease in the number of shots he was taking. Eva came down to pick Irene up for a visit and mentioned she knew a man who had overcome the drug by diluting the doses with water. "He's not a strong man, Susie. He doesn't have the drive to beat the problem himself. You see that, I'm sure. You have to take action, Susie or he will only get worse."

Susie wasn't convinced the problem was a lack of strength or drive. It was physical, she could see that and it scared her. She thought she would try it, maybe dilute his doses and increase by a little each day. She hoped it would be so gradual he wouldn't notice.

Two weeks into her plan, he was screaming from the bedroom. "Suuu-siE. SU-SiEEE!" She found him at the far corner of the room with a syringe in his hand trembling with anger. "What's happened? What did you do? Did you do something to the medicine?"

She considered a lie but instead stood silent shaking her head. "I just..."

"You just what? I have to go to the shop. Look at me." His hands shook violently, and his face was flushed. "What did you do?"

"Water," she told him. "I put water in them to help you."

"Help me? That's no help. You should know that." He went to the box. "How many? How many did you spoil?"

She pointed. "Just those. Just the five there."

Scrambling. "These?" He grabbed them and hurled them into the garbage pail. "This one and these here?"

"And that one." She handed him another and he threw it out too then took a full syrigette and injected it furiously into his arm. Susie stood motionless. It took a moment but his shaking subsided and he collapsed onto the bed.

"I'm sorry Garnet. I thought...I know it's hard and I thought that you won't be able to stop on your own."

He draped his arm across his eyes to shield them from the light and spoke calmly. "I'll stop, Susie. I will. I promise I will."

"I'll bring you something for your lunch today. I'll bring Jimmie down and we'll get the pages set."

"Okay," his breathing returned to normal. "When does Eva bring Baby back?"

"She didn't say but I'll call her before I come."

Out the door, he lit a cigarette and used his forearm to pull the sweat from his head. The crisp February air did its job to revive him on the two-block walk to the shop.

§

Susie wondered if Eva ever intended to bring Irene back home. It wasn't just that she missed her, but these long visits kept Irene from her brothers and sister. She decided to pay the long-distance fees and call Eva. "Hi. Listen, I can't afford to stay on, but we're ready to have Irene back home."

"Are you still spending your days in the Print Shop? Susie, you know that's no place for Margaret, she's only a toddler." Eva always seemed to forget Mrs. Chansky was at the house. The debt owed to Eva for the linotype was always top of mind for Susie, though Eva never mentioned it, she did make clear was how genuinely she enjoyed having visits with Margaret. "I've got her, Susie, you take care of the rest of your brood. God knows that's work enough for you." Never missing a chance to take a dig at him, "We both know Garnet's not doing any heavy lifting."

"Her brothers and sister miss her, Eva. Another week, then you'll bring her back down? Please?" Susie hung up knowing she was at her sister's mercy.

She met Garnet at the shop at noon. He'd gotten a lot done. "I'm productive when I'm not fighting withdrawals," he hinted and she got the message. "Check my pitch for Tenino to enter the Sawdust League:

> *It is time to begin planning for a baseball club if the town is to have baseball this season. Last summer the people went out of town every week to see ball games and it is reasonable to believe they will do the same this summer unless we have a ball club here at home. It probably would be a paying proposition for the organization to sponsor it.*

"Who would sponsor it?"

"I already met with Wilson at the quarry. He needs the good favor here. I don't think he can refuse."

The bell rang out as Gwen, Junior, and Bill burst through the door for their afternoon check-in and, if they were lucky, a nickel. "What have you been up to?" Susie asked.

"Starin' at alligators," Bill offered.

"Alligators?"

Junior confirmed. "On the fence, Mama. Me and Bill were looking for oil and Woody Wilson told us we should be diggin' at the sand quarry so we did and, on the other side of the fence, we saw eyes...looking out."

Bill curled his fingers, squinting, "Yellow eyes staring at us from behind the bushes, waitin' to take a bite outta one of us."

"And you think they're alligators," Susie challenged.

Billie's head bobbing, "Oh, they're alligators all right."

Gwen was losing her patience. "That's ridiculous." She had a proposition. "Papa, since I won the Bee yesterday, shouldn't I get two nickels?"

Susie intercepted. "Of course not, Gwen. One has nothing to do with the other."

Junior agreed. "Nothin' to do with the other. Hey, Mama. Are we still getting a party for our birthday?"

They hadn't had a birthday celebration since they'd moved from Napavine. "I think so." Then she checked with Garnet. "We can do that can't we Papa?"

He kept to his work but responded. "Sure. We can do that."

Garnet Junior clarified, "See I wanted to invite Bub Klein, but..." Billie's eyes narrowed, and he started pumping his fist. "Him and Bill..."

"He and Bill..." G.E. interjected, still not looking up from his work.

Junior went on. "He and Bill, well, the mechanics were offerin' nickels to any kid who could make another kid cry. So Bub picked Bill, and now Bill doesn't want him to the party."

Gwen poked at Bill. "Bill just wants Clara Davis to the party." Bill stomped down hard on Gwen's foot. She screamed.

"Hey, you don't know," Billie snarled.

"I do too know! Bill watches her over the yard fence. When she locked herself out of her house, she asked him for help." Billie's face flushed all shades of red. "She picked him up and pushed him through the window to unlock the door. Now Billie is her hero." Bill took off chasing her out of the shop and down the street.

Junior held out his hand out to his father. "Papa, can I have my nickel?" Garnet reached in his pocket and Junior snatched it from his fingers then skipped out of the shop satisfied.

Susie laughed. "Well, that was a lot of nonsense."

"Yes it was," Garnet agreed.

Nonsense felt good. She'd take more of that sort of nonsense over the last year any day.

Morning Olympian, July 13, 1923
Mrs. GE Parks charmingly entertained a few little folks at her home Saturday in honor of her sons Garnet and Billie. Games were enjoyed during the afternoon and dainty refreshments were served.

§

July ended with a familiar name on the front page of daily papers across the country, including the *Seattle Daily Times*. Garnet jumped up from the kitchen table holding the paper above him. "Susie, look. Look at this."

Pancho Villa let down his guard while traveling by car near Parral when he met his end. As his driver crossed a bridge, shots were fired from two sides and Villa was killed instantly.

Villa's demise provided an additional satisfaction to all that was going right that summer. G.E. succeeded in assembling a ball team that practiced Sunday afternoons at the Fir Tree Mill in Tenino. Out and about he could be heard calling out to his neighbors, "Count on Tenino to take the Sawdust League this year."

Tenino lost the bid to host the Thurston County Fair, but the Elks and American Legion organized a fabulous Tenino Community Fair for Labor Day weekend. There was a parade, contests with cash prizes, rides and a military band concert culminating on the final day with a Grand Street Dance. Susie called Eva with a perfect plan to get Irene back home. She would invite Eva and Jim down to enjoy the fair, cook them a delicious meal, then send them back to Kirkland without the baby. She coached herself before ringing her up. *Not backing down this time.* As a special incentive, Susie put Irene's name in for a Better Baby Contest they were trying for the first time at the Tenino Fair. Irene was two months shy of her 3rd birthday which qualified her for the Ages 1-3 years category. It was billed as less of a contest and more of a public health service. Irene was expected and Eva was excited.

> *Tenino Independent,* September 1923
> "Better Babies" To Be Featured This Year
> The object of the Better Babies department is not for the sole purpose of learning of the most perfect babies, but in case there is some slight defect that may be easily remedied by proper food or other care, that the mother may be told of the same so that it will be more fully developed as it should. Cash prizes are offered to those receiving the highest scores.

G.E. and Jim supervised the kids while Susie took Eva and Irene back to the examination tent. Naked babies being rotated, scrutinized, poked and prodded under bright lights was an off-putting spectacle. Some remorse set in for Susie fearing she'd lured Irene back home only to put her on display like a slopped hog. By the end of the day, two babies emerged with a score of 100% in the 1-3 years category. They were Thomas Churchill and, home just in time to be named the Best Baby in Tenino 1923, Margaret Irene Parks.

> *Tenino Independent* Personals, September 6, 1923
> Little Miss Irene Parks, who has been visiting for the past two months with her aunt and uncle, Mr. and Mrs. J.C. Cathcart of Kirkland, returned home Sunday.

§

Garnet was still waiting for a letter from Rex when he read a story in the Sunday *Seattle Daily Times* and learned his brother had also had a brush with death.

> *Seattle Daily Times,* August 26, 1923
> Starves 27 Days Before Rescuers Come to His Aid by United Press. Sacramento, Cal.
> Tired of life. C. R. Parks of Sacramento lay down on the bank of

a small creek at Rocklin in Placer County to starve twenty-seven days ago, according to word received here today. He was near death from lack of food and water when found last night. He said he had touched no food during the many days. The physicians said he will probably recover.

Garnet got on the phone with the *Times* news department to get more information. They were able to give him the name of a hospital but Rex had been released and he was refused a home address. He reached out to the Parkses in Virginia but found he knew more than they did. As months went by Rex and his new wife, Lena, managed to get in the news one way or another.

Oakland Tribune, February 20, 1924
Poison Taken by Jealous Young Wife
Despondent, according to the police report, because she had found a piece of paper in her husband's pocket with another woman's name on it, Mrs. Lena Parks, 840 Magnolia St., is said to have attempted to commit suicide by taking poison. She is recovering at the emergency hospital today. The alleged attempt at self-destruction took place last night. Mrs. Parks is eighteen years old. She is said to have gotten up after she and her husband retired and taken a quantity of poison. Her husband awoke and had his wife taken to the hospital.

Susie never had such an inclination to check Garnet's pockets, but his needle and the habit of it gave her anxiety. Especially on the Tuesday nights she left him and the kids to go to music rehearsal. *What if he takes a shot while watching the children.* She had tuned in to his movements and could tell when his body was readying itself for a fix. He had a way of slowing his speech and his steps to compensate for his urgency. She felt every step he took when he sauntered into the back room. It set her skin crawling.

Tuesday nights always started with this apprehension but, once her group was seated and began to play, she was transcended. The music took her to another place. There was nothing like those Tuesday nights working out the songs, finding the notes, and the shared satisfaction they felt when the sound came together just right.

9

Garnet had monthly check-ins with Dr. Wichman aimed at monitoring his healing, identifying any signs of returning trouble, and adjusting his pain medication. The doctor always started by asking Garnet about the cravings.

G.E. had little to lose and everything to gain by kicking his dependency. He'd beat death at only 32 and had the rest of his life ahead of him. He told Susie he believed the drug made him more productive but he came to realize that, in truth, it only relieved him of the distraction of wanting it. It dulled him and several times while doing business in the city he was caught not making sense. When Susie was with him, he could tell it embarrassed her. She never said it, but he was sure she thought he was weak.

"Last week I went two days without taking a shot. I had some sweats and had to work through the shakes. I've stopped keeping syringes at the shop. It was a busy week, and I didn't want to interrupt my workflow to go home. It was a test, I'd say. I shook and I had a wet shirt from the sweats, but I got through it." They agreed it was time to cut back more on his prescription.

Outside Dr. Wichman's office, he saw a post advertising a player piano for anyone with eight dollars and the means to move it. He'd have to call in some favors to get it transported to the house, but if anything would earn him points at home, he knew this was it.

Junior was in the yard having a catch with Woody Wilson and Billie was on the front porch. Bill was seated on a stump round, surrounded by milk crates and stacks of newspapers, with a handkerchief tied to his upper arm. The top half of his face was hidden under one of G.E.'s bolo hats. Garnet stepped out of sight and listened for a minute. "No excuse. Get it here in the morning." Billie slammed a block of wood on the crate, rearranged the stack of papers, and murmured to himself. "I need to set this typesetting and move this here like this...no time to waste." Garnet realized he was playing newspaper editor. It was a compliment he guessed but the awkwardness between them made him unsure how to proceed. He coughed, cleared his throat, and started up the steps. Billie pulled the hat off his head and straightened up. No words passed between them.

Garnet called into the house just as his helpers were backing the truck into the porch. "Susie. Where are you?"

"Coming..." she called back. She stepped onto the porch with baby Jim in her arms in time to see the blanket come off the Welte-Mignon Player Piano. She screamed, "A piano? Oh, Garnet."

The mechanics of a player piano added additional weight that made moving it extra challenging, but they got it set in the living room while the adoring family hovered over as if welcoming a new baby. Susie sat first and picked some tunes by ear with her right hand. The kids joined and banged noisily on the low notes. "Well, we need to get some music rolls."

She knew a drug store in Chehalis that sold piano rolls and sheet music. They jumped in the car and came back with rolls for *Toot Toot Tootsie*, Paul Whiteman's *Bright Eyes*, and *That Ol' Gang of Mine*. Gwen picked two pieces of sheet music, *Glow Worm* and *Daisy Bell*. Susie challenged herself with a new Louis Armstrong release called *Dippermouth Blues*.

The kids took turns on the pedals making the music fly while they fluttered fingers over the keys to make it look as if they were really playing. Before long, the challenge became more about trying to pump as fast as they could with less concern for the music. That got them sent outside.

When Gwen got *Daisy Bell* down well enough, they put a band together. The little ones played on spoons and blocks, Junior and Susie played violin and Billie danced. Garnet took his seat in the audience.

Daisy, Daisy, give me your answer do.
I'm half-crazy all for the love of you...
...But you'll look sweet
upon the seat of a bicycle built for two.

Garnet put his cigarette in his mouth so both hands were free to applaud. He knew he was going to take a shot that night, but the warmth he felt in that moment came simply from seeing them so happy.

§

An inch and a half of snow had collected Saturday morning before Christmas of 1924. Susie was feeling particularly grateful. Garnet was on the mend, she felt slow and steady progress in her efforts to catch up on the bills and, since the arrival of the piano, their house was more filled with music than ever. It was a perfect day for a trip to the city. "What do you say, Gwen? Let's go to Seattle and see Santa."

Gwen let out a scream, "We're going to see Santa! We're going to see Santa!" She had Irene and Jimmie jumping for joy, though at seventeen months, Jimmie had no idea what he was cheering about.

Gwen began peeling through drawers and closets. She pulled out a frilly red dress that was too small for her. "Irene, get in here." She found Jimmie a white shirt and wool shorts. "Mama, I need a bow tie."

Only Gwen, Garnet, and Bill had seen Santa before. Gwen remembered having a good talk with him and she hoped he remembered her. She explained to Irene as she dressed her. "Now, when you see him, he's going to ask you questions. Like he'll say, 'what do you want for Christmas little girl?' You need to think of what you will tell him."

Irene answered. "I want a rope and ladder so I can see what's in Bill's hiding place."

"No, no, Irene. Not a rope. You want something pretty, don't you?"

"Not if it doesn't take me up and see what Bill is hiding."

Gwen regretted the question. "Okay. We'll figure it out on the way there. Me, I want roller skates. Red ones."

"Oooo!" Irene cooed. Garnet and Bill came into the house having failed to gather enough snow for the base of their snowman.

"You have to get cleaned up," Gwen demanded. "Mama's taking us to see Santa."

They didn't believe her at first, but Susie's confirmation sent them racing to the bathroom sink to get cleaned up. Garnet entered from the back porch. "What's happening?"

"Santa," they shouted.

"Keep your coat on and get in the car," Susie told him.

Susie took the wheel so Garnet lit a cigarette and leaned back in the passenger's seat. "Wooo-hoo. Let's go see the fat old man." Susie hooted and they cheered from the back.

The sight of the grand Smith Tower looming tall over the city let them know they'd reached Seattle. Susie parked as close as she could to Fredrick and Nelson's. The city glowed, even in the daytime, with the twinkle lights that lined the store windows. Giant gold bells and fir garlands draped over electrical wires along Pine Street. They'd placed gramophones outside at the entryways with sound horns pointing out to fill the streets with Christmas music. "Look, Mama!" Coming up 5th Street, Bill and Irene spotted the Christmas streetcar lit up on all sides in electric stars. Jim ran to see and slipped on the slushy walkway.

They moved as a unit taking in the display windows. Each window had a special magic with animated dolls, soldiers, reindeer, and elves. Garnet lifted Jimmie on his shoulders to see the Lionel train that rolled across each scene from the North Pole to the inside of Santa's toyshop. It got him pointing and pumping himself up and down like a pogo stick on top of his papa's shoulders.

The smell of soft pretzels reminded Susie that they were in for a long line ahead and they wouldn't fare well managing five kids with empty stomachs. "Garnet, let's buy some to split." They were stocked with pretzels and napkins when they entered Fredrick's four football fields of floorspace. Extravagant displays and signs pointed to a hairdressing salon, a candy factory, an upstairs men's department, and another floor dedicated just to women and children. There was even a lounge for mothers with infants. Susie turned to Garnet, "Where do we start?" Gwen read signs then led the way to a line for Santa confirmed by two elves in green pointy hats. The pretzels occupied them on their wait in the entrance line. Once through there, benches lined the walls to Santa's burrow.

It would have been no surprise if impatience caused them to misbehave, but the anticipation made them perfect angels. The four sat quietly on their benches and Jim on Susie's lap. They scooted over a bit at a time as each child before them finished their turn. Finally, Santa's red suit came into view. Gwen played nervously with the lace on her dress and strained to hear the conversations of the children in front of her. She checked her siblings down the line for any signs they might embarrass her. Billie sat, hands folded, silently rehearsing a speech. Junior sat serious and stared straight ahead. The most active of them was Irene who wiggled and squirmed to control the butterflies in her tummy.

When their turn came up, they went in order from youngest to oldest. Jimmie and Irene went up together and each took a knee. As he turned to look at the man, Jimmie's eyes went wide, and he took Santa by the beard with both hands. "Feathers!"

Irene was mortified. "It's not feathers. It's his beard." Thankfully, Santa thought it was funny and let out a jovial Santa Claus *ho-ho-ho*. He asked Irene what she wanted for Christmas. She told him about the ladder and rope but caught Gwen's glare from the bench and added that a curly-haired doll would be nice too.

"And for you son?" Jim prepared to take another tug at his beard.

"He wants a train please." Irene smiled with pride in her conversation.

Bill asked Santa if he would ever give a kid a typewriter and Santa told him he'd have to think about it. Garnet Junior decided last minute that he wanted a kit to build a town around Jim's train. Gwen asked if he remembered her, and he said he definitely did. Then she asked if he could guess what she wanted. He said he believed he could, and he guessed wrong.

The event had taken a lot longer than they anticipated and it was time to go home. Garnet made a detour by the candy store and came out with a peppermint candy stick for each of them. They exited with Jingle Bells bellowing out to the street.

"Okay. Where did we park?" Thankfully, Junior and Gwen remembered and the rest of them followed taking turns to peel Jimmie up from the sidewalk until they found the car.

It was a happy drive home. They sang Christmas carols as far as Tukwila then began dropping off one at a time. Money being what it was, Susie and Garnet knew some Christmas wishes might not be granted, not by them, at least. If Susie knew Eva, and she did, the kids wouldn't suffer.

§

In January 1925 a new mayor of Olympia took his seat. Mayor Johnson wanted to clean up what he viewed to be incompetent leadership at the Capitol. This would have been of little consequence to the Parkes or Tenino if not for the rift the mayor started with his Chief of Police, C.H. Hansen. The mayor's first act was to appoint a replacement for Chief Hansen, the Fire Chief, and four other city positions. Chief Hansen refused to leave, so Mayor Johnson refused to sign his paycheck, then the fire chief and Hansen sued the city. This back and forth went on for months until the mayor offered to reinstate the fire chief and all the other positions if the city council would only agree to oust Chief Hansen. Hansen felt targeted and betrayed.

Garnet had followed the drama at the Capitol and was surprised when Chief Hansen show up at his office and asked G.E. to take his order for a print job. Hansen had a plan to clear his name and was taking out ads in local newspapers to nudge public opinion in his favor. He presented copy for some posters he wanted G.E. to have ready by Monday, but sometime late Saturday night he changed his mind. When Garnet went to the shop Sunday morning. he found the lock on the back door broken and Hansen's copy for the ad and the orders for the job missing from his desk. This pushed G.E.'s buttons and he talked about nothing else the rest of the week.

"I don't care who he is. He can't break into a private business. And use my employee to do it." It turned out, Hansen had entered the shop with the help of G.E.'s new assistant, Albert Dwyer, and another officer. Garnet paced the kitchen.

To Susie it made no sense. "Maybe he was investigating a crime or something. Did Albert tell you what he was after?"

"Oh no. He was after his copy and the posters, and he took the order ticket from my desk. He wanted to leave no trace that he was there."

Still perplexed, "So why didn't he just ask for it?"

Garnet pondered. "I should have read it more carefully. Albert was handling the job so I didn't pay it any mind. Maybe there was something in the copy that would incriminate him." Albert later told G.E. that he had wanted to alert him on Saturday before they entered the shop, but Hansen said no. He said Hansen was agitated and a little drunk and just pushed the door in. G.E. and Albert fixed the lock and checked the shop to confirm nothing else was taken.

Chief Hansen had taken liberties. This was a matter of principle, and Garnet was prepared to use the power of print to shame him for it. Thursday evening, Susie joined Garnet at the shop to finish printing and collating the May 15th issue of the *Independent*. That was when she read his front-page story, already in print, for the first time.

Tenino Independent, May 15, 1925
Olympia Police Chief Accused of Burglary Rear Door of Independent office Forced Open and Paper Stolen from the Shop Files.
The rear door to the *Tenino Independent* office was broken sometime Saturday night and the shop entered and some papers taken from

the files. The information available points to the chief of police and one of his officers of Olympia as the guilty parties.

According to the information at hand, plans were made in Olympia at police headquarters about twelve o'clock Saturday night to come to Tenino after the papers. Hansen, another officer, and a third-party drove to the city.

The papers taken from the office were copy for a poster printed in the shop several days before, the job ticket, and possibly the order for the same. They were of no value to this office and would've been furnished to the police chief, or anyone who would've asked for them during business hours.

Susie knew he was poking a tiger and considered telling him to pull the story. Then she thought, *Maybe Hansen would never pay any mind to what our little paper has to say.* In the next column to the right of the article was a framed, featured open letter to the Attorney General of Washington State from G.E. Parks and the *Tenino Independent*. *Oh no, Garnet,* she thought, *what have you done?*

Open Letter to Attorney General of Washington

May 15, 1925, *Tenino Independent*, honorable John H Dunbar, Attorney General, State of Washington, Olympia, Washington
Dear Sir:

Will you kindly inform me if a chief of police of a city of the third class has power to go to another town and break into a private business place in the middle of the night without a warrant?

My place of business was broken into last Saturday night and some papers stolen from my files and other damages done to the place. All I can find out about this outrage is from my employee of the *Independent*, who, in company with some prominent men of Olympia, including a county official, were taken in charge Saturday night by the Olympia police, and were all released by this employee who was threatened with a jail sentence unless he would deliver certain papers from the *Independent* office.

The chief of police and another police officer together with the employee above mentioned came to Tenino. They were unable to get into the shop without breaking the door, which they did, the officer doing the work and Chief Hansen holding the light, according to a sworn statement made by this employee. Then they entered the shop and took the papers they desired, returning to Olympia, but leaving the employee of the *Independent* in Tenino, who returned to Olympia the following day and had the articles returned to him taken from his person by the police the evening before.

Has the chief of police of Olympia a right to burglarize my place within the county without a warrant? Your office, I am sure, can tell me just how far a chief of police can go.

Very truly yours,
The TENINO INDEPENDENT,
By G.E. PARKS, Publisher

Hansen didn't share G.E.'s view of the incident. He also didn't appreciate G.E. dragging the Attorney General into it. Judging by the lack of response from the Attorney General, Susie concluded the AG didn't appreciate being dragged into it either. C.H. Hansen was now suing Garnet and the *Independent* for libel.

Oregonian May 31, 1925, Centralia, Wash., (Special)
Police Chief Sues Paper
A story recently published in the *Tenino Independent* charging that C.H. Hansen, chief of police at Olympia, broke into the newspaper's office and stole certain papers, is the basis of a $5,000 damage suit filed in the Thurston County Superior Court against the *Independent*. GE Parks is the editor of the newspaper.

§

Susie's musician friends buzzed with excitement at their Tuesday practice. Karl Moldrem, the respected Grays Harbor Orchestra conductor, planned to hold auditions in a couple of weeks for an all-southern Washington symphony orchestra. Susie wanted to be there.

Garnet Junior asked if he could go. "I'll be quiet, Mama. I want to watch." Susie and Junior left G.E. doing the crossword puzzle. He promised to pop some corn on the wood stove as a special treat, so they left the family to themselves and went together to the audition.

The Centralia Community Hall was filled with musicians from across the western region of Washington. They blew into woodwinds and brass, and plucked, banged, and clanged in magnificent discordance.

Many of the symphony's seats were already filled with Moldrem's veteran players, but he sought to add diverse musicians from the southern counties with this audition. Junior sat in the 3rd row surrounded by empty seats.

On stage, Susie felt an unusual bout of nerves. She was a little star-struck in the presence of Conductor Moldrem. He was efficient. He knew exactly what he wanted and he moved the players through quickly, hearing only a few bars before directing them either in or out. If they were chosen, he placed them in their seat prearranged on the stage. If they weren't, they were sent down to the audience. Moldrem had the violin section filled before Susie had a chance to play. It was disappointing but she accepted it with humility, descended the stairs and joined Garnet Junior to watch the rest of the auditions.

"How come you didn't get to play?" Junior whispered.

She whispered back. "He has everyone he needs. I'm a little disappointed, but it's okay."

Conductor Moldrem began auditioning the violas and pointed down to Susie and waved her up. He gestured to a viola player to offer her the use of their instrument. The novelty of the bulkier instrument required a concentration from her that served to calm her nerves. She played beautifully and Moldrem sent her stage right to the third seat in the viola section. Cheers gushed from a single spectator in the third row.

On the ride home, Little Garnet was a chatterbox. "You did it, Mama. I didn't know it was so big. All those people are going to play with you all at the same time?" It was as if he was seeing his mother for the first time.

Susie's face hurt from smiling. "It's a big group, isn't it? Thank you for coming with me. I'm so happy you were there."

They got home late and found the family sleeping, except for Garnet who was tackling another crossword puzzle. Junior bragged on his way to bed. "Mama's in the big orchestra. You should have seen her."

G.E. looked up from the paper. "No kidding?"

Susie was still smiling. "I wouldn't kid about that. I'm playing viola in a symphony orchestra."

Morning Olympian, Sunday June 7, 1925
Moldrem Orchestra to Have Premier – Has Eleven Thurston County Members
Eleven Thurston County people are members of the Karl Moldrem

Symphony Orchestra which will give its premiere concert at Centralia next Sunday afternoon. Arrangements are now underway to have the organization, which is claimed to be the finest of its kind in Southwest Washington, give a concert in Olympia at an early date. For ten months the 75 members of the orchestra have gathered in Centralia every Tuesday night for practice. The organization has been recruited principally from Mr. Moldrem's advanced pupils, augmented by many professionals and talented amateurs inspired by a sincere love for symphonic music. The participation of the latter class has been of great advantage to the orchestra as a whole. The number of performers has grown steadily from the inception of the orchestra over 75 now attending faithfully and enthusiastically weekly rehearsals.

§

Garnet received a court summons confirming that Chief Hansen was serious. It sent G.E. back pacing the floor. "We'll need an attorney, Susie. Hansen threatens our reputation and my integrity as a journalist and the *Independent* as a news source."

"Five thousand dollars," Susie said aloud then again quietly, to herself, lamenting his compulsion to always defend himself in print.

"We're in the right, here. This is not a police state where a police chief can just do as he pleases and break into a private citizen's place of business. We'll counter-sue for defamation."

"Isn't that what he's suing us for? Libel? Didn't you say libel is the same as defamation?"

She was legitimately asking. $5,000 was a big number. It would ruin them and they still hadn't sent a payment to Eva and Jim since Garnet was hospitalized. "He didn't mean to break the lock and it's fixed now. Just write a retraction, Garnet. Can't you just take it back?"

"What?" She offended him. He would never see the logic in it and could only hear her suggestion as a betrayal.

"For the paper Garnet. To keep the paper."

§

Oakland Tribune, July 24, 1925
Husband Likes Young Girls, Charges Wife
Shortly after marriage in January 1923, says Mrs. Lena M. Parks, her husband, employed by a local cookie concern, served nine months in jail at Stockton for contributing to the delinquency of a minor girl. Parks has too great a fondness for young girls, Mrs. Parks charges. Mrs. Parks asks custody of an infant daughter and $60 a month maintenance.

Other than the lawsuit looming over them, the summer of 1925 was the kids with the run of the neighborhood, working at the shop, Susie at rehearsals and playing concerts, and the family piling into the car to see Tenino's town team play ball. One Sunday evening, the Parkes returned home after Tenino eked out a win against the Fir Trees. It was a tight squeeze in the car for the seven of them, but the family had taken to baseball like it was their job and not one of them was willing to stay back with Mrs. Chansky.

At the game, Susie tracked G.E.'s condition. Despite the mild temperature in the stands, he had pulled his handkerchief out several times to wipe sweat off his neck and forehead. He drummed his thumbs nonstop on the steering wheel the whole ride back and wasn't talking at all. She knew there was nothing she could do for him but wait it out. "You okay?" He nodded and kept to his drumming.

In the back seat, Bill and Garnet took turns whacking one another over the head with their gloves. They took their lives in their hands by inadvertently smacking Gwen who was squished into the corner behind the driver's seat. Irene was happy enough with Jim in her lap until she felt warm liquid soak into her dress. She called out for help, "Ewww. Mama, can you get Jim off me?"

Jimmie yelled, "I didn't do it!"

"Yes you did!" Irene objected.

"Okay, Irene, let Papa get the car stopped." Garnet pulled up in front of the house.

Susie jumped out and Irene took off running to get her clothes off and spilled Jimmie on the grass. Susie took him by the hand prepared to spray him down. She didn't notice the shiny blue Chevrolet Superior parked at the curb or the man leaning against it.

He was in a mustard suit with matching shoes and a felt fedora. The boys and Gwen saw him. "Woa!" Junior and Billie dropped their gloves and the three moved in for a closer look. The man took a deep drag off his cigarette, stepped away from the car, and waited for his brother to see him. Garnet collected himself in the driver's seat, still dealing with his revved-up nerves and considered whether to take his shot early. He stepped out, spotted his brother, and pulled himself together. Almost as if he had been expecting him, he let out a chuckle. "There he is!"

Gwen stood between her brothers and whispered. "There who is?"

"Applesauce!" Junior's jaw hung open. "Papa knows this guy all dolled up like he is?"

Gwen elbowed him hard. "It's not called 'dolled-up' when it's a man, dummy. You gotta say he's like a 'Torpedo' in that get-up. Something like that, you know, like the wise guys in the movie."

"Yeah," Bill nodded. "He's hard-boiled, that's what he is."

Rex pulled his watch fob from his pocket. "What took you so long, brother? I've been waiting here over an hour!"

Their laughs were nearly identical. "Well, we thought you'd disappeared forever! It's great to see you! You look fantastic!" Garnet kept hold of him with one arm while he looked for the kids. "Kids!" They had already started in on the car, putting their paws all over the paint job of his stylish machine. "Come away from there, now. Stop touching the car!" They stopped and stood at attention.

Rex put them on notice. "You're touching a five hundred and twenty-five dollars piece of equipment there."

Garnet flinched. "I'll say! I always told 'em you'd be the one living the life of Riley! Kids, this is my brother. Your Uncle Rex. It looks like he decided to surprise us today." They nodded but didn't have the guts to speak. Gwen didn't remember him, but she stared at him with the same hard focus as the first time she saw him in Pittsburg. "You can say hello. Go ahead, say, 'hello Uncle Rex'."

"Hello, Uncle Rex," they parroted weakly.

"Hello, Garnet's kids." Rex preferred the company of adults and didn't care to make conversation with these impish characters. "As I was saying, Garnet, I've come to spend time with my favorite brother, meet the family and see what this little town has got to offer. Tun-i-no?"

"Ten-Nine-O. Named for the Northern Pacific rail car, number 10-9-0, is what I've been told. And yes, I'll show you around, you can count on that. Let's get in the house and get you something to eat. G.A.

says you've been in Oakland last he heard, is that right? Did you drive straight through?" Rex filled Garnet in on the details as they entered the house, leaving the Chevy to the mercy of the kids.

Billie had pluck enough to open the door and let them all inside. Garnet Junior sat in the driver's seat and went straight to moving the steering wheel back and forth. Gwen sprawled onto the backseat taking in the smell and feel of the smooth, black leather seats. Bill opened the glove box and pulled out a half-drunk bottle of bootleg gin.

"Put that back, Bill!" Junior pounced on him with the authority of an elder who wanted more time in the driver's seat of the car he wasn't supposed to be in.

Billie's find made Gwen curious and she started rooting around under the seats. "Oooo, lots of bottles down here. These are all filled up to the top!" She didn't know exactly what they'd found but something told her it wasn't meant for them. "Come on, let's get outta here!" She spat into her hand and rubbed her shoe prints off the seats.

Susie had Jimmie in dry clothes and was starting dinner. "Look who's here!" Garnet called as he and Rex entered the kitchen.

She was surprised and gracious, "Rex!" She made a note to herself of the incongruence between her tone and her gut feeling. It was the same gut feeling she had the first time meeting him at the Pittsburgh apartment. That he was unorthodox wasn't the problem. Susie embraced breaking the rules but she didn't abide breaking the law. She didn't know him that well but always hovering was this question of morality and her sense was that he had none.

For Garnet, Rex was a shot of adrenaline. His arrival was a welcome distraction from the sweats and agitation he'd struggled with only moments earlier. In Rex's company Garnet's laugh was louder, his speech livelier, and Susie noticed that he nodded in agreement to Rex's every word. They had some dinner and then took their cigarettes on the front porch accompanied by the roar of the street cleaning machine. Garnet raised his voice to be heard over the sound of the motor. "Well, it looks like they let Will out of jail again."

"What's that?" Rex yelled back.

"Our street cleaner, Will, runs a bootleg operation. He has a still in a shed behind his house. They haul him into jail almost every week and warn him to tear it down. Then the streets need cleaning again, so they let him out." Will and his machine turned the corner and the noise faded.

"He does pretty well, does he?" Rex asked.

"Who, Will? No, street cleaning doesn't pay anything."

"Not for cleaning streets, ya mug! I mean stilling hooch in the shed. What's he cookin' there, corn? Potatoes?"

"Oh, I'm not sure." G.E. butted his cigarette and lit another. "Let me take you up the street to see the shop." They walked Sussex Street and caught up on the details of Garnet's illness and his brush with death. Rex pulled news clippings from his breast pocket with reports of his starvation episode at the bridge and the goings on between him and his wife, Lena.

Rex elaborated. "Oh she's a looker all right, but she's a dumb Dora. It's always something with her. Every night I'd come in with her on me about something. Then she got pregnant, and she didn't know what to do with a baby. So, enough was enough and I drove north. I'm putting it behind me."

Garnet reached an arm around Rex in sympathy. "Well. I hope we can be a place for you to get some rest and regroup. You're welcome here as long as you are inclined to stay."

Morning Olympian, August 26, 1925
C. Rex Parks of Oakland, California arrived Wednesday for a visit at the home of his brother, G.E. Parks.

§

Billie bound into the kitchen with a white flower in his hands. "Here, Mama!"

Susie was touched and then horrified. "Oh! It's a trillium!" His eyes got wide and she realized she scared him. "It's pretty, isn't it?" He nodded. "Trilliums are for looking at but not picking."

"Why?" His eyes watered and she saw he might cry.

"It's okay, it's all right. Everyone picks a trillium once, and it's okay as long as it's only once. See, they're real special because it takes a long time for them to grow a flower. So, when you see one, when you see the three petals, say, 'if it's three, leave it be.' That's how I learned it."

He repeated. "If it's three let it be…okay, I won't pick it. But if it's four petals…"

"Oh, it's fine if it's four petals." She put the trillium in a bowl of water. "Where's Junior?"

"He took Uncle Rex over to Dee-Dum-Day-Ay's."

"To where?"

"The man with the pointy shoes that has two houses. One in front and a little one in back and he goes," and Billie sang, "Dee-dum-day-ay, dee-dum-day-ay. He sings that when smoke is comin' out of his little house."

"Are you talking about Will the street cleaner?"

"That's right. Me and Garnet call him Dee-Dum-Day-Ay, 'cause of his singin'."

"What would Rex want with Will the street cleaner?"

Susie knew there was something off-ish about Rex's interest in Will. Soon after he utilized Junior to make an introduction, a "friendship" brewed between Will and Rex. Then Rex announced that he was going to explore business prospects outside of Tenino. Garnet couldn't hide his disappointment but Susie's thinking was, if Rex was inclined toward trouble, and she was sure he was, *it's better he finds it away from Tenino.*

Garnet liked having Rex nearby. Rex bolstered him and helped keep his confidence up. He had a way of pumping Garnet up when he was down, like with the Hansen lawsuit. "You won't let these stiff shirts walk on you, Garnet. You're smarter than the whole lot of them. You'll never let these Brunos get the better of you. You can kill 'em with words!" Garnet wanted his brother in his corner, but Rex was cooking up something that sent him circulating outside of Tenino. Each time he visited, he made a stop by Dee-Dum-Day-Ay's.

§

Garnet refused to take the path of least resistance and simply retract his story about Police Chief Hansen and Susie made it clear she wanted no part of it. Now, with Rex otherwise occupied, it was up to Garnet to secure legal representation and dig himself out of this mess with Hansen. He hired Tenino attorney P.C. Kibbes and they spent several days in court. The judge allowed to Hansen that G.E.'s published article was libelous, but then advised the jury in a convoluted series of contradictions that left them all confused. The confusion was to G.E.'s benefit and the jury delivered a not guilty verdict.

Spokane Chronicle, October 07, 1925
Deny Damages in Libel Suits
A verdict was returned last night in the Thurston County Superior Court denying C.H. Hansen, Olympia Chief of Police, the right to recover damages from G.E. Parks, publisher of a weekly newspaper at Tenino.

Hansen appealed. P.C Kibbes stopped by the *Independent* to deliver the news that Garnet would be going back to court. He explained, "The appeal is going to be a harder one to fight this time, given the judge has already confirmed libel. I don't mind collecting from you, Garnet, but I feel a responsibility to remind you that I'll have to charge fees for the duration of my time. There's no telling how long it will take." With that he bid farewell and was off to another meeting.

"It's absurd!" Garnet yelled at no one. He paced the shop, pulled his hat off the rack ready to exit, then circled back and sat down at the typewriter. He set up to peck out the beginning of a story or a letter, he didn't know what. He typed out a few lines, pulled the sheet, threw it in the waste basket and started again.

Rex pulled up and found his brother working himself into a dither. "Come on. Get in the car. Let's get out of here." Rex drove him to a vacant quarry and parked. He reached under the driver's seat and pulled out a bag of vials filled with a clear liquid and a syringe promising a relief to an extent that Garnet hadn't felt in days. He hesitated at first to use it in front of Rex, but Rex's intention was for his brother to relax, feel comfortable and unashamed.

Garnet was a grateful, limp rag. "Where did you get it?"

"I've been connecting in the area around here. If there's something you want, there's someone willing to provide it. I've been worried about you, brother. So, I kept my eyes and ears to the ground, and I found a guy. I can keep you in the dope as long as you want it. You work hard, G.E. You deserve it." He reached into the backseat, pulled out a bottle, and handed it to him.

Garnet took a healthy swig. "This Hansen guy has it in for me, Rex. He's not going to let it go. I've been in tangles before but this one is vengeful. He's looking to take me down."

"We'll figure it out. I'll ask around and see what I can find out." It wasn't just the morphine that calmed Garnet's nerves. It was his brother having his back in a way that no one did. Susie had always supported him before, but this time he felt even she had abandoned him. Maybe it was selfish, but it felt good to have a brother, a friend, by his side willing to go the distance just for him.

§

The wind was blowing strong outside when Eva rang Susie up. She had been storing up opinions and frustrations over the several weeks they'd been out of touch, and she was ready to deliver an earful. Susie had to do her best to mask the nature of the conversation because Garnet was in the next room.

"I don't need any payouts now, or for a while, Susie. That's not my concern. What's bothering me is that I don't see that this paper is doing any better now than before he got sick. If this scandal he's gotten himself into is his idea of making a name for himself, he's doing it the wrong way."

Eva was keeping close tabs on the *Independent*'s money flow as it waned through and beyond Garnet's illness. He'd been back on the job long enough that she expected they should be seeing a profit, as he promised.

"I know what you mean, I definitely do. The *Tribune* did a good job keeping it going while he was away and..." She had to be careful. "We're excited about the future too!"

This annoyed Eva. "That's not what I was saying. I'm saying..."

Distractingly loud voices came in from outside. Susie stretched the cord as far as she could to get a look out the window. "Eva, something's going on outside. I have to go."

"I'm saying, Susie, this smells of..."

"We'll talk about it. Thank you for your ideas," she lied.

"Thank you for my ideas?" Eva repeated back, exasperated.

"I'll call you again. I have to hang up. Good-bye." She hung up and went to the window. Garnet was already there. Outside, Rex was at his car leaning in at the passenger side door.

"It's Rex," Susie reported the obvious to Garnet. "Who's he talking to?"

"I don't know..."

They stepped onto the porch. A slim, young leg kicked the door wide open, setting Rex off his balance. She wore a stylish pair of T-strap pumps and held a blue marble bag in the hand she used to take a swing at him. "Let me out, Rex, it's hot in here!" She pulled herself out and a gust of wind blew her and her powder-blue tea dress against the car. In the hand without the bag, she managed a cigarette and a bottle of rice whisky she let dangle between her thumb and pinky. Rex saw they had an audience and he scolded her in a harsh whisper.

Susie leaned over to Garnet, "Rex has a girlfriend?"

He studied the scene. "Not that he told me."

"Put it in the glove box!" Rex insisted.

The girl didn't realize right away that he was talking about the bottle. When she did, it struck her funny. "Okay, okay!" She fumbled with the glove box and tossed it in.

"Now, come on..." He had her by the arm trying to steady her and pulled her to the walkway. He was rattled. For the first time, Susie saw Rex lose his swagger. He actually seemed self-conscious, and she felt a little sorry for him. He tried to coax the girl toward the house. Susie and Garnet helped by coming down the stairs to greet them.

Susie reached out a hand, "Hello."

Still wobbly, the girl reached out but stumbled. Rex introduced her. "This is Lena, my wife."

Lena?! Your wife! What? This was unexpected.

Rex reset Lena's balance again. "Lena, this is my brother Garnet. And Susie."

Both Garnet and Susie were smiling but no words came initially. Then Susie said, "Lena? From Stockton?"

"That's right," Lena Parks confirmed.

Before, when Garnet told Susie about Rex and Lena, he had told her there was a baby girl. Susie craned her neck to check the car for any sign of a baby. There was none. Before they knew it, Rex was at the trunk of the car pulling out bags and a suitcase. To Garnet's delight and Susie's apprehension, it looked as if they were staying.

§

The next morning Rex and Lena slept in. With bellies full of pancakes the big kids fanned out to play in the neighborhood. Irene and Jimmie did somersaults on the living room rug which gave Susie and Garnet a minute in the kitchen.

Susie had questions and some thoughts, but Garnet was giddy and needed the floor. "The Frost house off Central is available. I know Rex and Lena are thinking they'll go to Seattle but why shouldn't they get a place here? The Frost house is a cozy little home." *Oh boy*, thought Susie. He continued. "I think he seems happy, do you? Happy to have her back?" *Oh boy*, she thought again and wondered if it was completely lost on him what a wild card this girl was. Since Lena's arrival, Susie was on high alert. He went on. "Lena said yesterday that she'd like to go for a picnic. I thought we could head to the coast at Arcadia. What do you say? Do you think Mrs. Chansky would babysit on a Sunday?"

Dear god! "I'm sorry, what was that?" There it was, coming from the mouth of her once sensible husband. She graced him with a correction in one stroke. "It sounds like great fun, Garnet. A day at the beach is exactly the kind of fun our kids would love...as a family."

He'd surprised himself with his thoughtlessness. "Of course. All of us. What was I thinking?"

Susie looked at him earnestly. "Don't leave us behind, Garnet. We almost lost you before. I know you love your brother, but we're still here."

"It was stupid, Susie." He took her hand. "I'm sorry."

She nodded then squeezed his hands back. "I'll do fried chicken and potato salad."

"Bratwurst! Do you have bratwurst?"

"We do! Why don't you tell the kids the good news on your way to the shop?" Garnet said he would, threw down his last swig of coffee, and headed out.

Barefoot and disoriented, Lena wandered into the kitchen.

"Coffee?" Susie offered.

"Oh, thank you, that would be wonderful." She rubbed her eyes. "Sally, right?"

"No, Susie." She handed her a cup. "So, are you visiting then?"

Lena cradled the cup as if it were a precious, restorative potion. "Well, as you can see Rex and I are back together. We had a bad fight, well, a few bad fights. He has this thing he does where he sees a girl and he can't seem to help himself." Her tone got stern, and she wagged her finger for emphasis. "I drew the line when they were too young...I mean really too young. I mean so young he went to jail! Well, he didn't like jail, that's the truth!" She chuckled at that one. "I just got to missing him so that I surprised him in Seattle. He was so happy he promised to never do that again. That's what love is. With me and Rex, once we set eyes on each other, well, we just can't help it, I guess." Rex walked in. Lena squealed with delight and wrapped her arms around him. "So, yeah, we're back together." Rex raised an eyebrow and accepted coffee from Susie.

"Well, you must be so happy. You'll have your family back together, then?" Susie prompted. Lena gazed up at Rex.

"Oh no. We do better without the baby if that's what you mean. She's with my mother in Sacramento." She stretched out for Rex's hand. "We learned our lesson. We won't let anything come between us again will we, Baby?" Rex confirmed.

"That's right, Babe." And there it was.

§

Tenino Independent October 9, 1925
Mr. and Mrs. G.E. Parks and family and Mr. and Mrs. C.R. Parks spent Sunday at Arcadia Beach.

It was beach day. Garnet Junior and Bill asked if they could ride with their Uncle Rex and got a firm no from Susie. The food and blankets would travel in the back seat of Rex's Chevrolet. Lena waited in the passenger seat and became an involuntary recipient of various tools and contraptions from the children. Irene skipped toward her with a bucket, a sieve, and several wooden spoons. "Do you have room for this?"

Junior offered a bat, a ball, and three gloves. "Here, Miss Lena, this can go in the back."

Jimmie handed her his bottle. "Here."

Garnet Junior grabbed it from him before it changed hands. "Not your bottle, Jim. That goes with us!"

The Parkses passed the three-hour trip to Arcadia Beach with a singing contest, several rounds of guessing games, and math quizzes. They crossed the great Columbia River by way of the Interstate Bridge. Papa announced, "We are in Oregon!" Gwen pinched them all in congratulations.

They arrived at Arcadia and loaded the kids' arms with food and gear to take over the rocky path to the beach. Twisted evergreens pushed up from the rocks like giant bonsais formed from years of holding their footing against the coastal winds. An enormous playground of tide pools and every shape of climbing stone waited for them on the stretch of beach.

"Look!" Bill pointed. Firmly burrowed in the sand and cradled by the tide was an enormous oblong stone covered in abalone and orange starfish. "It looks like brains!" They dumped their things and ran out for a closer look.

"Watch Jim! He's coming behind you!" Susie yelled after them. Remembering herself at age eighteen, Susie didn't expect Lena to be much help with food or set up. However, she was surprised that Rex had walked the entire way empty handed. Garnet and Susie unpacked while Rex and Lena reconnected with each other demonstratively. Rex was enjoying getting shrieks and giggles out of Lena with his playful tickling. Susie passed out plates with the goal of occupying Rex's hands. Gwen and Bill appeared before them just in time to catch Rex's hand slide up Lena's dress. Bill missed it but Gwen didn't. Her eyes doubled in size, fully locked in on Lena's crotch.

Garnet tried to divert. "Sister, what do you need?" Gwen stood transfixed. "Are you looking for your ball?" He held up the baseball, but she didn't answer.

Bill took it. "Gwen, catch!" He threw it at Gwen and broke the spell.

Lena was unfazed, "Oh Rex, you bad boy." She was all giggles and gave him a smack on the arm.

After the meal, Susie kicked off her shoes to join the kids at the water. They played tag, threw rocks into the waves, and took turns racing to the top of climbing rocks while Jimmie and Irene explored the shallow pools. Scaling those sharp points left their feet stinging with cuts. To the sun's glow, they slow-walked back through the seawater and soothed their sore feet.

Back at the blanket, Garnet was finishing an update on the Hansen lawsuit. Susie had the kids start packing things up to take to the car and set Jimmie up filling a bucket with utensils. In an effort to mix with the *grown-ups*, she offered up some news.

"Did you tell them about the play? The American Legion is putting on the play, *Patty Makes Things Hum*. I've never done a play before but Garnet's doing it and he got me a small part. Can you believe..." She laughed at the notion of the two of them as actors and expected them all to join her, then realized that Rex and Lena had gone back to tickling.

Rex brought out the whiskey bottle. It wasn't unexpected, but Susie was anxious about the lack of discretion. The children, who had proved themselves more responsible than these two, would be coming back for another load soon. Rex offered and Garnet refused.

"What's this? Are you worried about Mrs. Grundy here making

trouble for you, brother?" Rex tilted his head toward Susie indicating she was the "Mrs. Grundy" he referred to. Lena giggled in support as she took a generous gulp for herself. The comment was so mean it startled her. She had heard the term "Mrs. Grundy" at the movies referring to a stuffy, proper stick-in-the-mud. This guy didn't know the first thing about her. Whether he knew it or not, today on a blanket at the beach, Rex drew his line in the sand. Garnet should have been equally offended, but he was too concerned about Rex's charge against him to stand up for his wife.

"What? No, I'm not worried about that," Garnet assured him. "Maybe put it away though. Police do patrol here. I don't want you to get into trouble."

Susie felt the heat rise to her earlobes. By means of the adrenaline pumping through her, she had the rest of the picnic packed within minutes. Garnet attempted to engage her, but she was furious.

On the drive home, the kids drove the conversation. They chattered gleefully and recounted stories of the day. Usually, Susie would have been chattering and chiming in with them, but she was quiet. Deep in her thoughts, with her hands in her lap. *We have a problem.* She chewed her upper lip. *Rex and Lena are a problem. A serious problem.*

§

Rex agreed with Garnet that the problem with the *Independent*'s profit margin was that his outdated equipment failed to meet the standard he'd set with his modern Linotype. G.E. found an impressive printing press and folding machine that was just what they needed to perform and compete with the larger city papers. Their office on Sussex Street wasn't big enough to hold the machinery, so G.E. decided to move the shop to the next block of the newly built Mandery-Martin building.

Susie raised an objection. "No, Garnet! We haven't worked out regular payments to Eva and Jim and you still owe Kibbes. We've been folding papers ourselves for twelve years just fine! We don't need a machine to do that." Rex entered. "And while you're setting up a new shop, we can't put out a paper. What will you tell the advertisers?"

Rex answered her with the boldness of a co-owner. "You have to spend money to make money."

Her eyes stayed on Garnet, irked at his brother's gall. Garnet tried to calm the situation and walked her outside. "It's not what you think.

Rex is putting up the money for the down payment and I'll have an open house for the advertisers and the editors to come in and see the new office. It's going to attract a lot of attention. You'll see. I promise we'll be up and printing again in two weeks."

She took little comfort in his words. Sure, he might pull it off, but the bigger problem was that his judgment was off and he was distancing from her. Rex didn't have the skills nor the inclination to replace her at the job, but he was moving into position inside G.E.'s head.

It was usually fishing weekends when they hatched these schemes. Since Rex and Lena found an apartment in Seattle, Garnet started making the drive there mid-week to enjoy extra time relaxing with his brother. They indulged themselves in the variety of substances Rex always had on hand. Susie felt so personally rejected she didn't think to suspect the truth of the lure that attracted him there. Even though his manner was looser, and his thinking slowed down, when she questioned him, it was without an inkling of what he was actually doing and they argued.

"Garnet, he doesn't like me. He doesn't like the kids and then there's Lena's influence. Gwen watches her, Garnet. She's impressed with her, and she tries to emul...she tries to copy her. She calls her *modern*. Doesn't that bother you?"

"He likes the kids. He just doesn't know what to say to them. Not everyone is a circus clown like your brother Don." They went in circles, their voices got louder and the distance between them got wider.

Susie walked away to take some time to push past her jealousy and overall distaste for Rex and Lena. "Listen, Garnet. Let's ask Mrs. Chansky to come at night. We can go visit them together. I'll try to be more 'likable'." She raised her eyebrows.

This plan defeated his central objective, but he knew he couldn't say no. Realistically, Garnet knew he would eventually need to slow down this new pastime, if not give it up entirely. He was unrealistic enough to imagine this would not be a problem. The pleasure of using again had altered his memory of what coming off from it would entail.

They visited together a couple of weeks in a row. Of course, he abstained, and it was no time at all that he was back into full-blown withdrawals. He took to his bed with tremors, sweats, vomiting, and doubled over with stomach cramps. At the realization of what he had been doing, Susie marveled at the power of her own denial and at his capability to deceive her. It made her sick inside. It was scary.

Tacoma Daily Ledge, Locals and Personals, November 1, 1925
G.E. Parks is reported as being seriously ill.

§

The Hansen case went to Washington State's Supreme Court with G.E.'s attorney registering a counter-appeal to Hansen's appeal. Garnet had caught Hansen's lawyers in a delicious technicality in their brief. By Washington State rules of the court, an appellant brief must not exceed 8.5" on each page. Hansen's brief was 9 ¼", three quarters of an inch too long so, in a twenty-five-page appeal, G.E. and Kibbes argued that a retrial of the first case was unnecessarily costly and would prove nothing that had not already been proven. Besides, the brief was too long.

Motion to Strike Respondent's Brief
    Come now the appellant's and move that respondents brief be stricken for the reason that it is not the size required by section 4 of rule 8 of the rules of this court in fact that said brief is 9 ¼ inches from top to bottom instead of 8 ½ inches as required by rule.
    PC Kibbe, Tenino, Washington
    Vance and Christiansen, Olympia, Wash. Attorneys for Appellant

The judge was unimpressed with the Parks team's attention to detail and promptly set the retrial date of the Hansen appeal for the first week of June.

Rex and Lena visits were halted in the short term while Susie nursed Garnet through withdrawals and monitored his carefully prescribed doses of morphine. She now went with him to doctor appointments. Dr. Wichman offered him a tonic to take in between doses. The doc was a believer in the healing power of positive thought and, while Susie suspected it was nothing more than sugar syrup, she expressed confidence to Garnet and treated it as if it were a miracle drug.

On her way out the door to orchestra rehearsal, Garnet told her that Rex and Lena were moving to Tenino. "Why?" She didn't wait for an answer, she was running late and had no intention of compromising her night. She did double-check that the door was locked before she left.

Tenino Independent, January 29, 1926, Locals and Personals
    Mr. and Mrs. C.R. Parks have returned to Tenino from Seattle and

will reside here. Mr. Parks is a salesman and will call on the grocery stores in Thurston, Lewis and Grays Harbor counties.

When she got home, they talked. "Garnet, those two can't be here! You're not ready for him to be so close." Of course, he assured her that he was fine. He felt the syrup was working and he thought Rex was too busy drumming up a new business in outlying counties to be interested in starting up their old visiting habits.

Her eyes welled with tears. "Promise me, Garnet." She felt like a child, and she didn't like it. "Promise me you won't start up with him again."

"He and Lena are settling down. He likes the idea of a small town and she's been learning to cook. Who knows, maybe they'll start a family." The complete lack of awareness in that statement floored her.

"They already started a family, Garnet! They have a child in California. They never even mention her. They abandoned her!"

"Of course. But that's what I mean." She wondered if that was what he meant. "When they settle, maybe they'll go get her, raise her, and give her a brother or sister."

"He left the baby behind." Then, she made a connection she hadn't before. "In fact, both of your brothers walked away from a child. How did they do that?" The space between them was enormous. "The faith you have in your brother is..." *This is pointless*, she thought. "Just promise you won't start up with him again."

"I promise."

Either he didn't start up again or he did. These days, insurance of a promise wasn't holding up as it once had. Lena and Rex rented a small house with Rex away most of the time traveling western Washington on business. Lena took a lot of walks around town while Susie made a point of being too busy for her to comfortably stop in for a visit. In March, Susie would have a legitimate occupation to divert Lena. David and Jennie Gregg were on the train heading for Washington!

Tenino Independent, March 19, 1926
Mr. and Mrs. D.D. Gregg, parents of Mrs. G.E. Parks, arrived here Wednesday morning from Columbus, New Mexico. Mrs. J.C. Cathcart and Mrs. E. Berg also visited with Mrs. Parks Wednesday, Mr. and Mrs. Gregg returning home with them Thursday.

Susie took the children to stay over at Eva and Jim's so as not to miss a moment. The Parks kids enjoyed the status of being the older cousins to Don and George's little ones. They played hard. George offered Garnet his car so he could join them a couple nights and drive back to Tenino, provided he drop George and family off in Auburn on his way. Garnet couldn't fathom George's choice to live as he did in an off-road dirt floor shack. It was enveloped in such a thick layer of blackberry vines that George had to keep a knife on him to cut his way to the front door. Garnet appreciated the use of the car all the same.

On Rose Hill, Susie sat close on the couch with her ma. Jennie patted Susie's hand. "How old are you, honey?"

"I'm going to be thirty-one, Ma." She sighed and laid her head on Jennie's shoulder.

"Look at all those kids. They are fed and they all have shoes."

Susie laughed. "You and pa will come and see the orchestra play, won't you? We're playing a concert while you're here."

"Oh, won't that be wonderful! I love to hear your music." There at Eva's Susie took sanctuary from the life that waited for her in Tenino. It seemed she'd lived lifetimes since she'd last seen her ma but now, all she could feel was the warmth and sweetness of Jennie Gregg and she surrendered to it completely.

§

Rex banged at the door urgently. "Hey Garnet..." Susie started to make a move to answer, but his insistent banging stirred the rebel in her. The harder he pounded, the slower she moved. Finally, she reached the door. "Where is he?" He barked.

"He's in the back." Then with all sincerity she asked, "Are you okay?"

"Sure." He was impatient. "Is he coming then?"

"I haven't told him yet," *obviously*, and she smiled. "But I will," again, slowing her words in disobedience, "...now." She knew something was up and when it was up with this guy, chances were, it was not good.

Garnet joined him out on the front porch and Rex delivered a stream of words undetectable from inside the house. She meandered about the living room pretending to straighten things while she tried to hear. She picked up a dust rag and thought about how she detested the effect Rex had on her. Just the thought of him made her tense, restless, and uncomfortably suspicious. Gwen passed by, confounded by her mother's attention to housework.

"Mama, what are you doing? Is someone important coming over? Should I change my clothes?"

Susie laughed a little too hard. "No, just keeping things tidy."

"Tidy? Are we going to be tidy now?"

Garnet reentered. He noticed the dust cloth in her hand. "What are you doing?" Susie shot a threatening look at Gwen in case she decided to pile on. "Rex and I are going fishing. Just for a couple of days." He scratched the back of his neck self-consciously.

"No!" Susie said, annoyed at herself for always resorting to one-word objections that exposed how threatened she was by him.

"I know, Susie, I know but it's not like that. You know the money Rex was going to put to the printing press? Something's come up and we need to sort some things out, that's all. I told him it's just business and fishing. That's all we're doing."

"You can do that?" She hoped he could convince her that he could. "Are you talking about the press and the folding machine? He's backing out?"

"No, no, of course not! He's on board and he'll put in and get his share of the profit, just like Eva and Jim will get their share of the profit. All is going as planned." *No, he's backing out,* she knew it. "We just have some unexpected obstacles that need our concentration. I'll bring my tonic and coffee and cigarettes. That's all I'll need. You'll see."

"Okay then." She nodded then she added, "I'll expect a trout on the table for dinner. I'll have new potatoes and peas. You'll bring the fish!"

He promised her a fish for dinner and packed himself up for a fishing weekend.

Tenino Independent, June 11, 1926
GE and Rex Parks enjoy a weekend outing and fishing trip in the upper Skookumchuck country.

§

Eva didn't mind paying long-distance tolls when she wanted information. "What's going on down there?"

Like Susie, Eva had been steadily wound up by the goings-on

between Rex and Garnet, but she lacked Susie's incentive and restraint to keep a lid on her agitation.

"I'm figuring it out, Eva. I have a lot to sort out here. Garnet's gone away for the weekend. I figure it will give me time to go through the bills and see what needs to be done."

"Went away where?" Again, Susie was being barked at. She didn't want to answer. "Is he with that brother of his?"

"Eva, just let me get through the mail and sort the bills and the rest. I'll let you know when I have something I can tell you."

Eva didn't wait for Susie's confirmation. "He's with his brother, all right." She knew what was going on and she didn't like it.

Over the two days, between interruptions from the kids and meals, Susie sifted through uncollected advertising and print job invoices, outstanding bills from St. Peter's Hospital, P.C. Kibbes, and supply vendors. At the bottom of a pile was a promissory note signed by Garnet in August of '24 to Cole Printing. For what she wasn't sure, but payment on that would be coming due in two months. Garnet had been so distracted she couldn't remember the last time he'd gone out on an advertising call.

The way it looked to her, if he started making calls again, she could go to work recovering uncollected invoices and, if her numbers were right, they might be caught up by the end of the year. One concern was that there were several cash withdrawals unaccounted for and that was money not coming back. *It's just money,* she thought. Always more disturbing to her was his fast-talking brother who had Garnet's ear right now somewhere along the Skookumchuck.

Garnet returned from his trip to find little Irene carefully pecking out Glow Worm on the piano and Susie and Junior accompanying her on their violins. Bill had Gwen and Jimmie dancing.

Susie called to him over the neck of her violin. "There's a plate of food for you in the kitchen."

Gwen pulled at him. "Come here, Papa! Dance with us!"

"Okay, okay. Let me put the fish in the icebox."

Thank goodness, Susie thought, *there's a fish.*

§

The local papers printed an answer to at least part of what that fishing trip had been about.

Morning Olympian, July 1,1926
To the Creditors of the above named, C.R. Parks of Tenino, in the County of Thurston, and District aforesaid Bankrupt.

Rex had gotten himself into a deep financial bind so the brothers used the fishing trip to strategize how to get him out of trouble. Rex was thrilled when Garnet enlightened him about the miracle of bankruptcy. He learned he could keep his car while all the debts that threatened to take him down would simply go away. Of course, Garnet would be left holding the bag on the balance of the costly machinery Rex encouraged him to buy. Garnet told Rex not to give it another thought.

"What happened?" Susie asked.

"He said he got a bum rap by some distributors and ended up stuck with supplies of candy and pastries that he couldn't sell. It's hard to tell. He had several schemes he was working at the same time." *Scheme is the right word,* she confirmed to herself and doubted seriously that it was candy and pastries that had taken him down. "I think he'll go east of the mountains. There's a bakery there in Yakima. He drove a truck for a bakery before in California, so that's something he'll do while things calm down. I'm writing it up in the Personals that he's pursuing a business opportunity. You know, so he can start up there with his best foot forward."

Susie nodded. "You seem to be taking it all well, not too upset by the whole thing."

"My brother is a talented man. He works hard. Sure, he goes off the rails at times and gets in over his head. We're alike in that way. Is it courage or foolishness? I think it might be a little of both." Susie hoped beyond hope that this signaled Garnet getting more realistic about his brother.

From her little house in Tenino, Lena folded dresses and stacked shoes in a crate to be thrown into the back of the Chevy Superior. They were going over the mountains to Yakima where Rex hoped to be hired by a bakery. As his loyal brother G.E. Parks put it:

Tenino Independent July 30, 1926
C. Rex Parks left Thursday for Seattle where he will be given charge of one of the eastern Washington branches of Grandma Cookey Company.

In plain language, he would drive the cookie truck.

10

Garnet got lucky. Chief Hansen agreed to a $200 payout that ended the libel suit. It was more money than they had, but it was a lot less than $5,000. Less than two weeks since Rex left town, G.E. was surprised with a request from E.L. Keithahn and D.M. Major to buy the *Tenino Independent*. Keithahn had been an assistant to G.E. and Major was a Seattle printer and journalist ready to have a weekly paper of his own.

"Ten thousand, Susie. They'll pick up the mortgage on the linotype and I can pay the balance on the other equipment. We can pay Eva and Jim all that they are owed and have money in the bank to do what we want! What do you say?"

"Garnet, what do we do without a paper?"

"I'll work for Keithahn while we figure it out. These two are young and they're itching to get into the business and they'll need me to help get them started. They're probably offering us more than they should." Considering the offer again, he shook his head. "We're never going to get a $10,000 offer again. This is truly a one-time chance." His pitch was more effective on Susie than she expected. He was always better able to live with debt than she. It weighed on her and now he was offering up relief, so she said yes.

Garnet signed papers, deposited the check, and went to training Keithahn and Major how to run the paper he'd founded. He did it for three weeks, then he took a trip. The story in *The Chehalis Bee-Nugget* read:

The Chehalis Bee-Nugget, August 20, 1926
Mrs. G. E. Parks and children of Tenino visited Sunday at the home of Mr. and Mrs. C.A. Wood. Mr. and Mrs. Parks formally lived here. Having recently disposed of the *Tenino Independent,* Mr. Parks is going to Virginia to visit his mother. Upon his return

several locations await his consideration, but they intend to remain in Tenino until about October 1.

Without him, Susie hedged her bets on the reliability of their old Ford and drove the kids out to the last baseball games of the season. She made rounds to portion out the $10,000 to their creditors. Eva accepted her money but required answers to a string of questions that Susie agreed were owed to her. "Something's not right. You need to have a plan, Susie. I don't know what he's up to, but you need to have a plan." Then she asked suspiciously, "Why Virginia all of a sudden?"

"His mother is sick. He's seeing his ma." Beyond that Susie had no rationale to offer Eva. She knew it was true that she needed a plan.

In September, she prepared her four oldest for their first day of school. In October, Eva put a celebration together for Susie and Irene's birthdays. Garnet was still gone and she felt that in the form of concern and even sentimentality, but also, there was a noticeable ease she felt with his absence. He returned from Elk Creek with a lot on his mind.

"I've been thinking..." He told Susie he'd been thinking they could make a lateral move and relieve Ralph Noerenberg of the *Centralia Tribune. Did we not just sell the paper we had?* She unconsciously gripped the counter behind her and let him speak. G.E. thought Ralph would take a lowball offer and they could move the family to Centralia.

Gwen was in the seventh grade, Junior in fifth, Bill in third, and Irene was just starting first. After four years in Tenino, they had made real friends and real connections. Bill and Junior spent the last two summers building a lean-to fort in a corner of the quarry. It had sandstone chairs where the five kids conducted their own club meetings and did who knows what else. They called it "the office" and there, they told stories of fishing for trout and alligators. Even Jim was allowed to vote and contribute at "the office." After braving multiple scraped elbows and skinned knees, Gwen devised a perfect skating route along Park Avenue where she knew how to avoid all the bumps in the neighborhood. Their front porch of four years had a 180-degree view of all the goings on in that neighborhood. They had secrets and had concocted back stories about almost everyone who passed them on Sussex. Further, the kids had learned more than one way to get a nickel. The porch was Billie's newspaper office, its steps were Junior's ball return and, on many nights, Irene and Jimmie would just sit on those steps looking up at the moon. Irene would say, "There it is."

With his chin in his hands Jimmie answered. "Yup that's the moon!"

G.E. did put the bid in for the *Tribune* and Noerenberg accepted. Susie moved the family into a little house by the trolley tracks in Centralia, two towns south of Tenino. G.E. set up his first issue of the *Centralia Tribune* in December of 1926.

Oregonian, December 03, 1926

Centralia Paper Sold Centralia, Wash., (Special)

Announcement was made today that the *Centralia Tribune*, a weekly publication, has been purchased by G.E. Parks. Mr. Parks several months ago disposed of his interest in the *Tenino Independent*. Mr. Noerenberg, ex owner, has not announced his plans for the future. He has made many friends here during his ownership of the *Tribune*.

§

A week before Garnet would take over the *Tribune* he hummed like a revved engine at dinner. "Centralia is a much bigger town...more money and more commerce potential. Of course, I had to come in higher than I planned, but I think it will pay off. The folks here are looking for an alternative source of news. I'd like to change the name of the paper, maybe to the *Centralia Independent*. You know, give them a paper that represents an independent voice..."

Irene spoke softly. "Papa." He didn't hear her.

"A progressive voice like one that's not been heard in this area. Olympia controls the thinking of the region and it's a detriment."

"Papa," Irene said louder, and finally got his attention.

"Yes, Baby."

Smiling sweetly. "Can I have some applesauce?" The bowl of applesauce was by his elbow.

"Oh, sure. Here you go." He scooped her up a helping then Jimmie, Bill, and Gwen all held out their plates, so he doled out a spoonful for each of them.

His anxious rattling-on had the quality Susie recognized when he was ramping up to withdrawals, but this seemed even more frantic.

Susie offered, "Do you want me to go in with you Monday? Do you feel ready? Maybe Chas or Albert is free and can help get you started."

Garnet shook her off. "Oh no, there is a whole staff in place already. I'll call if I need you. I just need to find my way around, you know, write my first piece, just get in there. Dig in."

"Papa," Jimmie interrupted. His arm was fully extended with a serving spoon dripping over the sides with applesauce. "Applesauce?"

Garnet winced. "Oh no, son," he answered. "That's yours."

§

While Garnet was away the girls and Jim had been enjoying the luxury of sleeping in Susie's bed. The Centralia house was much smaller, so Susie set Gwen, Irene, and Jimmie up in the second bedroom and Garnet Jr. and Bill on the couch.

"Ahh, Mama!" Gwen complained. "I can't sleep here with Jim's legs kicking me in the face!" Jimmie giggled and did it some more.

"Jim! Okay, we'll figure it out." Susie pulled the quilt off the bed and considered their options. "Irene, where's the best place for you?"

"I want to sleep out on the porch. Over the tracks." The small apartment had a tiny balcony that overlooked the street. Irene excited Jimmie with her ingenious idea.

"Can I go?" he pleaded.

"Okay, you two find pillows to make a bed. Take your quilt. Sister, you take the couch, and the boys can sleep in the bed." Gwen frowned. "Or I can cancel the bed-making on the porch."

"Okay, okay," Gwen conceded. She pulled up her blanket and pillow and went to the couch and Junior and Billie leaped happily into the bed.

Susie went out to help the little ones, but they had already built their bed and were snuggled under the quilt. The chilly air and the bright show of stars above them made Susie a little jealous.

"Look at you two. You're going to get a good sleep tonight!" She gave them each a kiss. "Count the stars for me!"

"Yes, Mama." Irene was all grins. She reached out through the gaps of the railing toward the electric wires. "Look, I can almost touch the wires from here."

"Ooh, you almost can! You won't, though, right?"

"No, we won't," Irene promised and wriggled down under the quilt. "We'll be here to see the trolley come in the morning."

"Oh boy!" Jimmie hollered. "We have the best bed, don't we Mama?"

"I think you do!" She pulled the quilt up over his shoulders and went to her room.

Under the stars, Jim filled Irene in on his solitary life while she was away at school. "I got four frogs out at the creek behind the bank." She didn't comment. "Did you hear me? They're in the cigar box in the kitchen cupboard. I gave 'em leaves and two worms and six flies...I coulda' caught more flies but we had to get ready for Papa, but tomorrow I'm gonna get..."

Irene bumped Jim's side. "Hush." She was trying to make out the words being whispered from their mama and papa's room. Maybe it was a fight.

"But I..." She sent Jim a stronger jab to the ribs.

"Can you shush. It's Papa! Listen." She knew that would get him if she told him it was papa. Jim put his best effort forward to be a listener.

"Come on Susie...come here," their papa said from the next room. It sounded fun and Irene thought maybe they should get up and join them. Their mama answered.

"No, Garnet, no, stop, now!" There was a string of muffled words then she said, "They're just right outside on the porch."

Jimmie weighed in. "Well, I listened. It sounds like a whole lot of nothin' to me."

"SHusSH!" Jim put his head under the covers. It wasn't very often Irene put her foot down with him and he didn't like it.

Papa spoke a little louder. "I've missed you Susie and I'm nearly feeling my old self again!" Susie marveled at his capacity. After all that they'd been through, knocking on death's door, still, to him, sex was always a good idea.

Jim was more than four now. This was the longest Susie had gone without a pregnancy since she and Garnet met. She was naïve in their first years together and didn't necessarily understand what was causing them. She would never discuss the question with friends and certainly not with Eva. She did notice how Garnet's enthusiasm for the babies dwindled a notch with the birth of each one. When his illness affected his ability and inclination for sex, she stopped getting pregnant. That's when she put together what was causing it. She loved every one of her babies, but she knew there was stress in adding more. This discovery made her realize she might have a way to control the size of the family.

Jim was still under the blanket recovering from Irene's reprimand. She felt bad and shook him. "Hey Jim, so all you caught was flies?"

He came out from under to explain. "No, I told ya. I caught flies and two worms. And I put some leaves..." Then he got worried. "...but I didn't put water!"

"It's okay. We can do it in the morning. I'll help you. Hey, did you use the toilet? We don't want to be changing this bed tomorrow. Did you?"

"I tried, but I couldn't." He stalled.

"Go on then, go do it." He didn't move. "Go on, Jim, go potty!"

He plodded off to the bathroom which was right next to Mama and Papa's bedroom. Susie lay next to her playful husband and pushed off the irksome voice of Eva in her head. *You need a plan.*

Garnet urged, "Susie, come on a little closer." She had no *plan*. Garnet would be starting his fifth paper and they still did not have his addiction under control. "Susie..." The truth was it calmed her to be wanted again. *Tonight is tonight*, she would make her plan tomorrow.

Jimmie came back to Irene excited. "Mama and Papa are wrestlin'! Let's jump on them!"

Something told Irene to stay under the night sky and leave her parents to themselves. "Come on, Jim," she told him. "Let's count the stars."

§

The Ford died Tuesday night at Susie's orchestra rehearsal and she had to ask an oboe player to give her a ride home. E.L. Keithahn offered them a ride to the car lot where they put down money enough to purchase a 4-door, silver bullet Oakland Six motor car. They drove it home that day. The kids were beside themselves crawling in, out, and around it. Unable to suppress his unbridled joy, Garnet warned, "No scratches now!"

G.E. wrote the editorial for his first issue of the *Tribune* that weekend while Susie rode the trolley with the kids. He filled it with sentiments of hope and faith in the community, in the way he always started his relationship with new readers. He promised unbiased reporting, fair subscription costs, and expressed his solemn belief that, 'This town of (fill in the blank) is, in my opinion, the very best town of its size in the nation.' Next to it was an introduction from Ralph Noerenberg extolling his faith in G.E.'s abilities.

> *Centralia Tribune,* December 03, 1926
> With this week's issue the management of the *Centralia Tribune* is assumed by G.E. Parks recently of the *Tenino Independent*. He took charge of the entire organization, printing plant and newspaper on December 1. Mr. Parks is an experienced newspaper publisher and should give the patrons of the paper and excellent journal.

G.E.'s issues went out on December 3 and December 10th of 1926. Friday afternoon after the release of the second issue, Susie found him on the bed alone, drained and despondent. "I'm a fraud. I can't do it."

He had never started a newspaper with anything but optimistic jubilance. "Why? What happened?"

"Nothing! Don't you see? I'm finished. I can't do it! Look at me." She tried to see it. If he'd lost his confidence, what was she to do? This struggle of his made her feel nothing but helpless, but she could see he was in no condition to run a newspaper. Deflated Garnet Parks confounded her. "Garnet, you don't have to do this. You need time to get your strength back. What if you don't do it? What if you rest?"

She convinced him to ask for a meeting with Noerenberg. Ralph was a compassionate man. He agreed to subtract expenses covering the transfer of ownership out and then back again then returned the remaining cost of the sale to Susie and Garnet. He let them out of their agreement and, for himself, considered it a long vacation. He was back in his publisher's seat by February of 1927.

§

Garnet continued to struggle. During the day, Susie left him to his thoughts hoping he'd find a way to sort himself out. He took walks, read the papers, and smoked. The children couldn't keep his attention for more than a moment. The kids said, "Papa's sick again." They knew it when his eyes were wrong. When he was apathetic and distant and not as careful about tucking in his shirt or straightening his tie. "Sick" was the term they used. Christmas came and went. Garnet shirked his high-profile club meetings and planning committees. When he was home, he was tired and distracted. He was away from the house more often and vague about when he would return. He refused to go back to the doctor. Susie was no match against the grip his poison had on him and she couldn't blame Rex this time.

At night in their bed, he lamented and sometimes expressed concerns about his family. The only letter he mustered the energy to write was to Rex and he asked for a phone number but he didn't hear back. Then one day, he opened the *Seattle Daily Times.*

> *Seattle Daily Times,* December 23, 1926
> Two youths in a big sedan at 6:15 o'clock last night crowded C. R. Parks, a bakery truck driver, off the highway near Yakima and robbed him of $73 after threatening to beat him up. Parks told officers the young men were armed and that they suddenly crowded in front of his truck and stopped as he was attempting to make a turn.

Garnet knew Rex had been involved with some shady characters before leaving western Washington and he left owing many of them money. He suspected some had learned Rex was in Yakima and came to collect.

While visiting with a neighbor Susie shared her love of farming and, without revealing too much, she shared that they were having difficulty making it work in town. The lady suggested, "I know a woman who lives here and owns a farm near Vancouver. She's looking for someone to live there and take care of it. I can put you in touch with her if you'd like."

Mary Price had 80 acres in Sifton, Washington just north of Vancouver. She offered the Parks' a three-year lease with an option to buy. Included with the farm were eight head of cattle, an apple orchard, and a full plumbing system running off a windmill. It would cost them $900 a year, $450 to be paid up front. They could afford that. As part of the lease agreement, they would own one of the milkers, a Holstein named Mickey's Cow who had a calf. Susie didn't ask Garnet, she told him. "We're leaving. We'll lease this farm and you will rest." He didn't like the idea, but he knew he had forfeited his vote.

The kids piled into the Oakland for their first look at Mary Price's farm. After three-hours they passed a spit of a town called Orchards then followed a long rail fence that paralleled the road. They knew they'd found their farm when they saw a windmill stretching upward from inside an apple orchard. Eight cows and one little calf stood in a line eying them curiously. The place was neglected. Fruit trees needing pruning, fallen boards needing repair, and slippery wet leaves needed raking but it was nothing they couldn't handle.

Susie was struck by the magnificence of the main house. Built from old-growth fir, it stood as tall as the barn. She had never imagined she would live in a home so grand. A port off the barn housed a steam tractor, a rusty plow, and every kind of tool they would want for planting and caring for livestock. This had been a productive farm at one time. Garnet couldn't deny its potential and the kids fell in love.

In Centralia, Susie sat alone on the balcony over the trolley tracks. Finally, she had *a plan*. It was their best chance at recovery. The kids had only been in school for four months. They had no attachments but as she looked over the lights in town, she was hit by an overwhelming grief. It had her by the chest and a pressure from her throat pushed out a torrent of tears. She held herself and rocked. It had been so hard, all of it. How could she know if she was doing the right thing?

It was more than that, though. Someone might think she was petty, or selfish, but at the center of her pain was the fact that she would have to give up her seat in Moldrem's Orchestra. The injustice of it hurt her whole body and she rocked herself hoping if she cried hard enough, it would let go of her.

It finally did enough that she could stand, but it didn't go away. She was now carrying something into this new chapter that was not selfless. It was a sacrifice that brought with it resentment. *It better work,* she thought. It was time to get packing. At rehearsal, she told them she would be turning in her viola. She pushed off their protests and contrived an urgency to get out the door.

Susie and Garnet signed the lease, pulled the kids out of school, and were at the farm by the first week of February.

§

It took weeks for the big house to warm up. It was Bill and Junior's job to keep the heat going. They braved frozen hands and damp feet to pull out the driest chunks of wood from a disheveled woodpile. The thrill of having an indoor water faucet in the country was short-lived. They found several bursted pipes along the line to the windmill which wasn't running due to missing parts. It meant hauling water in buckets from the well to the house and the well to the barn which was flooded by winter rains. Those first few months were hard work. Once they steadied the heat in the house, they found the stillness of a northwest night with not a soul but them for miles made for a peaceful night's sleep.

Mickey's Cow produced milk by the gallons and they put it on everything. Bill thought Mickey's Cow's baby needed a name. "We should call him Mickey's Cow's Calf?"

"Who's Mickey?" was their running joke that was never answered.

There was plenty of work to do but the farm itself was also their private playground. The windmill was perfect for climbing and playing pirates and shipwreck. The kids screamed with joy as they flew from the barn rafters into piles of straw. Since the old Orchards School had been condemned as a menace, lessons were conducted out of a storehouse seven miles away. Susie told Garnet she thought the kids should take the rest of the year off. He deferred all decisions so there was no objection from him, but the decision made Garnet Junior anxious. "Mama, Irene is behind, she can't read. She was behind the other first graders in reading already."

"Oh. Really?" It embarrassed Susie that her ten-year-old son knew more about Irene's schooling than she did. He was like that, though, always watching and worrying about the younger ones. Susie thought about what to do.

"Don't we still have Bill's first-grade reader? Maybe I'll get it out for her."

"Give it to me, Mama. I'll do it with her." Junior set up a schoolroom in a corner of the barn. He took Irene by the hand like a proper teacher and together they went through it page by page. They also worked out addition and subtraction problems and read storybooks together from the family library. The two would put in about two hours before joining the others to play.

Most days Jimmie was on his own just running, arms outstretched like a bird released from its cage. Gwen and Bill invented contests like milkcrate races off the roof or a rope and straw bale obstacle course in the barn. Even with chores that occupied half the day, it beat the devil out of sitting at a school desk for five hours.

Delicate sprouts on the fruit trees signaled to Susie she had better get a garden going. She planned to find a horse to pull the plow that sat off the barn. Garnet rested as directed. The kids thought he looked better, not as sick as before and noticed he was starting to joke again. He pitched in when he was needed. "Garnet, I'm getting dinner finished. Can I get you to move those planks out of the pasture to the side of the barn?" With a smile and a salute, he'd start up the tractor. It was funny, G.E. Parks in his jacket and bow tie bouncing high atop that rusty old tractor. As he passed her, he tipped his derby hat in her direction. The air was clean and there was still some money in the bank. Susie hadn't breathed this easy in years.

§

The ground was hard at the site of their would-be garden. They had chickens happy to help with the tilling and Susie found a mare strong and smart enough to do the bigger job. She reverently called her Sam II. With the kids, she pulled the rusty plow from the back of the barn, cleaned it up the best they could, and went to training herself and Sam II in the use of the awkward contraption.

Gwen, Junior, and Bill took on the job of digging a trench around the perimeter of the barn to deter the rain. Jimmie flew by several times a day with a chicken under each arm. He kept busy uncovering the best worm spots for the hens who he believed couldn't be trusted to find them on their own. Back and forth he persisted, carting them one or two at a time to his wormholes. It took up most of his day.

Sometimes, Garnet took the car out to get familiar with the area and put out some feelers. He was never gone long and by all appearances was keeping himself away from temptation. He met a pair of brothers who ran a small newspaper along the Columbia River called the *Camas Post* and offered to lend them a hand a few days a week for a modest wage. They were thrilled to have the advantage of a seasoned newsman like G.E. around.

At dusk, Susie sat on the porch. She watched Bill's silhouette skid across the grass to a high spot in the barn where he could read his book uninterrupted. Inside, Jimmie was planted beside Junior who was building a birdhouse from scrap wood. Gwen and Irene took turns on the piano.

Garnet brought Susie out a cup of coffee. He lit a cigarette and took a slow drag. "It sure is quiet out here, isn't it?"

"You seem so much calmer. Do you feel better?" Of course he did. She just wanted to hear him say it.

"I do. I had gone to a poor place. I don't know that a hospital bed would have done me better than this. You've done a great job here, Susie. It's astounding how you've developed the place in such a short time." Through the open window, Irene's much improved Glow Worm trickled out to the porch.

Garnet had to know they were better for the change. He had only to look at how the children were flourishing. As far as she knew, he hadn't had a shot of morphine in weeks and didn't seem to be looking for one. She wouldn't say it out loud, but she felt better in control. Garnet had carried a weight too heavy, and the pressure thwarted him. She took control out of necessity, but she felt no burden. It is what they needed.

"It's not hard for me," she said. "I can manage us here. You can concentrate on your rest and writing, and you can take your time to decide where you want to go from here. You shouldn't have the pressure anymore. It wasn't good for you or any of us." He blew out a line of smoke and pulled at his collar.

"Well, I've always been able to take the pressure." He tightened a little, injured by her implication. "The *Courier* had its share of pressure, and I handled it. I mean, where would we be if I hadn't negotiated such a good price on the *Independent*?"

Well, we would be in Tenino, she thought. "You're right, but you weren't counting on being sick. It took its toll."

Susie's rationale worked to settled him again and he melted back into his chair. Gwen played Pacabel. "This is good right now. Slowing down. We'll take our time."

§

That summer Jimmie tried to hatch an egg. Bill put him up to it. He found Jim in the coop petting chickens and collecting eggs. "I hatched some once."

"No, you didn't," Jim snapped back.

"I did. Just sat every day until I felt one of 'em move. You have to stay on 'em all day and even overnight or they get cold. You probably couldn't sit still that long, I'm guessin'." Bill swaggered off sure Jim wouldn't be able to resist at least trying.

With Bill out of sight, Jim arranged some straw where he placed three eggs and situated himself cross-legged over them. At about the three-minute mark his leg began hurting, and he felt a sloppy wetness of egg seep in through his shorts. He jumped off and marched out to the barn to confront Bill. "How long did you sit on those eggs?"

"I don't remember. How did you do?"

"I broke one."

"Yeah, come to think of it, I did too," Bill admitted grinning. "I wonder if I didn't ever hatch those eggs after all."

G.E. found another opportunity to fill in at the *Washougal Record* for a printer, McCabe, who was on vacation. Working the press gave him a chance to feel the ink on his fingers again and the autonomy to be in his own thoughts, and deal in occupations of the mind that didn't involve cow pies and tractor grease. The job inspired him to inquire about a clerking job at the Harlan Printery in Vancouver where they put him to work part-time. On his off days, he honored his agreement to rest and continued his reading ritual in the mornings. He received newspapers in the mail from Washington, Oregon, and New Mexico. He usually had a lot to say about the editors' content in opinion articles, both favorable and not-so-favorable. He followed politics and sports news religiously. He did not expect to see Rex's name show up in the *Spokane Chronicle*, but somehow Rex had gotten into something involving an altercation and a shooting. From the sound of it, it seemed to be a complicated series of events.

> *Spokane Chronicle,* May 20, 1927
> Authorities investigating the accidental shooting of Major S. W. C. Hand Wednesday night in the armory here reported today that they had nothing definite for the publication regarding the case. When they searched Major Hand's office, where his body was found, they found bloody fingerprints upon the telephone.
>
> According to Olaf Sandvig deputy prosecutor, Hand called up his wife near Selah after he had shot himself. According to Sheriff L. D. Luce papers in a $10,000 heart balm suit were served upon Hand yesterday evening just before the shooting. C. R. Parks, bakery wagon driver, who is bringing the suit, reported to the police that he and Hand had an altercation on the street about 8:15 o'clock. The heart balm case has not been filed in Superior Court.

Garnet pondered it. An accidental shooting? He wondered what kind of soldier accidentally shoots himself. Rex served the man with a heart balm suit, which meant the soldier was involved with someone in a way that Rex didn't want him involved. Lena, of course. The Spokane paper was far enough from Yakima that Garnet knew this was more than Local News. He dug through his stack of papers spanning two weeks back to see where else it was covered. Sure enough, there was a story in the *Bellingham Herald*:

> *Bellingham Herald,* May 20, 1927
> Disclosure in alleged love triangle and of a fistic duel on the street between the enraged husband and the suspected "other woman" followed yesterday the mysterious shooting last night of Major Samuel W. C. Hand, 161st Infantry, Washington National Guard.
>
> Major Hand was at first believed to have shot himself accidentally. It is now hinted that he attempted suicide. A military investigation of the whole affair is expected as a result of the report.

A suicide attempt! He found stories in the *Seattle Daily Times*:

> *Seattle Daily Times,* May 21, 1927
> Mrs. Lena Parks was seriously ill today from two poison tablets she swallowed yesterday in her room in a hotel here. The attending physician told authorities Mrs. Parks took the poison in an attempt to end her life.
>
> Her action came less than two days after Major S. W. C. Hand, Washington National Guard Officer, of Selah, was wounded by the discharge of his army automatic pistol. Major Hand, who probably will recover, said the shooting was accidental.
>
> Mrs. Parks' poisoning was made known when Kathleen Gray, sixteen-year-old daughter of Mrs. Dolly Gray, proprietor of the hotel in which Mrs. Parks resides, heard groans from the woman's room. She was found to be ill and a physician summoned.

As if he were trying to cover up a crime scene, Garnet tore out the articles, stuffed them in his jacket and threw out the remaining pages. He had to find a way to contact Rex. It would be no benefit for Susie to know any of it. Rex might need his help and he felt he should be able to see to the health and well-being of his own brother without his wife's permission. He would send a letter to G.A., in case Rex had given him a phone number, and then he would visit the telephone exchange in Vancouver and engage the help of an operator to locate him.

In the meanwhile, in the world of cow pies and tractor grease, his family thrived. Between the fresh vegetables, the cow's milk, and the chickens providing eggs and meat, they ate like kings. Junior learned to drive that tractor and the boys built a second port off the barn to stack the towers of firewood the two had cut up all summer. Flowers on the trees turned to fruit and the sunsets came earlier. It was apple picking time and Susie was sewing because, this Fall, they were going back to school.

§

G.E. put in some hours at the Printery then stopped by the telephone office where he was connected to a Yakima operator. She was able to locate Rex's last known address at the Pacific Hotel, but when they rang up the proprietor there he was gone. Before heading back home, G.E. swung by Washougal to check in with U.R. Gibbs and his friends at the *Record*. Gibbs alerted him to an opportunity in Oregon at the *Eastern Clackamas News*. "The editor has to sell. I published that paper for six years before I came here. It was successful. The community there likes their local news." Gibbs encouraged G.E. to take a drive over the bridge to Estacada and meet him.

He was going to be late getting home but he crossed the bridge that same evening and spoke to Mr. Haynes, the editor at the *Eastern Clackamas News*. Haynes had accepted an offer in Milwaukee. He had already moved his family to Wisconsin. He needed to make a sale quickly and told Garnet if he wanted to buy him out, the *Eastern Clackamas News* was his.

This was going to be a tough sell for Susie. He took the hour drive home mulling how to set up his proposition. The kids were at the radio listening to the Children's Hour. Garnet helped Susie clean up the dishes. When the program ended, the children made dibs at the wash basin then were marched off to bed. The night's music program was brought to them by KPO's Dance Orchestra. Susie listened while working on a sewing project in her lap. Garnet skulked into the room then stood before Susie and pulled a Hershey bar and a Milky Way from his jacket pocket. He held them out to her. "You pick." Susie was scandalized! She scanned the room for signs of a child who would be livid if they saw it. When she was sure the coast was clear, she picked the Milky Way.

The indulgence made her a little lightheaded. "What did we do to deserve this?"

He waited till the chocolate was melting in her mouth before delivering his statement. "Well, I have ulterior motives." He told her about Gibbs and how he had come to learn about the paper in Estacada then laid out the terms Haynes at the *Eastern Clackamas News* presented to him. She laid the half-eaten Milky Way in her lap as she listened. She'd lost her taste for it. She could see he believed he was telling her a new story but how many times had she heard it before. She'd been free from this pressure for almost a year.

She wanted to tell him no straight out. They were just starting to set up a rich, full life on this farm. They had put the hardest months in already and next year was going to be much easier. He hadn't even given it a chance. It had renewed him and now, *he's gained a little energy, and it's back to the same thing all over again.*

She said it plainly. "I can't do it."

His regained health restored his powers of persuasion. "I understand it. Of course, you have every reason to object. I'm just concerned, given that we know that I will eventually get back into the editor's seat, that the terms Haynes' has offered won't come around again." He went on to explain about Haynes leaving for Wisconsin on little notice, forcing him to offer Garnet ridiculously easy terms. "He's even willing to accept payment over time."

They moved the conversation into the kitchen and continued talking late into the night. At the kitchen table, they discussed potential compromises, from the unrealistic to the unacceptable. "Maybe you don't come with me right away. Maybe I get the paper started and you stay here with the kids. I'll come home on weekends." They both knew they wouldn't be able to buy a newspaper, afford rent on the farm and have another place in Estacada during the week. It was unrealistic. Then he offered, "If Eva put up the money, we could…"

"No!" Susie stopped him. "No, we won't do that again." They continued to lay out scenarios. The longer they talked, the more it illuminated the magnitude of their losses. Over their years together, every step forward resulted in a deficit. Would they now add this farm to their tally of losses? It was the Greggs who uproot, her pa who moved the family every time he has an itch. She thought Garnet was different. He spoke differently and he dressed differently, but then she was seventeen. At seventeen, she believed his fancy words would take her somewhere beyond what she'd known as a child. Now, here she was with a brood of children and the difficulty of a man asking to pick up and move again. She was no different from her ma. She couldn't feel more strongly that walking away from this farm for another newspaper might be the step backward that breaks her.

Then it occurred to her. For Garnet, the farm itself was a symbol of failure. It wasn't his victory, it was hers. If she held to it and refused him another chance to succeed as a newsman she would win, but she would stand alone. Alone wouldn't be so bad for her but, she didn't believe she had permission to make that choice for his children. What an unfortunate place they were in. This farm or the acquisition of another newspaper. *Someone loses,* she thought. *One of us must choose to lose* and she knew who it had to be.

§

Garnet vowed to find a place in Estacada that would house some of the animals and Susie got packing. This time, she completed each task with ceremonial sentimentality. She milked the cow and told her, "Well, Mickey's Cow, you're too good to lose. He'd better find a place for you." She stopped by and gave Sam II a thorough scratch on her neck and rubbed her muzzle. "We won't be doing this too many more days. You're a good girl." She sighed and then called out reminders to the kids before they left for school.

"Bill, bring some wood in before you put your school clothes on!" Gwen and Junior already had the hay out to the cows. Jim slow walked into the kitchen with his belly hanging over his britches and a shirt full of eggs.

It was oatmeal and eggs for breakfast. The kids claimed their sack lunch from the counter and the four went to the tarp covered truck that would take them to school. Susie's packing was interrupted by a call from Eva who was in a particularly good mood.

"Jim and I were thinking that we would come down to you this Thanksgiving. I've got a good turkey ready for butcherin'. I know you've got squash, potatoes, and corn. Did you can beans?"

"I did some but only green beans," Susie hedged. "The house will be upended, though."

"Well, I've got enough I can bring down. George still doesn't have a phone, so I guess I'll have to send Don down to pull him and his family out of the briers."

"That's not nice, Eva." Susie shifted her balance and Jimmie passed by.

He heard Eva's name and copied his big sister Gwen by wagging his head from side to side, "All Aunt Eva says is, 'Nah, Nah, Nah." Susie put her hand over the mouthpiece and shooed him off.

Eva didn't hear. She was occupied in defending her remark about their brother. "Ah, I'm kiddin'. George doesn't want to go anywhere these days is all I'm saying. He just sits in his house dreaming about diamonds in those hills. So, I'll have Don grab them and bring them all. We'll have a regular Gregg family Thanksgiving!"

It was unavoidable. Eva was going to have to know the truth of it. "What I mean to say, Eva, is that I've started putting things in boxes."

"What do you mean, *putting things in boxes*?"

"We're making a move."

"You're what?!" Susie held the handset away. "What in the Sam Hill are you talking about? You should be doing no such thing! After all you've done at that place in ten months? Settling on that farm is the best decision you've made since you came up here. Is this another pie-in-the-sky notion of Garnet's, Susie? You are not moving. As long as I live and breathe you will not move from that place!"

She lacked the strength to be diplomatic. "Well Eva, it's not your farm, not your marriage, and not your husband. I'm not saying you're wrong, but it's not your decision to make."

"Maybe it should be!"

"I have reasons for going along with this that you can't understand. I've given it a lot of thought and I know it's the right thing to do." What Susie wouldn't have given right now for some of Maggie's unconditional support. Blind acceptance was a thing she never got from Eva. Her fierce loyalty came as a package with her intrusive eruptions.

"I wonder if you've just completely lost your senses!"

Susie shouted. "What do you want me to do, get a divorce?" They both knew the gravity of an idea like that. Susie would never forget her mother's face when they learned that Ida was divorcing Joe. It was beyond a disappointment. It was foreign. Unspeakable. It was daring of Susie to even say the word out loud.

"Well, it's beyond me how uprooting your kids and leaving behind all the hard work you put in for ten months of your life is the right thing to do." Eva was fishing for information but Susie met her with silence. She had no defense and no interest in providing Eva with fodder to spout more opinions. It would change nothing.

"Eva, this is costing you money, we should hang up."

After several more seconds of costly silence, Eva spoke. "Okay. What do you need? I can help you pack. Would that help?"

Susie exhaled. "Yes. That would help. Thank you. Really, thank you."

They disconnected and Susie went to the barn where trunks were stacked still yet to be unpacked. She knew at least one of them had baby clothes and blankets inside. She wanted to go through and pull out what was still usable because, among the many reasons for going to Estacada that Eva would never understand, there was this one. A baby was coming in June.

§

Garnet offered to write the announcement of his acquisition for the brothers at the *Camas Post*:

Eastern Clackamas News, Farmer-Printer, December 12, 1927
G.E. Parks of Orchards was among the list of *Post* callers while in the city the first of the week. Mr. Parks, newspaper man and linotype operator by profession, perhaps by way of doing penance for his sins committed in this calling, has been reveling in the dreams of the rancher and the dairyman at Orchards for the past year. In the meantime he was employed for a few weeks on the *Post* machine and later at the Harlan Printery in Vancouver. He is now re-entering newspaper work, this time at Estacada, Oregon, and is moving to that city. *Camas Post.*

When the older kids learned about the move, they were hardly fazed. They had moved six times in six years so, as much as they loved it on that farm, picking up and leaving was as natural to them as their mama having another baby. However, it was different for Jim. No sooner did the words leave Susie's mouth that he was out the door. She caught up to him in the coop where he laid in a heap in the corner, crying.

"I'm sorry, Jim. I know how much you love it here." He wiped a long line of snot across his forearm.

"Do...do I have to wear those itchy tight long pants and go to school now too?"

"You will have to go to school next year. But no itchy pants, I promise. I will make you soft long pants. Also, you can pick which chickens we bring. We can't bring them all, but we'll take your favorites."

He burst out in sobs. "They're all my favorites!"

He was crushed and, though she wanted more than anything to give him comfort, she knew who had the best chance of soothing his broken heart. She went back to the house and sent Irene out to him. After about a half hour she checked out the window. Irene had him at the giant maple, pushing him on the rope swing with a chicken in his lap.

§

The exit from the farm got a little messy. They had paid a plumber $157 to repair the broken pipes and the windmill back in April. To save Mary Price the trouble of writing them a check for the repair, Garnet simply deducted it from their quarterly payment. Maybe she was confused or just stingy, but Mary Price demanded full payment and wasn't interested in hearing about their plumbing troubles. G.E. stood his ground and didn't pay. Mrs. Price took them to court for restitution owed, arguing the Parkes had been squatting on the property for 59 days. The judge ruled in her favor so, if saying goodbye to their beloved farm weren't injury enough, they were fined $354 for the privilege of doing so.

U.R. Gibbs wrote them a piece of goodwill on his editorial page.

Washougal Record, December 27, 1927

Good Luck to Him (From *Washougal Record*, U.R. Gibbs, editor and publisher). G.E. Parks who worked in this office last September while R. McCabe was on vacation, has bought the *Eastern Clackamas News* at Estacada and moved to that city with his family. That paper was published by the editor of the record for six years immediately prior to his coming to Washougal. This was nearly three years ago, and in that time the *Eastern Clackamas News* has change management about twice a year on average. We wish Mr. Parks success in this new field, for which we retain a very friendly feeling. He can give them a newsy up-to-date paper if they will give him the necessary support.

The new house in Estacada sat above town, across from some railroad tracks. It was a walk from shops below but quite a distance from the nearest neighbor. Beyond the tracks was a huge field of strange bushes that put off a foreign, earthy smell Susie had never experienced before. It was called ginseng and to Susie, it was a symbol of the strange and uncomfortable feeling she hadn't been able to shake since they arrived.

She made a conscious effort to maintain a positive attitude. One thing she tried was to introduce a new routine of standing at the door before school to hand out lunches. In this way, she would give each of the children her full attention to start their day. She had seen an image of a mother doing this in a magazine, and she felt it was the sort of thing that was missing from her parenting. Garnet Junior approached her. The leaves she brushed off his shoulder revealed he'd been climbing trees already that morning. She tweaked his nose and handed him his lunch bag. Bill always prepared himself independently for his school day and would have handled his lunch just fine. Nonetheless he indulged her, stopped to collect his lunch, and took a kiss. Irene gave a dramatic curtsy, accepted her kiss, and allowed Susie to straighten her bow. When Susie tried to fix an out-of-place curl on Gwen's forehead it was more fussing than she could tolerate, and she threw her hand away. "No Mama! Stop!" Gwen exited leaving Susie welling up in the doorway.

It still weighed on her that Irene might be behind despite the help Junior gave her at the farm. She meant to speak to the teacher at the Orchards School but before she knew it, they were packing to move away. Susie watched them make their way up the street and called out to Gwen. "Sister." Gwen didn't turn. At thirteen she was socially anxious about facing her second day in a new classroom. Also, Susie knew Gwen was mortified these days by the volume of her voice. "Garnet! Bill! Be sure that Irene finds her classroom today. She wasn't sure yesterday and had to ask for directions. Will you walk her?"

Bill turned and answered. "I will, Mama. I'll walk her." Irene turned too and waved.

Susie took on setting up the house while Garnet established himself at the paper. She converted the carriage house into a stall for Mickey's Cow and Jimmie's chickens. Every room in the house was filled with untouched trunks and crates. Also, her belly was going to be impossible to disguise before long and she had yet to tell anyone a baby was coming. All this anxiety made her extra sensitive to indications that she might be failing, which was why the well-dressed mother in the magazine held such weight. *We'll see how long I can keep that up*, she thought and she went into the kitchen.

There Jimmie was at the table next to Garnet who was seated in his customary fashion with a cigarette and coffee, orienting himself to the area's local newspapers. Jimmie shoveled spoons full of oatmeal into his mouth, talking straight through it.

"Mowah serruupp, pleeese?" Garnet looked up to Susie for help.

"Woa, Jim. Swallow your bite." He swallowed a little. "No, swallow it. All the way. Now ask for syrup."

That was an eye-opener to Garnet. "He was asking for syrup?"

Jim swallowed most of it, then spit a wad back into his spoon and said, "More syrup please!"

Garnet choked in disgust. "Awww, no, son. Not in the spoon!"

Jimmie grinned boldly. "Sorry, Papa."

Susie poured more syrup into his bowl while Garnet read from *The Oregonian*. He was in good spirits. "Well look at this, Susie. Your vaudeville star Frank Crumit has married an actress…the twice-divorced Julia Sanderson."

"Oh, shucks. I thought I still had a chance with him." She grabbed a wet rag to intercept Jimmie licking his sticky fingers. She wiped his hands and he asked to go outside with the animals.

Garnet folded his paper ready to start his day. He was in full form, sharp and ready. "I'll be calling on *The Oregonian* today. I thought I could make a presentation at the Editor's Convention. Get our name out there."

It was time to tell him about the baby today, to give him time to digest it. "That's a good idea. A long trip, though."

"That's why I'm leaving early to get back to the shop by afternoon."

Tell him now, quick and over. "So, Garnet." She waited for him to turn. "There's a baby coming." He took a final sip from his coffee cup and set it on the counter. He took a breath as if he were about to speak, but he didn't. "Garnet, did you hear me?"

There was no detectable quality in his body or tone. He seemed to have put himself in neutral. Nodding, "I did. I did." He did not meet her eyes and left the room for his hat and coat. "I'll, um, speak to you tonight." *Oh dear*, she thought.

That night they had dinner, listened to a radio show, and when the last of the children were put to bed, Susie unpacked a trunk.

Garnet said, "Another baby, huh?"

She stopped and faced him. "Yes. A baby."

"We'll be having number six then?"

"It's not ideal. But we haven't had a faulty one yet," she joked.

"I suppose I was thinking you would work in the shop while the kids are at school."

"Well, Garnet, it's not like I've never worked the shop with a baby on my hip."

"It's true. We'll see how it goes. I'm on the schedule for the Editor's Convention. I shook some hands today. It was a good call."

Is it irresponsible to want to celebrate and share the joy of a new baby? His passive posture felt bad. It made her feel foolish.

He took a long, thoughtful pause then a puff on his cigarette. "I think Estacada needs a baseball team."

§

It was evening. Susie and the kids cleared dinner dishes and Irene asked if she could switch on the electric lights in the living room. Gwen and Garnet Jr. were in a standoff at the sink about whose turn it was to wash and whose turn to dry. Bill flinched as he squeezed between them, hoping to get his job done without incident. Garnet was writing in the back bedroom when a knock at the door sent Irene and Gwen flying to answer. Gwen opened the door. It was Rex.

Neither of them greeted him. Gwen let out an involuntary *uh oh* knowing more than she should about the potential impact of a visit from her Uncle Rex. Irene spun around and shouted. "Papa! Mama! Uncle Rex is here!"

Susie came from the kitchen for confirmation. It was him all right.

Garnet heard and rushed in to greet him. "There he is! I've been looking for you! Where did you disappear to? And how on earth did you know we were here?"

Susie thought the floor was rocking beneath but then realized the tremors were coming from inside her. She pulled the nearest child to her to steady herself. He hadn't changed in a year and a half. He wore an over-coordinated, tropical-colored suit with all the subtlety of a neon sign. She knew his "how-the-hell-are-ya'" handshake and that cunning grin and how it was designed to engulf the ones, only the ones, he deemed worthwhile. Others he would discard quickly and without a thought. She was amazed at his skill in garnering loyalty, and she had no illusions about which side of his line she was on.

"Susie," Rex said with a nod.

She nodded back. "Hello Rex." *Where's Lena*, she wondered.

They put Gwen and Irene on a mattress with the boys and Rex took Gwen and Irene's room. The next day, Garnet took Rex to the *Eastern Clackamas News* office. They spent the afternoon and all that evening catching up. Rex shared details of the goings on in Yakima with excitement about the pending lawsuit against Major Hand that he expected to come through in his favor and bring him a $10,000 windfall.

"What do you say we get back to the house for dinner?" Garnet suggested but Rex declined. He had someone he was meeting in Portland and, he winked, didn't expect he'd need a place to sleep tonight.

Garnet laughed his hearty Rex-laugh. "All right then. I'll leave you to it, my good man." He gave Rex a slap on the back. "You're never long for landing on your feet and finding a new young lady, are you?"

Rex nodded. "Young is right!"

"So, I'll expect you at the house tomorrow night then?"

Rex confirmed, tipped his hat, and was on his way.

Garnet got home as Susie and the kids were finishing dinner. He dished himself a plate and offered her an answer to a question she didn't ask. "So, Rex left Yakima in November, at the time of that ambush we read about in Yakima, remember? It was a terrible thing, it was Klan remember, they killed the Filipinos at the boarding house? It was in every paper. A violent, ugly thing that was."

"Was he involved?" It might have been unfair, but she put nothing past Rex.

Garnet corrected, "Oh no, of course not. I don't know why I lead with that. I mean he and Lena split also. That was the main reason." It was an odd tangent, but Garnet was trying to cover for Rex and the embarrassment that had put Rex and Lena on the front pages. He hoped a KKK boarding house ambush might have magnitude enough to overshadow his brother's spectacle. "I just thought you were wondering why he is here. He and Lena had words, so he left town to keep the peace."

"He left to keep the peace, huh? That was big of him." She could tell Garnet was covering, and she wasn't much interested in what or why. Clearly the inevitable had come to pass. Rex and Lena were through. Susie's larger concern was about what Rex was up to now. She knew if he planned to involve Garnet, he'd have no thought of its effect on her or the kids. This concern was compounded by the fact that she knew she couldn't count on Garnet to resist him.

"He'll be back here tomorrow night," Garnet added.

"How long?" She asked.

"Oh, I told him he's got a room here as long as he needs." He lit a cigarette and settled on the sofa in front of the radio.

"You what?!"

"Well, I did it, Susie. I convinced my brothers at the American Legion to sponsor a baseball team in Estacada. I'll be managing finances. They'll be called the Legionnaires. It's catchy, isn't it? It's time to start warming up Garnet's arm for the junior team. I think it's all right to tell them that he's fourteen. You know, bump him up two years, don't you? He's good enough."

"Sure," Susie called from the kitchen, but still echoing in her head were his words...*he's got a room here as long as he needs.*

Eastern Clackamas News, March 9, 1928
Support the Baseball Team
Estacada is duly entered in the Portland Valley Baseball League for 1928. *The News* believes that this is a good move for the young people of the section, for the baseball fans, and for the town and community in general.

§

The five Parks kids were now squeezed into the boys' room so that Rex could settle in comfortably into the third bedroom of the house. Nights, he showed up in the early morning hours unable to maneuver himself in the dark without tipping over a table or vase. One morning, he was still sleeping when Susie confronted Garnet at the breakfast table. She held two empty bottles of hootch she'd found in the bathroom sink.

"What am I supposed to do with this, Garnet?"

"What?" He glanced up and with false indifference he said, "Put them in the garbage?"

"You know what I mean. This shouldn't be lying around the house for the kids to find. They hear what goes on in that room at night. You think they don't hear it?"

"He tries to keep it down. It's the girl that..."

"I don't care if it's him or," she spit the words out like poison, "his *girl*...it doesn't belong here in our house. You will tell him to leave, or I will!" She was shouting.

"I will not put my brother out!" He shouted back.

"It looks like it will be me then!"

He cursed, "Good night, Susie!" and threw his water glass in her direction. It just missed her and shattered against the wall. She stood stunned, then sensed the presence of an innocent onlooker. Irene was there in bare feet with eyes wide, watching from the living room. Garnet saw her, mumbled to himself, and butted his cigarette. Susie shoved the liquor bottles at him and went to Irene.

"Mama's all right. We're all right. Are you all right?" Irene looked at her Papa and he nodded.

"Uh-huh," she answered and let her mama hold her. To Irene's relief, Susie sent her off to get dressed before breakfast, then she took the broom to the spattered glass on the floor. "This is not working, Garnet. I won't be housing stray girls and picking up after him." Still intent on making her point about Rex, it escaped her that she'd just dodged a water glass hurled at her by her husband.

It was early, but Garnet started gathering what he needed to leave for the day. He didn't look at her. "I'll talk to him." He tucked his watch into his breast pocket then shook his head and picked up the dustpan. "I'm sorry I threw it. I wasn't trying to hit you."

"Who were you trying to hit? Are you a hitter now?"

He shook his head no. "I was frustrated."

"It's not glass flying at me that's going to hurt us. I mean it would have but I'm quick and the glass we can sweep up. It's this other thing, this permission you give your brother, that I don't know what to do with."

He must have scared himself because he had no comeback. "I know. I'll talk to him."

§

Garnet did talk to Rex who agreed to do his courting away from the house moving forward, for his brother's sake. Garnet promised Susie that Rex would keep a no-booze and no-girls policy in the house. Garnet sweetened his proposal to Rex by inviting him to work part-time at the newspaper. This allowed the two of them to spend more time together and succeeded in blurring the lines between business and brothers having fun.

When Junior and Bill weren't at school, they were at baseball practice.

Garnet Junior was a talented second baseman for Estacada's junior team and his sights were set on a spot with the Estacada Legionnaires one day. Billie practiced on alternating days with the younger boys' team. The family spent every Saturday that summer in the stands at the boys' games or at Legionnaires' doubleheaders.

It was a school day and Garnet and Bill decided to get their wood chopped in the morning so they could have more time to play in the afternoon. Inside, Jim had positioned himself at the table for a breakfast that wasn't yet ready.

"Mama," Jim poked at her belly. "I want to name the baby Calvin."

Irene disagreed, "That's a terrible name! Mama! That's the name of the caterpillar-killer-boy at Aunt Eva's! I like Alexandria."

Susie praised her. "Ooo, that's a stylish name."

"I know it is. I named one of Jimmie's frogs that. It's Alexandria and he keeps changing it back to Hank!"

Before Jim could launch a counterargument, Bill burst through the door. "Mama! Garnet's bleeding! He's bleeding all over."

She ran out and found Junior holding up a bloody, four-fingered hand. He wasn't crying, he was just standing there holding it up like a torch. "Irene, go get towels. Bill, get ice!" She pulled off her apron and wrapped it around his hand, keeping her words calm while she scanned the ground for the finger. "Hold it tight as you can." His eyes stayed fixed on her, and he nodded. He didn't cry.

Irene returned with rags in her arms and a trail of them behind her. Susie replaced her apron with a clean dish towel and put Irene in her place to help Garnet hold it. Sniffly and shaken, Irene did as she was told and Bill held his bowl of ice and watched. Susie made circles in the dirt like a chicken pecking scratch. Suddenly she spotted the finger and grabbed it off the ground, then wrapped it in a rag and buried it in Bill's ice. Irene had not blinked once. She was beginning to look pale.

Garnet had taken the car that morning. Susie went to the house to make a call to him but there was no answer at the paper. She decided they would walk Junior down the incline to Doctor Gilbert. She held Junior steady, minding not to move him and stimulate the bleeding. "Bill, can you take him on the other side. Give Irene the bowl." However willing Irene was, she was still wobbly from the seriousness of her previous job.

"I'll do it!" Jimmie offered. Bill handed the bowl to Jim and took his brother's arm on the right side. Gwen, who had been inside getting ready for school, came out the front door to find them starting down the hill. Susie put her in charge of getting the color back into Irene. Jimmie embraced his ominous responsibility taking careful steps down the incline. They all moved steadily together toward the doctor's office.

They delivered Garnet Junior to Dr. Gilbert. Jim presented the floating finger to the receptionist and the boys waited outside until they were allowed to come back and see their brother.

"I can't say it's every day I'm presented with a finger by two brave boys such as these, Mrs. Parks." The doctor went on to explain why he did not reattach the finger. "Make no mistake, it sometimes works. In this case, he severed it down to the second knuckle. Once healed, he would have had trouble bending it." He turned to Garnet Junior. "You're a ballplayer, right, an active boy? I'm afraid I couldn't sew your finger back well enough for you to still throw to home. You're better off without it." He ruffled his hair. "In fact, this might improve your knuckleball!" He chuckled.

Junior stared down at the giant mass of gauze. "Well, it's my catching hand. Do you really think I'll catch just as good as before?"

"I can almost guarantee it," the doctor assured him. Susie put another call to the *News* office, but the assistant said G.E. was out. Before they left the doctor's office, Susie rang him up again. Still no answer. The doctor lifted the bowl of water with the floating digit. "Now would you like to take this home? Maybe have your mom pickle it for you?" This doctor was a hoot, all right. Being such a serious boy, Junior might have been sensitive to a ribbing like that, but he smiled and seemed to appreciate the distraction.

At home, his brothers and sisters surrounded him with uncharacteristic charity, all vying for position to help him in the house. They set him up on the couch in the main room and, after dinner, Gwen tuned the radio to the five o'clock Children's Hour and they situated themselves in a semi-circle on the rug to watch the radio. Susie tried Garnet again but no answer.

None of them made it to school that day. Though she planned to send them tomorrow, Susie let them stay up and listen to *The Town Cryer* past 8:30. She was about to send them off to dress for bed, when Garnet made his entrance.

"Susie, kids!" he bellowed. "Papa's home." Gwen and Jim jumped up quick, making sure they were up front and center in case there was a treat. Sure enough, he had a piece of bubble gum for each of them. "Well then, I thought you might be looking for a treat. Here you go, Sister,

Jim..." Irene and Bill waited behind for their turn. "Hey now, where's Junior? He's not usually one to lag behind."

An involuntary gush of words flowed forth from Bill. "Garnet's on the couch! We went to the hospital 'cause he was choppin' wood and when I went to the pile to get him another log, he was just yellin' and bleedin' all over..."

"What?" Garnet looked for Susie to get confirmation. Jimmie chewed his bubble gum to the speed of Billie's story.

Bill continued. "We walked him to the doctor with his finger in a bowl!"

"I carried it, Papa, all the way down the hill." Jim stretched his gum through his teeth in a long string for emphasis. "Didn't drop it the whole way!"

"And I had to hold his hand up while Mama found his finger," Irene offered, paling again at the thought of it.

"Susie!" Garnet called out. She was coming up the hall with a fresh ice bag. "What are they talking about? What is all this about?"

Susie's concentration was on positioning Junior's bandaged hand over the cold, cloth bag but she answered. "He told it about right, I'd say."

"Why wasn't I called?" He complained and that annoyed her.

"You were called. You didn't answer. You were out. I called you from the house to bring the car, then the doctor's office and then from the house again several times and you were out." She went for another pillow.

"I was? Yes, I was." He approached the couch and took a chair next to Garnet Junior. "So then, you were chopping wood?"

"Yeah. I was chopping, and there was a snag, so I went for it. I was holding on with my left and chopping with my right. I know to use the wedge and I was using it like Mama taught me, but when I went to take a second slice on it, the ax went down on my... I wasn't thinking, I guess... I shouldn't 'a done it like that."

At the foot of the couch, Bill added more. "The doctor said that we were brave to bring the finger to him...but he didn't put it back on. I figure maybe that's good cause now you can't be pointing and blaming me, right Garnet? And also, he'll be able to still play ball."

Garnet echoed. "He said you'll still play ball?"

There's no doubt Junior was worried about this part of the story and disappointing his father. "I don't know how long I'll be out."

Garnet shifted in his seat. "Well, you don't worry about that. You just get better. They'll cover the infield in the short term."

Billie offered, "He likes warm milk, don't you Garnet? I can getcha some if you want."

"No, I'm all right," he answered then, without warning, his eyes closed.

Susie returned with the pillow and whispered to Garnet. "There's food in the kitchen."

"I ate. I went out after a long day of calls and then got a bite to eat with Rex." That information landed on Susie's last nerve. She could see his mood was high and he was working to control the conversation. "Well, you've all been through a lot today, Junior. I'd say you deserve a treat. You know, they are rebroadcasting Friday's *Hoot Owls* tonight. What if we stay up and listen? It's a *Hoot Owls* night if there ever was one. I'll even pop some corn!"

"They've already stayed up, Garnet. You got here way past bedtime."

But the kids had launched into a chorus of jumping up and down and chanting, *"Please Mama, Please!?"* Garnet Junior's eyes opened at the suggestion of popcorn and *Hoot Owls* on a school night. "Please Mama?"

Garnet appealed to his injured son. "You have earned a special night, I think. You'll close your eyes if you feel tired, won't you son?"

"I will." From his position on the couch, his body made its best attempt to jump for joy.

Susie conceded. "Okay. Get your pajamas on." They ran to their room.

Papa brought them bowls of popcorn and gave an introduction. "Have you heard this show is broadcast to over one million listeners? It's bigger than Amos and Andy!"

They were pajamaed and plopped in position in time for the *Hoot Owls* introduction. Gwen and Irene took a spot at the end of the couch on each side of Papa, forcing Junior to fold his legs up to accommodate them. Jimmie sat at his papa's feet and Bill stretched out on the floor chomping popcorn with his eyes glued to the radio.

This is KGW radio coming to you from Portland, Oregon and it's time for "The Order of Hoot Owls Roosting in the Oregonian Tower... Remember everybody, "Keep Growing Wiser!"

When we gather for the meeting
And they put us on the air
We will send a friendly greeting
To the people everywhere.
So accept our invitation
Hear each merry jest we bring
Turn your dials and get the station
And listen while we sing:
Hello, Everybody,
Here we are again;
Growing wiser, Hoot Owls,
Friday, half past ten.
Everybody's happy
No use feeling blue
So Hoot, Hoot, Hoot Owls, Hoot!
From KGW.

Junior was in a deep sleep only ten minutes into the show. Garnet kept up a steady routine of looking over at Susie, grinning, and nodding at every punchline. She studied him, his behavior, and his manner. *He was out for more than dinner.* Usually, Susie loved the entertainment and fun of staying up late with the kids, but the timing of it tonight unnerved her. She couldn't stomach the uncommon, almost silly, interest he suddenly took in their children tonight. It smelled of deceit and manipulation. To the background noise of *Hoot Owls* merriment, dark feelings circulated inside her, invoking a wave of anger so strong she thought she might burst. Suddenly her family busted out in piercing laughter and it caused her physical pain. She felt dizzy.

Jimmie was the second to nod off. His body went limp and puffs of popcorn floated out of his hand onto the floor. Irene collapsed over the arm of the couch. Only Gwen and Bill made it to the end of the show. Garnet carried Jim to bed with Gwen keeping pace alongside him and repeating all the best lines from the program. In a daze, Irene dragged herself behind them to the room.

Billie stayed with Susie while she reset Junior's hand position and tucked his blankets. "Will he sleep here tonight, Mama?"

"I think it's a good place for him."

"Where will you be?"

"I'll put some pillows down here on the floor, in case he wakes up."

"I'll stay with you," Bill said. "In case he wakes up and you don't hear him."

"How about you sleep in your room tonight? You can let me take a nap tomorrow and look after him then." He yawned a big, long yawn.

"Okay, I'll stay with him tomorrow. I'm gonna read to him from Babe Ruth's Own Book of Baseball. I promised him I would do that tomorrow."

"Then you will definitely need your sleep. Come on." She guided him down the hall to his room then went to her room to get pillows and a blanket for her night on the floor. Garnet was getting ready for bed. He was smiling.

"Well, that was fun, wasn't it? The kids sure liked it." His glee sickened her.

"It's a good show. I'm going to go tend to my son now." Her reminder snapped him to attention.

"Oh, yeah, did you check on him? How is he doing?"

The vacancy revealed in the question turned her stone cold. She spoke harshly. "How is he doing?! Well, one minute he was using his two hands with ten fingers to chop wood for our family...doing his part to keep the stove on, to keep us warm at night. The next minute, he is covered in blood with one less finger and he's hoping maybe it can be reattached because a twelve-year-old boy should have all his fingers. Even so, he still hasn't cried about it. That kind of thing can take its toll, in several ways, I would think." She couldn't remember, even in their worst times, ever thinking less of him. He had brought his brother back into their lives and into their house, thoughtlessly, blind to how it was sure to tear them apart. Blind or indifferent, did it matter? Now she and the children had managed this crisis without him, while he made himself unavailable. Even then, he couldn't maintain his attention to the top story in their lives that day.

Instead, he was defensive. "What are you implying?"

"I'm not implying. I'm saying it. Why were you late coming home? Why didn't you answer the telephone?"

"I resent the question. I was calling on businesses. For advertising. That's the truth. Rex had gone to Seattle, and I had to cover for him. It kept me there late."

"Didn't you say you ate with Rex?"

"Oh, I did? Yes, I did. He telephoned when he came back from Seattle and we..."

"He telephoned you? So, you took his call." She was getting no joy from catching him in lies. "I'm going to sleep in the main room tonight. I won't be up to make you breakfast." She turned to leave. He leaned over to pick up a sock and a sound of tin hit the wood floor. It was no cigarette because it landed with a clack. She knew what it was. He dropped his syringe.

Oregonian, March 9, 1928
Boy, 7, Cuts Off Finger, Estacada, Or., (Special)
Garnet Parks, 7-year-old son of Mr. and Mrs. G.E. Parks, cut off the index finger of his right hand to the second joint, Wednesday morning. He was splitting kindling wood when the accident happened. Mr. Parks is editor of the *East Clackamas News.*

The Oregonian got it wrong because he was 12 years old, not 7, it was his left index finger not his right and it was on Tuesday, not Wednesday. However, G.E.'s assistant, who had taken Susie's call that day, got it right.

Eastern Clackamas News, March 9, 1928
Cuts Off Finger
A most unfortunate accident happened to Garnet Parks, son of Mr. and Mrs. G.E. Parks, Tuesday evening when he cut off a part of his index finger on the left hand while splitting kindling. The wound was dressed by Dr. W.W. Gilbert and he is getting along so far very nicely.

§

Days of rain may have pleased the Estacada farmers and gardeners, but it brought unease to the locals who were anticipating the first game of the season for their Legionnaires against Vancouver. In the Parks house, things were tense. Evenings were thick with silences that were only broken when Garnet or Susie responded to one of the kids. Susie needed Rex gone, but the divide between her and Garnet made communication impossible without igniting more trouble. The cold war between them provided latitude for Rex to express himself without censor. He was back to stumbling in drunk and entitling himself to the crudest talk in front of the children. He felt freer than ever to bring his girls in and out of what Garnet had come to call, "Rex's Room." The few words that did pass between Susie and Garnet happened in the bedroom after the children were in bed.

Susie whispered forcefully while struggling to lean over her stomach to pick clothes from the floor. "Are you surprised that you started using the minute your brother showed up?"

Garnet stood defiant. "What makes you think that's when I started? What makes you think I ever quit?" Susie stopped cleaning and tossed her chin at him for clarification. "Rex has nothing to do with it. I've obviously been handling it just fine because you couldn't tell."

The recklessness in his tone activated a violence in her. She threw the wad of shirts at him and left the house with no coat or shoes. The chill of the night penetrated her bones and rain soaked into her nightgown. She felt a strange relief from the sting of rocks on her bare feet for how it matched the pain she was in. Collapsing against an oak tree, she surrendered herself to its soggy wet roots and held her belly between her knees.

She remembered twelve years before, in her nightgown crawling on their floor and dodging bullets. Then she didn't dare venture out where raiders would shoot her dead as soon as look at her. Tonight, the threat came from inside her home. She was safer here out in the night on the cold, wet ground. She cried.

Glaring bright lights hit her in the eyes. It was the headlights of the Chevrolet Superior. Two figures ambled from the car and meandered up the walk, grappling onto each other for balance on their way into her house. Too tired to feel contempt she thought, *Great, what's next?* She wrapped her arms around the unborn baby she was bringing into a home that was crumbling. It wasn't her home. It wasn't her life and she considered curling up and sleeping at the base of that tree in the rain, but five children in the house who were no threat to her needed whatever was left of her. She had to go back.

She stayed out in the rain long enough to give Rex and his girl time to get in the room and close the door. When she went in, she cleaned herself up and found a dry nightgown. Garnet was on his side of the bed, sleeping soundly. She tucked a pillow under her belly to support the baby, then laid awake, without a plan and powerless to escape the noises coming from the next room.

§

On no sleep Susie was the first to rise, hoping to have coffee in the quiet of the morning. She lit a fire under the percolator and yawned which caused her jaw to snap and sent a shot of pain through to her head. It was probably the result of a new habit of clenching her teeth in the night. She rubbed her jaws to relieve the tension then ran her fingers along her forehead, over her mouth, cheeks, and eyes trying to read her own expression. It felt like anger and she wondered if her face would set like that permanently. Coffee was ready, she poured a cup, then heard rustling in the hall.

She anticipated Rex's shuffling feet but when she heard a click, click, clicking she knew she was about to encounter the girl. At the sight of her, all she could think was, *Oh my, she's barely more than a child.* The girl lacked the maturity to curb the volume of her voice in a sleeping household. Amid a rattling of unintelligible nonsense at Rex, she spotted Susie.

Susie had planted herself at the counter gripping her cup in her hands. She said nothing. Rex gifted her with his artificial grin then presumptively, and unsuccessfully, reached around Susie for a cup. She stood rooted in her spot, unyielding.

"Oh!" The girl squeaked uncomfortably. Rex chuckled and tried again. Susie didn't budge.

"Well, Clara, it looks like our host is stuck to the counter here."

"Sarah," the girl corrected.

"What?" he said, disoriented.

"Sarah. You called me Clara."

"Ha, no I didn't," he lied. "So, what do you say we go on into town and get some breakfast?" Susie stared them down as Rex took his hat and jacket from the rack and guided his jittery girlfriend out the door. He slammed it on the way out for emphasis.

Once she was sure they were gone, she went to the room. Vodka and whiskey bottles, cigarette butts, and magazines lay across the floor. The blankets and sheets were piled in a wad at the center of her daughters' beds that had been shoved together to accommodate Rex's purpose. She set out to clean and launder the place so Rex would fully understand he was being evicted. When she pulled at the bedding it came up bloody and sticky with God knows what. "Oh, God!" She threw them off then got herself a rag for protection from the despicable goo. The bedding and the rest of the garbage all went into a crate and out to the back. It took her several trips.

In the backyard, Susie gathered enough kindling and dried fir branches to get a fire going. She used an old pitchfork to serve the remnants of Rex up to the sacrificial blaze and threw the crate on top.

She scripted a speech for Garnet that left no room for alteration or interpretation. Garnet would deliver Rex's clothes and tell him he was not to come back because she had a baby's room to get ready, and she added, *good luck to him.*

Rex was gone and David Lyle was born on June 18, 1928. Rex took an extended vacation to British Columbia and the Legionnaires took a big win against Sherwood. Eva came to help with the baby and took Irene back to Kirkland for a month.

> *Clackamas News,* August 31, 1928
> Mrs. J.C. Cathcart and Mrs. Ilone Beaman of Kirkland visited Mrs. Cathcart's sister Mrs. G.E. Parks, in Estacada a couple of days first of the week. Little Irene Parks, who has been visiting the past month with her aunt, returned home with them.

§

When she returned Irene, Eva took Susie and their Aunt Sophrie for a movie night in Portland to see Al Jolson in the Jazz Singer. The dark theater and drama of a Jewish kid's rise to success in New York City was worlds away from Susie's life and it was a sweet escape. When Jolson said the words, "Wait a minute, wait a minute I tell yer, you ain't heard nothin' yet!" his voice synced up perfectly with his mouth and the audience let out an audible gasp. Song after song was delivered with the miracle of synchronized sound. Susie didn't want it to end. Afterward, they took the long way back to the car and linked arms singing Blue Skies and Toot, Toot, Tootsie in the night along Portland's city streets.

Rex's absence didn't improve the mood in the house as Susie had hoped. Ties were severed between her and Garnet. She stopped going to the shop altogether. It was hard to care about the paper anymore. It had always been their work together, but this Clackamas paper was just his. *Did he even miss her or the kids?*

Here, in this new home, there wasn't nearly as much work to do as on the farm but this thing between them made every task so heavy, it was like moving through wet concrete that she was determined to plod through to keep it from setting to the point where she could no longer move at all. Garnet spent more time than ever at the shop and then at his "stops" that were now part of his routine before making it home at night. The only thing they still had together was baseball.

She thought she couldn't be surprised anymore but when Rex returned from Canada, Garnet decided to expand the paper and name Rex his Advertising Manager. He billed him on the same credit line with G.E. Parks, Editor. The bottom was falling out from under them and, in response, G.E. expanded his reach and his circulation, firming up his ties with his brother Rex.

Clackamas News, August 31, 1928
C. Rex Parks and Mrs. J.M.C. Miller will be in charge of the office at Sandy. An application has been made for a permit to enter the *News* as second class mail matter at the Sandy post office and subscribers in that section of the county will receive their paper on Friday morning at the same time it will be received by subscribers in Estacada and vicinity.

Susie had long ago given up on her receiving line ritual with the kids before school. They got themselves off in the mornings independently. Jimmie was in first grade, so it was just Susie now at home with baby Lyle.

Garnet never lingered in the mornings these days. "I'm heading out. The championship game is tonight against Lake Oswego. I think we have a chance to beat them. See you there."

The bigger truth spilled out of her involuntarily. "We're in trouble, Garnet. We need to talk." She had no idea what she would say that could be helpful but it didn't matter because it only succeeded in hastening his exit.

"We'll go to the game. You'll bring the kids," he called back.

At the game, Susie held the baby in her arms and watched her family watch the Legionnaires lose their championship game to Lake Oswego in a shutout. She missed the whole thing. The Parks family exited toward the outfield, kicking dirt and recapping the team's errors.

"Hey!" Bill shouted at Gwen. He threw a ball to her and Garnet Junior intercepted.

"Over here!" Their papa yelled and caught Junior's throw barehanded. For a little while, they ran and played on the grass. They laughed and squealed and, in that moment, the joyful sounds of her family permeated the icy wall that separated them.

Garnet spent most nights "in meetings" with Rex. Susie was confident he was well supplied in morphine knowing Rex was just that kind of brother. His American Legion kept him away when Rex didn't. It was the American Legion that forged a friendship between Garnet and a man named L.D. Meade who admired the work he was doing as a newsman plus, he just liked G.E. All the boys down at the Legion Hall liked him and they had fun ribbing each other.

> *Clackamas News,* March 13, 1929
> During the show a few nights ago a fellow walked up to the door and asked Bill Perry if G.E. Parks was inside. "I'll look and see," replied Bill. He stuck his head inside the door for a moment and said, "No, he is not here."
> "How can you tell in the dark by just looking inside?"
> "There's only one bald head in the house and that's Atlee Erickson," replied Bill.

Garnet expanded the paper with Rex and shook hands and joked around with the boys. Most of his Legionnaire buddies in Estacada weren't familiar with his wife. Susie wondered if he were to pass their baby Lyle on the street if he'd even recognize him as his son.

§

Saturday night, Susie was up with the baby and checking out the front window for any sign of Garnet, who had not come home. On the one hand, it was just nicer when he wasn't there. On the other, he was her husband, and she was supposed to know where he was. The next morning, Gwen and Bill fixed breakfast. Susie wasn't hungry. Their living room was in shambles from the last of the boxes still to be unpacked from more than a year ago.

She lifted the lid on a crate of back issues of the *Tenino* and *Lewis County Independent*s and uncovered a stack of select issues of the *Courier*. *He was always so excited and so hopeful,* she thought. *He never gave up.* Wrapped in an August issue of the *Courier* were her gold watch and Gwen's silver cup.

> *To Gwenyth Parks. Commemorating your mother's heroism at Columbus, N.M., March 9th, 1916.*
> *from Mary C. Prince*

She set them aside and then went to throwing things out. Stacks of legal papers from the libel and debt suits. There was a box of tubes and syringes that set her gut churning. She started a burn bin and picked up her pace discarding things with such focus she hardly noticed the kids blowing through the house threatening each other with torture and bodily injury. She figured they'd be fine, plus the chaos worked to keep her going. She didn't hear him come in.

"Sorry, Papa!" Gwen was out of breath and circled around Garnet Junior who was after Jim. Garnet must have kept the door open because, on their next pass-through, the whole lot of them were ejected out the front door.

He was muttering something that ended with, "...so I decided to stay over."

Susie looked up. "Oh, I didn't see you."

"I was telling you why I didn't come home. I met with a man, C.E. Sparks, about a radio in the afternoon, so then I worked late and..."

"Don't do that, Garnet. I'm looking through these boxes here remembering a time when you were too big a man to lie to me." He flailed his arms in an exaggerated display of outrage and stormed into the kitchen looking for coffee.

"I don't know why I try with you!" He yelled back to her.

"See, Garnet? I'm here without you and I can't help but notice that the job I have to do is easier when you're not here. You don't have to lie about why you're out. It's easier when you're gone." That would hurt him and she knew it. "You were out shaking hands, growing the paper? Really? I've always been in your corner, Garnet. Next, you'll tell me you're buying another Linotype. Doing another expansion? How long before you tell me you want to sell and start over?"

"You've been talking to Eva!"

"I haven't. I've defended you to Eva at every step. Why don't you come home anymore?"

"Because I can't breathe here! Because I feel you judging me. Scrutinizing me. You've got me on a hot burner every minute!"

"That's not coming from me! It's because I can't give you what you want! I don't have what's in that needle. Why do you prefer Rex to your family?!"

"Because with him I can breathe!" he screamed.

Susie stood up. "You can't breathe? No, I'm the one who can't breathe! I can't!" She tried to pull in a breath, and it was true, she couldn't.

"I'm pregnant!" Garnet slammed his mug on the table splattering coffee all over the walls. It woke Lyle who now cried from the bedroom. Neither responded.

"You can't have another baby!" he commanded.

"I can't? You're telling me I can't? Really? Who are you to tell me I can't?" she countered.

"You shouldn't have had the last one! You shouldn't keep having..." She pushed past him on the way to the baby.

"Don't ever say that to me! You can't...don't you ever say a thing like that to me... ever again!"

The kids were all outside and probably missed that fight. Nothing more was said until that night. They left Gwen in the house to watch the younger ones and took a walk. It was a beautiful night for a walk. The sky was clear, and the air was crisp. A perfect night for a walk, but neither of them noticed.

Garnet was composed. "Meade wants the paper. He has a house in St. Helens that he signed over to me. I'm going to go get treatment."

"Where?" she asked.

"I don't know. There's a sanitarium over on Stark Street. Morningside Hospital."

"We'll go then." The humility in what he was suggesting dropped her defenses instantly. She'd been closed off for so long she didn't know there still existed a crack in the door but there it was.

"No, I won't be able to do it. I can't do it with you." He wouldn't look at her and she could see his shame. She knew he was right. He wouldn't be able to do it with her or with his children nearby. He needed to put distance between them if he had any chance of beating the hold this monster had on him.

Susie nodded. "I understand. It makes sense." They talked logistics, money, and how Susie would manage while he was away. They were quiet, then she spoke. "You need to sign the house over to me. If you're away, I need the house. For the kids. It can't be in your name while you're away. I'll have no rights under the law." Of course, she was right. She would have no recourse if their only possession was in his name. He agreed. He was deflated. They returned to the house with no fight left in them. They joined the kids in front of the radio and seated themselves on different ends of the room. She couldn't quite make out how she felt. She wondered if she was scared. She remembered her response to the reporters after the Raid thirteen years earlier.

"I don't know whether I was scared or not. You don't know when you're scared like that. You're not thinking about being scared."

Clackamas News, May 31, 1929
Estacada Paper Sold. ESTACADA, Or., May 30-(Special.)
L. D. Meade of Saint Helens this week purchased the *Eastern Clackamas News* from Garnet Parks. Mr. Parks has been the editor and publisher for about eighteen months.

§

A day after L.D. Meade signed his St. Helens house over to G.E., G.E. signed it over to Susie. No announcements were made to acquaintances. Garnet briefed his assistants and associates. Susie didn't know how he dealt with Rex, who hadn't been around for days.

That first Saturday in June 1929, Susie sat up in bed. Her chest was tight, and she was having trouble getting hold of her breath. No one was up yet. *Where are the papers?* Garnet had packed his bag the night before and told her he was ready to drive to the city. She remembered just tossing that quit-claim deed for the St. Helens house like it was a scrap on top of some newspapers, but now she couldn't find them. Her breath was fast, shallow, and panicked. She rifled through the piles and found the deed at the bottom. She paced and read the legal language of the document to herself:

> "...*by these presents: That Garnet E. Parks of the city of Estacada, county of Clackamas and state of Oregon, in consideration of the sum of one dollar and other valuable considerations.*

"Other valuable considerations? What are those?" she muttered, worried she was supposed to have given something in the transaction besides the imaginary dollar. *That can't be right,* she read on.

> "...*to him paid by Susan A. Parks of the city of Estacada, county of Clackamas, and state of Oregon the receipt whereof is hereby acknowledged...*

Hereby acknowledged. So then it's acknowledged? Is it though? I don't know!

> ...*does hereby remise, release, and forever quit claim to the said Susan A. Parks heirs and assigns forever, the following real estate situated in*

the county of Columbia in the state of Oregon and in the township of Saint Helen's and founded and described as follows:

"So, that sounds right. It's done then." Again, muttering to herself. "...Lot number 18 in Block 148 and so on. Okay..."

"Mama. Pancakes! It's Saturday!" Susie was jolted back into the present by Jimmie and looked up to find the five of them gawking at her from behind the kitchen wall. The baby cried and Gwen took care of him. Susie put the papers in a safe pocket of her handbag and shifted her attention to breakfast and the children.

The kids gobbled up the eggs and slathered syrup over stacks of pancakes. Susie took a bite but couldn't take another for fear it would come back up. She wondered why Garnet hadn't come to the table yet and why he hadn't said anything yet to the kids. She knew she couldn't do it and shouldn't. It wasn't her place, and besides, she was afraid of what she might say if it were left to her.

He came in stoic. *Why won't you talk to them? They know you're sick. Just tell them you're going to get help.* The little talk there was, was about baseball. Susie kept her commitment to letting this be his time and said little. Finally, he said, "You'll be driving me into the city today. All of you."

Susie put the dishes in the sink and Garnet returned to the back room. Susie brought Lyle out to the kids in the car and squeezed herself into the passenger seat. *Why am I always pregnant, shoving myself into a car?*

She watched Garnet lock the door. Every moment of this day had the sense of some sacred ritual. Like when she left the farm. Like the gears of time were shifted into a profound slow motion. He took care of business with no detectable emotion. He had said so little, so why did she still have a sense that he was lying? What was there left to lie about?

The forty minutes into Portland were of Irene and Jim filling the space with chatter. Susie's thoughts were on logistics. Would she move the kids to St. Helens and wait for him? Would she get a job in Estacada? Who would hire her, six months pregnant? How long would he be away? Garnet pulled to the curb. "I'll get out here."

Susie leaned to him and whispered, "Garnet, you haven't told them anything. You're just going to get out?" He shook his head and said nothing, but her expression implored him that he must. So he did, but he didn't look at them.

"Susie, I'm no good for you and the kids right now. I'll check myself in and come back when I'm cured." He got out of the car.

This is too much for them. She checked their faces and saw their bewilderment. "Good-bye Sister," he said, and then, "Good-bye kids."

They watched him walk away but Susie couldn't sit still. She knew she had to get moving or the concrete would set and render her immobile and she knew he was lying but she didn't know about what. "Gwen, take Lyle and get in the front." She turned the car around. *He's leaving for good.* She wasn't sure about it, but it felt true and the thought of it brought on relief and pain all at once.

Their sixteen years together came at her like a hard wave threatening to take her under. It sapped her strength, so she pulled the car to the side and resorted to crying. Bill leaned over from the backseat. "Mama. Why are you crying, Mama?"

"I'm all right, Bill." She felt Gwen on her like glue. "See, I'm all right. We'll go home and figure things out."

11

Fifteen years and five months before, almost to the day, Susie and Garnet had driven a borrowed car to the Deming courthouse and got married. Now, Susie drove their Oakland north to Rose Hill, followed by a sympathetic Jim Cathcart who drove his truck and trailer carrying some furniture, crates, and Mickey's Cow. Susie hoped the trip wouldn't dry the cow up. They squeezed into Eva and Jim's carriage house for as long as they could stand it. Then she found a modest old house, cold on the inside with yellow paint chipping off the cedar plank exterior, and moved them in. Six months pregnant with no job, no indoor plumbing or electricity made the days and months that followed hard on all of them.

"If Papa knew what's happening here, he would come back!" Gwen insisted. She was unapologetically unhappy with her mother for, "... driving him away with all the fighting."

"My letters come back *return to sender,*" Susie defended. "I don't know where he is."

After a month, he did send a letter. The return address said General Delivery, from Valencia Street in San Francisco. He was brief and gave little information about his plans or why he was in California. He did ask about Gwen. *Please send Gwen, I'll raise her.* It was an appalling kick to the gut where his unborn baby lived. Susie thought she'd sooner take another bullet than let her children see what was in that letter.

Then another letter came. This time it was addressed to Gwen. *I have a nice place here in the city. I can buy you a train ticket. Come and live with me.*

When Eva got wind of it, she was livid and let Gwen know it. "You would abandon your mother and go live with that man? It's despicable!"

There was a part of Gwen that would do that and Eva had no

influence with her shame tactics. Gwen wondered how much better her life would be down there with him as an only child. Out loud but soft enough to avoid confrontation she answered, "Why not? Why shouldn't I?" Then she told Susie, "It would be no different than what Irene's life is, living with Aunt Eva, with all her toys and dresses. Here we're just freezing in the dark." It was cruel. Susie believed Gwen was goading her to tell what really happened and on that she wouldn't budge. Susie wouldn't risk biasing them against him, especially when and if he were to come back. Besides, Gwen had no intention of leaving.

The baby was a month away when Susie took a job hoeing Patchel's strawberry field which was a walk from the yellow house. Gwen would be fifteen in December, which made her a desirable housekeeper and nanny to the well-off Marsh family of Kirkland, so she quit school and went to work. Susie went into labor and Eva and Irene drove her to Mrs. Brown's Sanitarium in north Kirkland. Susie delivered a baby girl and gave Eva a letter addressed to General Delivery Valencia Street, San Francisco. It said simply:

October 1, 1929
Garnet,
The baby is born. Please come home. She's a girl. I named her Barbara Jane. Jane after our mas.
  Susie

§

A well-dressed man entered the *San Francisco Chronicle* off the corner of Mission Street and 5th and addressed the man at the front desk. "Good afternoon. I'm here about a job. Having worked as an editor and publisher myself, I would think it appropriate that I speak directly to Publisher Cameron about how my skills can best be utilized."

His boldness was startling to the clerk. "Sign in here and I'll see what I can do."

He picked up the pen, licked the tip, and signed his name.

George Sparks

§

The census takers knocked on doors in the spring of 1930. In a Portland boarding house, Rex reported his name to be C. Rex Parks, a single salesman born in 1901, (reducing his age by five years from his factual birthdate of June 4, 1896). In San Francisco, George Sparks reported from his home at the Colonial Apartments on Valencia Street. It said he was a single printer born in 1895, (reducing his age by five years from his factual birthdate of August 3, 1890).

North of the brothers, in a yellow house on Rose Hill in Kirkland, Susan A. Parks reported herself as married, a printer, and head of household with six dependents ages 0 to 13. She got no response from her husband to the letter she sent about the birth of the baby. Susie knew the fate of a married woman who waits for a man. She didn't have much, but she knew that if he decided to come back what little she had would be his under the law. So, in March she took the ferry into Seattle and did what, to her, was unspeakable. Through gritted teeth and with her ma's disapproval imminent, she filed for divorce.

In the Superior Court of the state of Washington for King County
Susan Parks, plaintiff alleges:

I
That the plaintiff and defendant were married in Deming, New Mexico, February 6, 1914, and are now and ever since have been husband and wife, and the plaintiff has been a resident of King County, Washington.

II
That there is no community property.

III
That there are seven children as a result of said marriage: Gwyneth, Garnet, Billie, Margaret, James, Lyle and Barbara.

IV
That the defendant left the home of the plaintiff without any cause whatsoever, on June 1, 1929, and has never returned.

V
That the defendant has failed, neglected and refused to support the plaintiff and their minor children, and she has been compelled to support said children since June 1, 1929

VI
That during the last two years, that the plaintiff and defendant were living together, the defendant treated the plaintiff in a cruel

and inhumane manner and it is impossible for the plaintiff and defendant to longer live together.

VII

That the plaintiff owns the following describes separate property: "Lots Numbered 18 in Block Numbered 148 in the city of Saint Helens, Oregon, as per plat on file and of records in the office of the clerk of Columbia County, Oregon", an old model Oakland car, one cow and some household furniture.

Wherefore the plaintiff prays for an interlocutory order entitling her to a divorce and granting her the custody and control of said minor children and declaring said property to be her separate property free from any right title or interest of the defendant and for such other and further relief as to the court shall seem just and equitable.

She only told Eva what she did. The thought of it filled her with shame and the action of it felt like failure. After six months with no response from Garnet, the judge granted her a divorce. She did what she had to for their security and she was surprised by the relief it brought her.

Comes now the plaintiff and moves the Court for an order entering the default of the defendant, Garnet Parks, herein on the grounds and for the reason that said defendant has failed to file any answer, demurrer, motion or pleading of any sort herein for more than six months.

I

That the plaintiff is entitled to a divorce from the defendant.

II

That the plaintiff is entitled to care and control of the said minor children.

III

That the plaintiff is entitled to the property which is her separate property free and clear from any commitment community interest of the defendant.

The pursuit of money replaced play, rest, and often sleep. Susie had yet to find a dependable job. She and the boys sold berries and baked goods out of the back of the Oakland and she sold off furniture and other valuables from out of the crates brought up from Estacada. Garnet and

Bill learned to strip and dry cascara bark which brought in fifteen cents a pound. Eva stopped in often with armfuls of food.

Gwen couldn't tolerate *the squalor*, as she called it. When the Marshes paid her, she turned most of it over to Susie. Susie would have loved the luxury to refuse her, but she and Gwen knew that wasn't an option. Within a month of Barbara's delivery, the stock market crashed. Susie would now have to compete with men for available jobs in a declining economy. Her situation seemed impossible and any pathway out improbable, but hope came to her in the form of a neighbor lady named Elva Adams. Elva had it on good authority that Kirkland's Lincoln Ferry needed a lunch counter waitress and urged Susie to get right down there. It would mean early and long hours, but it paid three dollars a day! Mrs. Adams offered to take the baby, Barbara, which made working those hours a viable option. Susie took the job. "If you keep her, you'll need to feed her." With the baby in her arms, Susie walked Mickey's Cow over to the Adams'. It wasn't ideal, in fact it was heart-wrenching to have her eight-month-old baby living with someone else across the street, but it meant they would survive.

So that's how it was. At night she returned from working on the ferry, collected Lyle up from Gwen at the Marsh House, and stopped by the Adams' to hold Barbara for a bit before going home. The walk with Lyle from Elva's gave her talk time with him before facing the challenges that waited inside the house. Most nights, dinner was beans and potatoes.

"Yuck!" Jimmie complained at dinner.

"Shut your mouth, Jim. Be happy with what you get!" Garnet Junior's temper had gotten shorter since Gwen left the house and it was shortest with Jim who just didn't have an off switch.

"I hate beans. Every night, beans, beans, beans..." Garnet smacked him on the side of the head. Irene flinched and Bill took Jim's plate.

"Here, I'll take them. You can have my potatoes," and he scraped the beans off Jim's plate and traded for the potatoes on his.

More than any of them, Jim missed a warm house, good food, and the safety of a Mama and Papa in charge. He was ashamed that they had become poor. He followed his brothers around sometimes, but they were always working. He wasn't a worker by nature so he spent most of his time alone. He skipped school, wet the bed, and sometimes swiped things from the store. Susie couldn't give her troubled son what he required and he was floundering.

When rooting through the Gregg's old log house that Eva used for storage, Susie found a guitar. It wasn't a replacement for her attention or for his papa, but she knew music in any form was the best therapy she had ever known. She collected enough change to buy strings, cleaned it up, strung it, and brought it to Jim.

"Jim, what do you think?" He lit up. "Would you like to learn to play it?"

He nodded. It was the first light she'd seen in him since they left Estacada. He gripped it awkwardly then looked up appealing for help. "Here," she said. "Your left hand goes here." She showed him the chords Don had taught her and left him to practice, which he did. He practiced and practiced. He learned to play the Gus Cannon song *Walk Right In* which she loved too and, when time allowed it, they played together. There were nights after dinner they got the instruments out to sing and play. He was such a lonely, dissatisfied boy. In the few moments she had, that guitar was how they connected.

§

George Sparks walked along his small-town street greeting folks he passed then stopped at a vendor. "Good evening to you, George! The usual bratwurst and sauerkraut?"

George savored the familiarity he enjoyed as a regular customer. This man offered up the best bratwurst around, though the sauerkraut lacked the full flavor he remembered from his past.

"Yessir. Pile it on." George paid then continued down the sidewalk taking big bites as he approached the path leading to his home. He entered and went directly into a side room, which looked to be his office.

"George?" called out a woman from the next room. He didn't answer. He put what was left of his bratwurst onto the desk, then reached into a drawer and pulled out a box. Inside were syringes and the ingredients he needed for an injection. "George?" the woman called again. She spoke to someone, probably a friend. "Sorry, Vickie, it sounds like George is home, but he usually goes into his room to take his shot. He takes it once or twice a day for his diabetes."

§

One night on her stop at the Adams', Elva gave Susie a proposition. "Now that Barbie is two, we'd like to adopt her." Feeling such gratitude and appreciation, Susie kept her smile and continued handing blocks to Barbie for stacking. Her throat was tight as she told Elva she would talk to the family and get back to her. She walked on to the house and considered her options. She was still keeping long hours on the ferry and that didn't allow for taking care of her little ones. She knew Gwen couldn't keep both Lyle and Barbie during the day, and Elva was a good woman, a good person. Maybe it was the only choice she had.

She entered her house, stark and utilitarian. It contained only the most necessary furniture with few photos to indicate that a family lived there. They were all there visiting with Gwen and her new boyfriend, Cliff the milkman. Someone had started dinner, which allowed her to sit. She shared Mrs. Adams' proposal and Gwen laid it down. "No. You can't let her have her. Bring her home, Mama. We'll figure it out."

They did. They took turns caring for Lyle and Barb while Susie worked. Jim continued to have a knack for trouble and at four, Lyle was showing signs of the same talent. Susie decided they needed to buy some land in the country, where they would have space and sustainability and get the boys away from town. She sold the St. Helens house and bought five acres in the country between Kirkland and Redmond. She also bought a buzz saw and, with some help from her friend, Crisco, she, Garnet, and Bill cleared the land and built a log house. Garnet was a workhorse. He quit high school to focus on finishing the house and watching Lyle, Barbie, and Jim full-time. The hard work of it took its toll. Susie's night terrors were back. Just like after the Raid in Columbus, she'd shoot out of bed and run through the house in a panic until Bill and Garnet wrangled her back into bed with Lyle and Barb.

The pressure took its toll on Garnet Junior as well. His hard work and devotion to caring for the family came with a price. He had developed an unpredictable disposition and an explosive temper. Jim got the worst of it. Just before his thirteenth birthday when it was more than he could take, he grabbed an oversized coat, some bread, and whatever money he could find, and took off hitchhiking to get as far as he could from his brother and all things attached to his family.

§

Susie carried her family knowing that no matter how well she did, someone would still suffer and important things would be left undone. Each day she got up at four in the morning to make the ferry. Some days the truck wouldn't start so Garnet would strap Barb to his back and he and Bill would grab Susie by the arm and run her up the hill from the log house to Eva's. If there was one thing the Parks kids knew, it was how to pull together to solve a problem.

Lyle and Barbie had a game of jumping onto the running board of the truck any time Garnet drove home. After picking Susie up from the ferry dock one night, Garnet slowed on the driveway. Lyle jumped on but Barbie missed and fell. Lyle jumped off screaming as the truck dragged her through the gravel. Garnet applied the brakes, and Susie jumped out to find Barbie bloody and raw under the back wheel. She snatched her up into the cab and Garnet floored the gas to the Kirkland clinic. Jim was gone and it looked like Barb might not walk again. It was a tough summer.

Every day Susie earned, she built, she sewed, she cooked, and she took every side job, but still, for every triumph someone's needs went left unmet. Sometimes it was hers. Those bullet fragments were shifting position in her neck and causing her serious pain, but it had to wait. Even so, she seized any available opportunity for joy. If it happened that food was in surplus or a surprise visitor showed up at the door, she threw a party. Susie was never so tired she couldn't muster the energy to put something on the stove and get a band together to play. It was her gift.

§

At a kitchen table in the little town of Winton, George Sparks reads the baseball scores in a cloud of smoke with a cup of coffee and a stack of newspapers beside him. The woman, Cherie was her name, joined him. She was visibly pregnant. Their oldest daughter, Joyce, played with paper dolls on the floor. "George, you've had your face in those newspapers all morning! What's so important that you must read every paper in the county?"

"I have to stay current. I may decide to buy one of these paper's out. I bet I could turn any one of these publications into a daily paper inside of a year."

Puzzled, Cherie said, "Why would you want to do that?"

§

Susie rented an apartment in town to be closer to medical care for Barb and left Garnet and Bill to themselves at the log house. Irene enrolled at Kirkland High and moved back with Susie to help with the little ones. She was upset by Barb's condition. "You're not walking right, Barbie. You're limping something terrible!" Irene knew nearly everyone in town. She got the word out about her little sister and was advised to try a chiropractor. Over the course of several visits, the woman was able to put Barbara's left hip and six vertebrae back into place. She was walking again.

Over the two years since Jim ran off, Susie tried to reach him by phone. He kept in contact with Gwen and Irene but wanted nothing to do with his brothers and wasn't ready to communicate with his mom, but that winter that Barb walked again was the same winter that Jim finally agreed to come home for Christmas.

Susie poured herself into preparations. She made all his favorite food, bought presents, and filled the small apartment with family. It was a Christmas bash to beat all. He drove himself down from Bellingham in a borrowed jalopy without a license. Susie didn't tell the family he was coming and when he walked through the door with his guitar in his hand, the screams of joy about took the roof off. Proud to be earning his own money, he brought presents. Christmas Carols were sung accompanied by George's banjo, Don and Susie's fiddles, and Jim's guitar.

The repair of that broken summer lit a fire in Susie. More than ten years after saying goodbye to Moldrem's Orchestra, she revived herself and started a little orchestra of her own.

> *Seattle Post Intelligencer,* February 5, 1937
> For the benefit of the Red Cross flood relief fund, the Rose Hill community club at Kirkland is sponsoring the old-time dance at its clubhouse tomorrow night. Mrs. Susan Parks and her Orchestra are donating their services and the club is donating the hall.

She also saw a doctor about her neck. They couldn't extract all the fragments since some of them were still too close to her artery, but they took enough to relieve some of the pain. Of course, she was asked how she came to acquire the fragments in the first place, and her answer inspired another call into the *Seattle Daily Times*.

Seattle Daily Times, May 10, 1937

After twenty-one years, bullet fragments that embedded themselves in her throat during Pancho Villa's historic raid on Columbus, N. M., have been removed and Mrs. Susan Parks of Kirkland, now has only her memories by which to remember that night of terror March 9, 1916.

Mrs. Parks returned home yesterday after the operation was performed at a hospital here. She was the town's telephone operator when Villa and his Mexican troops crossed the border to raid Columbus. Her husband was out of town. Bullets shattered her windows, but Mrs. Parks reached her telephone switchboard and stayed there until she had called United States troops to the rescue. The wife of New Mexico's governor rewarded Mrs. Parks heroism with a gold watch.

12

Some Newspaper Man!
1929, in those first months in San Francisco, G.E. wrote a letter to G.A. in Chicago saying he'd sold his business, acquired a new car, and wanted to come out for a visit. That was the last letter anyone received from him. When Rex didn't hear from him for over a year, he contacted a Seattle detective. The Seattle Police Department returned their conclusions:

> Mr. C Rex Parks
> 310 Corbin St.
> Portland, OR
> Dear sir:
> Replying to your letter of February 23, we made inquiry for the whereabouts of your brother, G.E. Parks, but have been unable to find him. He is not known to the Typographical Union, and the last information we can secure regarding him is that in December 1929 he was receiving mail at General Delivery, San Francisco, California.
> Yours very truly,
> Louis J Forbes, Chief of Police

No one would have thought to conduct a search for George Sparks. He knew that. His last summer in Estacada, G.E. had called on a radio man named C.E. Sparks. Maybe he'd planned a name change before he ever left. Maybe Rex helped him, the two had a lot of time to talk that summer. Even so, Rex never saw him again either.

If even one of their children had acquired G.E.'s habit of reading several newspapers at the breakfast table, they might have happened upon a March 14, 1957 issue of *The Atwater Signal*. It was the community weekly in Atwater, California where George Sparks worked and near Winton where he lived. They would have seen a three-quarter page feature article with a photo of George Sparks, who possessed an undeniable likeness to their father. They would have seen photos of his family and read an interview filled with colorful descriptions of a life that vaguely resembled the life of their papa, Garnet E. Parks, though it would be inflated, reconstructed, and overall much improved. *The Atwater Signal* reporter seemed to have genuine affection for his friend, George Sparks whom he referred to as "Mr. Newspaper." The tone suggested he respected him and believed everything his friend and colleague told him.

Atwater Signal – Atwater, CA, March 14, 1957
This is Mr. Newspaper
Have you ever wondered how much experience is required to qualify the men who produce your newspaper? And, have you ever imagined how much building is needed to form a city? Or how much promotion is necessary to establish a business?

George Sparks, *The Atwater Signal* linotype operator, might be considered typical of required experience in our industry and may very well reflect the basic interest necessary to laying the foundations of a successful city of businesses.

Mr. Sparks is a native of the Blue Ridge Mountains of Virginia. He received his higher education in Emory and Henry Col. After leaving college, he taught school for two yrs., and in that time when seven-month terms were required, he was "Master" at three different schools during the two years.

Pressures brought about by teacher shortage in those days were quick to convince Mr. Sparks that there must be other ways of making a living, so he jumped feet-first into the weekly newspaper by becoming owner of a small Virginia newspaper.

There is an incurable infection to this business which drives its victims into public service with a compelling force.

From this early success in the paper business, Mr. Sparks moved to Kansas City, Missouri, where he became a reporter on the *Kansas City Post*. After some months of observing that printers were better paid than reporters, he took his mechanical talents to the newspaper's metropolitan shop and became a printer.

His next move took him to Albuquerque, N. M. and the *Herald*. With the outbreak of border dispute wars between the U. S. and

Pancho Villa, Mr. Sparks became a reporter for the Associated Press. In this field his co-workers were such famous people as Bugs Bear, who is still with Hearst Papers; Webb Miler of the United Press, and Floyd Gibbons, of the *Chicago Tribune*.

Along with all these duties he also operated a weekly newspaper at Columbus, N. M. for a short time.

George was sold on the great southwest – even became a homesteader near Columbus. It was while he was keeping all the irons hot, reporting for the AP, publishing a paper and homesteading that Pancho Villa raided the town of Columbus and left seventeen townspeople dead.

This incident was marked as a serious turn in the war and Mr. Sparks was invited to accompany the U. S. Counselor to Mexico to a rendezvous with Villa at his camp 50 miles below the border.

As a result of this expedition, a mighty scared reporter turned in a 2000-word story that hit almost every newspaper in the nation over wires of the national AP service.

Two years of this life was enough, so George worked his way northward to Oregon and Washington, and into Canada. He worked on such papers as the *Portland Journal*, the *Seattle Times*, the *Vancouver, B. C. Sun* and other newspapers in Vancouver Province.

During World War I, he returned to his old stomping grounds with the U. S. Cavalry to patrol the border between the U.S. and Mexico. Following the war he joined the American Legion and retained active membership in that organization for twenty-five years.

In the early 1930s he moved to California, working on the leading newspapers in San Francisco and Los Angeles.

He then struck out again in the anxiety to build and develop a part of the state as he established the *Santa Cruz American*.

A fiery editor of the "old school," Mr. Sparks emerged victor from two libel actions in the courts of Stanislaus County, when he lashed out against corruption at Oakdale. A highly respected citizen of that community, Mr. Sparks owned and published the *Oakdale Enterprise* for eight years and also established the *Jamestown Enterprise*, which he sold three years later.

Throughout more than half his life Mr. Sparks has owned and published newspapers in our America. He just smiles and waves aside a question to the number of papers he has worked with – "I can't count 'em."

Mr. Sparks came to *The Atwater Signal* in 1951 from Walnut Creek. In the steady stretch which he has served in this community, his machine has set literally miles of news stories about Atwater and Winton and the world as people here and at Castle Air Force Base read these incidents weekly in *The Atwater Signal* and *Valley Bomber*.

Since his first days of residence here, Mr. Sparks and his family have made their home on Cypress Avenue near Winton. His daughters, Beverly and Joann attended schools in Winton and high school at Livingston. His older daughter, Mrs. Joyce Stanley lives with her family at Merced, while Beverly, now Mrs. Barnes, lives in Sacramento.

How many community newspapers have flourished under the assisting hand of men like our George Sparks, and how many George Sparks' are even today earning their living contributing to the business and social welfare of Atwater and Winton?

In George's story, he got that job with the AP, he worked at some of the best-known publications and alongside the top journalists in the nation. In George's story he represented the US in a face-to-face meeting with Pancho Villa himself! George Sparks lived his young adult life untethered by a wife and family. In George's story, he emerged the victor in every challenge a man of his stature might face along the way. George Sparks lived a life of adventure and accomplishment to be admired by all who heard it. He could really tell a story.

§

The Parks children grew up, went to war, married, worked, ran businesses, had children, and settled in various states around the country but they got together when they could to eat, play music, and tell stories.

Gwen could talk any one of them under the table. "Remember when we were in Estacada and there was that big maple tree hanging over the woodshed? We said, 'Wouldn't that be a great place to sleep?' We got two apple boxes and put them up on the shed, remember?" She hit Lyle sitting next to her. "Well, you wouldn't remember, you weren't born." Then she pointed to Jim. "Oh no, you wouldn't remember. Well anyway,

Uncle Rex got things wholesale in these tin boxes that were the size of an apple box. So, Garnet and I got the tin box for me, and we decided he and Bill would use the apple boxes. When our parents' light went off, we knew it was time to go. We got pillows and we got Bill. We always had to carry him by the hand."

"No, you didn't!" Bill was the only one who dared to challenge Gwen.

She went unfazed. "I tossed the pillows and Bill up to Garnet and we put him in the apple box and got him all comfy. Garnet got in his apple box, and I got up and got in the tin box and my tin box starts..." She began laughing to the point of incoherence. "I'm sliding off the roof, down the slope, and yelling 'Ohhhhh!'" She had to catch her breath. "I fell out of the box, and it went off the roof and almost took me with it! The lights went on and we stayed up there all huddled together. Papa comes out in his pajamas, and he's got the flashlight shining on that tin box lying on the ground. He didn't look up at us. He didn't see anything, so he went back into the house and turned off the light. Then I said, 'The heck with it. I don't need a box.' I put the pillow down and slept on the roof." Still laughing through her words, "That's the truth."

All the best Parks stories ended with *that's the truth*. The stories were of a childhood marked by mischievous adventures and always with an emphasis on entertainment over accuracy. They loved to make each other laugh.

"I was always leaving my bed. I'd climb out my bedroom window and go sleep in the garden. My mother..." Gwen called Susie *my mother* when talking to her brothers and sisters. "She'd come in to make the bed and say, 'Where did all these beans come from?' They were all stuck to the blanket. I don't know why I never wanted to sleep in my bed!"

"I got up on the roof too at night, but I was sleepwalking," Jim remembered.

"That was you?" Lyle said, "I thought that was Bill! All I remember was looking up at the roof of the log house and there he was hanging down with no pants, bare ass!"

Gwen pointed at Jim. "When he was a baby, we played with him just like he was a doll. I dressed him up and put him to bed. Mama would come home from work and say, 'Where's the baby? Where's the baby!' and I'd have to stop and think, *where did I put that baby?*" Looking around theatrically, "Oh, that's right, he's in the dresser drawer!' One night they came home, and I had you in a trunk!"

Irene remembered her father. "I remember I asked, 'Papa, why are you bald? Where's your hair? He told me 'the wind blew it away.'"

Jim nodded emphatically. "Our father was funny, and he belonged to the best clubs and always dressed in the finest suits. We had money, remember? Dad worked hard and he was respected. My first-grade teacher told the whole class, 'the Parkses are a well-to-do family.'"

Barb countered. "What kind of teacher says that!"

"Well, we were. Our mother was more interested in her social life, running around going to her clubs or whatever."

Garnet defended her. "She was playing music. You didn't know she was playing...in the orchestra."

Jim corrected. "Oh, she was a talented musician, so she went out nights and we had that hired woman."

"That was Mrs. Chansky." Bill decided Jim needed it mapped out for him. "Mom was working, that's why. Listen, when we came up from Portland, our mother said, 'Let's see here. I got six kids I gotta take care of and one on the way.' So, Irene decided to go to Aunt Eva's."

Now Irene corrected. "I didn't *decide to go to Aunt Eva's*. I left home on day one! The reason was Mama was ill when I was born and they didn't want me to get what she had, so they sent me to Eva's."

Bill said, "Nah, you wanted to go."

Irene threw him a tender glare. "I was one minute old, Bill!" Then she continued. "Anyway, they sent me to Aunt Eva's. She didn't have any children and," Irene fluttered her eyelashes. "I was kinda nice, you know." She winked.

Bill continued. "So, then Gwen said, 'I'll go downtown and get a job at somebody's house.' That left us. Me, Garnet, and Jim. Garnet worked like the devil, and I did my share and took Jim berry pickin' and cascara bark peelin'. That's how it was."

Irene opposed with a smile. "Well, I also had to pick...stuff. Strawberries and hops and apples. All that good stuff. Jim and I were outcasts. That's the truth!"

"You always say that." Barb couldn't believe it because she loved Irene, cried whenever she left and was happy to her bones whenever she came home.

Barb asked, "So how long did I live with Mrs. Adams?"

Bill told her, "You were there about a year and a half. You would have been there longer, but the cow went dry."

Irene held her heart and cooed. "Remember when we got the

babies' picture taken? When Mama made an appointment for Lyle and Barb to have their first photo in Kirkland?" Those first years on her own in Kirkland didn't allow for indulgences like baby photos, but when the family decided to deny Mrs. Adams her adoption, a rededication to family was sparked in all of them. They hovered around the two little ones, spitting in their hands to plaster down stray hairs. Bill found a man's tie and Garnet tied it for Lyle then stuffed the extra length of it into his little shirt. Susie and Irene put Barb in a dress and a bow in her hair. "They were so precious."

Lyle giggled, "We might have been *precious*, but we could get into trouble. We used to roll coffee grounds into toilet paper and smoke 'em!"

Barb nodding, "Mom tried to spank us for that but the dog, remember Carl? He wouldn't let her near us so she had to give up."

Barb told about a time just before Jim ran away. "We were all at the log house celebrating birthdays and having fun eating corn in the yard. Garnet told Jim to get the water and, of course, Jim said no. Garnet went after him but Mom got between them and put up her dukes like Jim Corbet. Remember she used to box like Jim Corbet? She said, 'Don't touch him!' and Garnet put his fists up at Mama. We were so scared! Jim was twelve and he hid and was crying. Irene fainted and that scared Lyle and me, so we started crying too. That's probably what stopped the fight. When Irene fainted, Garnet quit and left. He was trying to fill the shoes of our father...it was too much for him. He needed treatment but back then people didn't get help for what was wrong with Garnet. He was hurt and he hurt Jim. It wasn't fair."

There were conflicting views among the Parks kids:

"Our mother was strong."
"She was spoiled."
"Papa was a respected newspaper man."
"Mama worked hard."
"I don't think my father liked me."
"Mama was a socialite, always had to go to things and play her violin."
"Our father was weak."
"Nothing was more important to Mom than her kids."
"I have wonderful memories of Mama. She was my friend."
"Papa made Mama laugh."
"Our mother worked her fingers raw to keep us together."

"She was loud, she rattled windows when she laughed."
"Mama embarrassed me, but I loved her."
"He wanted to be someone, make a difference."
"She was fearless."
"Papa was the smartest man I knew."
"I was his favorite."
"Our mother didn't have favorites."

Whatever Susie knew about his leaving, she never told their kids and she never pursued the truth of what became of him. They told their children a version of the story that was filled with holes, but it worked in the absence of the truth: *he must have been the victim of a violent crime that prevented him from coming home.* If she felt pain or rejection, fear or resentment, Susie didn't tell them. She put out the fires, dodged the bullets, held her post, and made space for joy and music.

He may have confounded her. She might have exhausted him. She never said it but maybe she decided to let him have his story in return for her freedom, the freedom to prevail where together they failed. The question of "What happened to Papa?" was a prevailing theme throughout their life. Once it was answered, consensus was it was probably better left as a question.

BIBLIOGRAPHY, RESEARCH, AND ACKNOWLEDGMENTS

Bonnand, Sheila. "The Bisbee Deportation of 1917 - Sheila Bonnand." *libcom.org*, 1997. https://libcom.org/article/bisbee-deportation-1917-sheila-bonnand.

Brandon, Morgan. "Columbus, New Mexico, and Palomas, Chihuahua: Transnational Landscapes of Violence, 1888–1930." University of New Mexico, UNM Digital Repository. September 5, 2013. https://digitalrepository.unm.edu/hist_etds/56/.

Bryan, Howard, and Howard Bryan. "J.R. 'Chief' Galusha: Recollections of a Pioneer Lawman." Essay. *True Tales of the American Southwest: Pioneer Recollections of Frontier Adventure*, 191-250. Santa Fe, NM: Clear Light, 2009.

Donnelly, Jim. "In the Air, On Land, On Sea." *Hemmings.com*, 2006. http://www.hemmings.com/stories/article/in-the-air-on-land-on-sea.

Finley, James P. "Buffalo Soldiers at Huachuca: Villa's Raid on Columbus, New Mexico." *Huachuca Illustrated,* vol 1, 1993: Villa's Raid on Columbus, New Mexico. Huachuca Museum Society, 1993. https://net.lib.byu.edu/estu/wwi/comment/huachuca/HI1-12.htm.

Hardin, Jess Wolf. "Pancho Villa Attacks Columbus, New Mexico." *Legends of America*, February 2021. http://www.legendsofamerica.com/we-panchovilla.

Harris, Larry A. *Pancho Villa and the Columbus Raid.* Whitefish, MT: Kessinger, 2007.

Hopper, James. "What Happened in Columbus." *Collier's The National Weekly*, April 15, 1916.

Hays, Michael Archie. *No Pretty Picture: Maud Hawk Wright and Villa's Raid on Columbus.* Santa Fe, NM: Sunstone Press, 2016

Hurst, James W. *Pancho Villa and Blackjack Pershing: The Punitive Expedition in Mexico.* Westport, CT: Praeger, 2008.

Hamm, R. (1982, October). Wild Old Days! Heroic Susan Parks. *True West*, 29(10), 56–57.

Jackson, Rhonda A. "The Columbus Raid." *Historical Review* 2000, 2010. https://donaanacountyhistsoc.org/.

Katz, Friedrich. "Pancho Villa and the Attack on Columbus, New Mexico." Current links for DOI: 10.2307/1865904. *University of Chicago Press Journals Division*, 1978. https://doi.org/10.2307/1865904.

Laemlein, Tom. "Blood on the Border: The Battle of Columbus." *National American Rifleman.* NRA Publications, December 4, 2017. http://www.americanrifleman.org/content/blood-on-the-border-the-battle-of-columbus.

Lannon, Albert Vetere. "Arizona History: The 1917 Bisbee 'Deportation' of Striking Miners." *Arizona Daily Independent*, July 13, 2018. https://arizonadailyindependent.com/2018/07/11/arizona-history-the-1917-bisbee-deportation-of-striking-miners/.

Lehr, Dick. "The Racist Legacy of Woodrow Wilson." *The Atlantic.* Atlantic Media Company, May 4, 2021. http://www.theatlantic.com/politics/archive/2015/11/wilson-legacy-racism/417549.

"Libel Hearing Set." *Tacoma News Tribune*, June 18, 1925.

Mahoney, Tom. "The Columbus Raid." JSTOR. *Southwest Review*, 1932. https://www.jstor.org/stable/43466150.

McGaw, William C. *Southwest Saga: The Way It Really Was*. Phoenix, AZ: Golden West Publishers, 1988.

The Morning Olympian. "Moldrem Orchestra to Have Premier" *The Morning Olympian*. June 7, 1925.

Moseley, George B. "The U.S. Health Care Non-System, 1908-2008." *Journal of Ethics | American Medical Association*. American Medical Association, May 1, 2008. https://journalofethics.ama-assn.org/article/us-health-care-non-system-1908-2008/2008-05.

Naber, Kara. "Columbus Remembers: Switchboard Operator Signaled Raid to Rest of the World." *The Deming Headlight*, March 4, 2016. https://www.demingheadlight.com/2016/03/07/columbus-remembers-switchboard-operator-signaled-raid-to-rest-of-the-world/.

Ortiz, Willie. *Attack on America: Pancho Villa's Raid on Columbus, New Mexico*. CreateSpace Independent Publishing Platform, 2016.

The Press Democrat. "Seeks Death By Starving Self." *The Press Democrat*. August 26, 1923.

Quesada, Alejandro de. "March 9, 1916: Pancho Villa and the Villista Raid on Columbus." *The History Reader*, May 8, 2020. http://www.thehistoryreader.com/historical-figures/march-91916-pancho-villa-villista-raid-columbus.

Ravel, Abarbanel S. "Pancho Villa and My Grandfather." *Tablet Magazine*, August 27, 2019. http://www.tabletmag.com/sections/community/articles/pancho-villa-and-my-grandfather.

Ross, Steve. "Ninety Years Ago in Washington, a Wave of Anti-Immigrant Sentiment Resulted in Horror for Filipinos." *Slate Magazine*. Slate, August 4, 2017. https://slate.com/news-and-politics/2017/08/ninety-years-ago-in-washington-a-wave-of-anti-immigrant-sentiment-resulted-in-horror-for-filipinos.html.

Sharp, Jay W. "Pancho Villa Raid of Columbus, NM." *DesertUSA*, 2019. http://www.desertusa.com/desert-people/pancho-villa.html.

Sherman, J., and B. Sherman. *Ghost Towns and Mining Camps of New Mexico*. Google Books. Google, 1975. http://www.google.com/books/edition/Ghost_Towns_and_Mining_Camps_of_New_Mexi/AeLucnQnl5QC?hl=en#v=snippet&q=Columbus&f=false.

Smyser, Craig. "The Columbus Raid." *Southwest Review*. JSTOR, 1983. https://www.jstor.org/stable/43469529.

Sneddon, Matthew, ed. "II. Historical Context and Essays." *Center for the Study of the Pacific Northwest*. Northwest Homesteader A Curriculum Project for Washington Schools. https://www.washington.edu/uwired/outreach/cspn/Website/Classroom%20Materials/Curriculum%20Packets/Homesteading/II.html.

The Spokesman Review. "Say Major Hand Will Recover." *The Spokesman Review*. May 20, 1927.

The Tenino Independent. "G.E. Parks Goes to St. Peters Hospital." *The Tenino Independent*, November 24, 1922.

Vazquez-Lozano, Gustavo. "The Night Pancho Villa Attacked Columbus." *The Daily Chela*, December 18, 2022. http://www.dailychela.com/francisco-pancho-villa-attacks-columbus.

W. H. Horne Co., ed. "Burning the Bodies of Dead Bandits at Columbus, N. M." *The Douglas Archives*, a collection of historical and genealogical records. W. H. Horne Co., October 21, 2021. 21http://www.douglashistory.co.uk/history/articles/burning_bodies_new-mexico.html.

Welsome, Eileen. *The General and the Jaguar: Pershing's Hunt for Pancho Villa; a True Story of Revolution and Revenge*. Lincoln, NE: University of Nebraska Press, 2007.

White, E. Bruce. "The Muddied Waters of Columbus, New Mexico" *The Americas*, Vol. 32, No. 1." Cambridge Core. Cambridge University Press, December 11, 2015. https://doi.org/10.2307/980403.

RESEARCH:

Barbara Brutschy: Reference Librarian, Fern Ridge Library

Katie Bush: Public Historian, Clark County Historical Museum

Chris Chrzan: Librarian, Timberland Regional Library

Ed Clayton: Researcher, Troutdale News Consultant

Ryan Cohen, MLIS: Customer Service Librarian Contractor, National Library of Medicine, National Institute of Health

Susan Coutts: Deputy Clerk, Courtroom Clerk to Commissioner Mitchell – Dept. 4

Richard Dean: Columbus, New Mexico Historian

John Derby: Retired Bureau Chief for the *Merced Sun Star*, Editor Publisher of *Winton Times*

Laura Edmonston: Deputy Law Librarian (Reference), Washington State Law Library

W. Michael Farmer, Ph.D.: Western Fiction Writer, westernfiction@aol.com

Kian Flynn: Geography & Global Studies Librarian, University of Washington Libraries

Elizabeth Gassman: Publishing coach and editor, eggedits.com

Loita Hawkinson: Research Specialist, Kirkland Heritage Society

Renee Lang: Executive Secretary, The Telecommunications History Group, Inc.

Marni Larson: Chief Deputy Clerk, Lewis County Clerk's office

Sarah Lim: Museum Director, Merced County Courthouse Museum

Denise Merz: Legal Records Coordinator, Thurston County Clerk's office

Stephanie Mohr: Collections Manager, Eastside Heritage Center

Jonathan Potter, MA, MLIS: Assistant Director, Spokane Academic Library (Eastern Washington University & Washington State University) Washington State University Health and Sciences

Eileen Price: Reference Archivist, Washington State Historical Society

Ollie Reed: *Albuquerque Journal*: Fact checker

Peter Schmid: Visual Resources Archivist, Providence Archives Sisters of Providence | Providence Health & Services

Gerry Settle: Administrative Assistant, Alumni office Emory & Henry College

Heather Thomas: Reference Librarian, Serial & Government Publications Library of Congress

ACKNOWLEDGMENTS:

Tom Borener: Proofing and editing

Lory Wolgamott: Proofing and editing

Jill Robinson-Wolgamott: Fact checker Veneta, Oregon

Manuel Medina: Consultor Español

Vickie Robinson: Postal Clerk and resident of Winton, California

Joy Wilde: Health Specialist and astrologer

Contributions of personal stories and documents:

Irene Parks Hill, Barbara Parks Gay, Dann Wiley Gonyea, Collis Hill, Lory Wolgamott, Pam Parks, Valerie Vroom, Kelly Parks, Kristy Lunga, Joe Friars, TR Mathis

READERS GUIDE

As you read make a note of your response to any of these general prompts:

> What was a vivid picture you had while reading?
> What in the story was confusing?
> Describe a strong reaction you had to a character.
> What was interesting or surprising?
> What connections did you make to your life, another book, or the world?
> What are the author's biases?
> What themes did you find?

Author's note:

> Would a person be able to successfully keep a secret today like the secret G.E. Parks kept for so many years?
> Have you or someone in your family discovered a family secret and, if yes, how did the family react?

Preface

> What about the introduction to the family makes you curious to know more?
> What about the siblings' perspective stands out when recounting memories of their father?

Chapter 1

> From this interaction, what do we know about Susie? About Garnet?
> What predictions can you make about how an experience like this will impact the children later in life?
> Is Susie angry? Does she love him? What could she have done differently?

Chapter 2

> How does Susie's pa compare to a modern dad?
> The Gregg's took risks without a safety net. How were they advantaged or disadvantaged compared to generations that came after them?

Chapter 3

> Do Garnet and Susie seem compatible or are they an unlikely partnership?
> To what ideals does Garnet aspire?
> Is Susie a feminist?
> Why didn't Susie hold her ma accountable for her pa's behavior?
> What are some of the ways Susie shows feelings of inadequacy?

Chapter 4

> Why, despite her condition and the condition of her baby, was Susie so determined to stay by the switchboard?
> Why is Garnet split between feelings of guilt and envy?
> What are the factors that dictate a group's response to trauma? Is the response the same when elements of nationality or race are involved?

Chapter 5

> Attention Susie got regarding her actions during the raid embarrassed her. Why would she shy away from this kind of attention?

During Susie's interview in the *Courier* office, what does Garnet's behavior tell us about him as a journalist, a businessman, and a husband?

Chapter 6

Garnet shows passionate loyalty and pride in his community and the people in it. How is this an attribute? How might it be an Achilles heel?
While in Pittsburg, what does Susie's attitude toward the city reveal about her?

Chapter 7

Describe Eva as a sister, as a person and as an influence on Susie, Garnet and the kids.
Did the reminder of Susie turning 27 come as a surprise? Does she seem older or younger than her age?

Chapter 8

Is Garnet's positivity toward his business and his town genuine or strategic?
What factors contribute to Garnet's special attachment to his brother Rex?
What is Susie's responsibility to support his relationship with his brother? Should she push back harder?

Chapter 9

Does Susie make a fair assessment when she decides to leave the farm or is it a rationale?
How does the sting of the rocks on her feet offer Susie relief?
What symbolism does the Linotype hold in the story?
What makes it hard for Susie to identify when she's feeling fear?
What does the second telling of Garnet's exit reveal about that day?

Chapter 11

> What inference can you make about the brothers' reports to the census takers?
> Why did the Greggs have such strong feelings about divorce?
> What factors determined the Parks childrens' reactions to challenges after their father left? Why were Garnet Jr. and Jim more adversely affected than the others?
> How does Jim's return symbolize a shift for Susie?

Chapter 12

> What role, if any, might Rex have had in Garnet's disappearance?
> Do you think Garnet contacted Rex after he left Oregon? Why or why not?
> What was the power of storytelling in Garnet's life?
> How did storytelling shape the Parks children and their worldview?

www.ingramcontent.com/pod-product-compliance
Lightning Source LLC
Chambersburg PA
CBHW051122160426
43195CB00014B/2300